D1165855

WILLIAM FAULKNER'S
LIGHT IN AUGUST

GARLAND FAULKNER CASEBOOKS
(Series Editor: Noel Polk)
VOL. 2

WILLIAM FAULKNER'S
LIGHT IN AUGUST
A Critical Casebook

François L. Pitavy

GARLAND PUBLISHING, INC. • NEW YORK & LONDON
1982

Library of Congress Cataloging in Publication Data
Main entry under title:

William Faulkner's Light in August.

  (Garland Faulkner casebooks ; v. 2)
    Bibliography: p.
  1. Faulkner, William, 1897–1962.   Light in August.
I. Pitavy, François L. II. Series.
PS3511.A86L58   1982   813'.52   81-48416
ISBN 0-8240-9385-2

Printed on acid-free, 250-year-life paper
Manufactured in the United States of America

Contents

Series Editor's Preface

Work on the writings of William Faulkner shows no sign of slackening. Articles and books reflecting an ever-widening range of interpretations and critical approaches continue to appear with such frequency that the thickets of Faulkner criticism are in some ways becoming even more tangled and bewildering than those of Yoknapatawpha County itself. In spite of several excellent bibliographical guides, the problem, even for veteran Faulknerians, of keeping up with, sifting through, and evaluating the field, are formidable; for the non-specialist—the student, the professor who simply wants to be a better teacher of Faulkner—these problems are frequently overwhelming.

Garland's Faulkner Casebook Series is designed to come to the aid of both specialist and non-specialist; each volume, devoted to a single Faulkner work, is designed to provide, as it were, a place to start, as well as a place to come back to. Each volume in the series is edited by a scholar who has specialized knowledge of, and, in most cases, who has been a principal contributor to, the scholarship on a particular Faulkner novel. Each editor has been asked to select "the best and most useful" of the available scholarship on that novel for inclusion in the volume, as well as to commission new essays to fill gaps in the scholarship. Writers of previously published essays being anthologized in a volume have been invited to re-write, correct, or simply to update their essays, in light of developments in Faulkner scholarship since the essay's publication.

Each volume will contain (1) an editor's introduction, designed to provide an overview of scholarly study of the novel; (2) an essay, new or old, which brings together all of the available information about the novel's genesis—the inception, the writing, revisions, publication— based upon examination of manuscripts and upon other biographical data; (3) the body of essays described above; and (4) an annotated bibliography of criticism of the novel. The bibliography is *highly* selective for the years prior to 1973, the cut-off date of Thomas L. McHaney's *William Faulkner: A Reference Guide*, in order to provide a key to "the best and most useful" material; an effort has been made to be *complete* for the period since 1973.

Noel Polk
Series Editor

INTRODUCTION

François L. Pitavy

   Light in August has long been recognized as one of
Faulkner's major works. In spite of its large cast of characters (nearly seventy in all, more than in *The Sound and the
Fury*, *As I Lay Dying*, *Sanctuary*, and almost twice as many as
in *Absalom, Absalom!*), its chronological disruptions, its
unresolved tensions and ambiguities, its ironical recurrences
and reversals, the shifts in meaning in its major characters
and symbols, this long novel (Faulkner's longest after *A Fable*
and *The Mansion*) reads more easily than, say, *The Sound and
the Fury* or *Absalom, Absalom!*: its style and technique seem
relatively straightforward, and the story is not too difficult
to understand.
   Yet, if accessible to understanding, the novel has appeared resistant to *comprehension*. It is indeed divided into
two major blocks of material, each with its own protagonist,
Lena Grove and Joe Christmas--the two poles of the novel--
the distance between them being spanned, albeit incompletely
or uncertainly, by Gail Hightower. Hence the unity of this
proliferating novel has seemed faulty--a major stumbling
block for criticism, one of whose solid tenets is that beauty
in a work of art resides in the harmonious adequation and
interrelation of its parts, as in a Racine tragedy or a
Mozart quartet (vide the embarrassment of the critics before
The Adventures of Huckleberry Finn, or even *Moby Dick*, and
to this day the almost obsessive concern for "the great
American novel," a concern shared even by such contemporary
novelists as Norman Mailer and William Styron in their recent
productions). Consequently, the general trend of the criticism
of *Light in August* has been to search for unity in the rich
and complex themes of the novel, to emphasize one of them and
make it into the ordering principle of the work (it is sufficient to look at the first or second footnote of a large
number of the articles or essays on this novel to be convinced
of the prevalence of this critical approach).
   It would be foolhardy for this brief introduction to
attempt discovering the "key." The success and high critical

reputation of *Light in August* is proof enough that it functions
as a work of art. But the history of past criticism suggests
that one should stop the search for unity and *perfection*--a
way of immobilizing a fiction which keeps on *revolving*, a text
where the sense keeps on *circulating*, as appears, for instance,
in the last three chapters, in which new movements or cycles
originate: the luminous, rocket-like ascension of Christmas's
pent-up black blood, the ceaseless revolution of Hightower's
wheel of thinking, and the narrative momentum of the last (but,
in a way, not ultimate) chapter, where the narrator, by telling a narrative about desire and frustration, engenders in
his "impatient" young wife, the narratee, a desire for a narrative which cannot be dissociated from desire itself--a metaphor for the desire of the writer, and of the reader. This
narration within the narrative ("en abyme") here points at
once to the open, ceaseless functioning of fiction, away from
closure and perfection, and to the circularity of an otherwise
fractured text in which the discrete elements and the opposed
and complementary meanings never cease exchanging senses and
changing signs.

· · · ·

Trying to reconstruct the genetic history of *Light in
August* may help us to understand not so much the author's
design (do we ever know it, or even does he ever know it precisely?) as the (ill)logic of the text, the (un)reason of the
discourse. To this end, one has to go back to the extant documents, giving indications as to the history of the writing.
Partial indications at best: in this case at least, total reconstruction is impossible. As has often been remarked, and as
any attentive student of Faulkner's papers knows, the author
generally discarded first drafts or worksheets, taking pains
to save only finished, or almost finished, work.[1] Here is a list
of documents available so far (for this and further research):
  · the Virginia manuscript: a complete, 188-page manuscript
in the Faulkner Collection in the Alderman Library at the
University of Virginia. The original title, "Dark House," is
crossed out and the definitive title is written above it. The
flyleaf also bears this information: "Oxford, Mississippi/17
August, 1931." At the bottom of the final page, appears:
"Oxford, Miss./19 Feb. 1932."
  the Texas manuscript (Academic Center Library of the
University of Texas at Austin): three unnumbered sheets bearing the title *Light in August*, possibly an early version of
the opening of the novel, describing Hightower at his window
and sketching out his life (now the basis of the beginning of

Chapter 3 and part of Chapter 20), and one untitled page with
a few lines describing the arrest of a man called Brown.

· the Oregon manuscript (University of Oregon Library):
one page with eighteen lines roughly corresponding to pp. 332-
34 of the published novel.[2] The page, obviously an early
version, is numbered "12," a possible indication that Faulkner
at one time may have intended to open his novel with Joe
Christmas on the day of his capture (now Chapter 15).

· the typescript setting copy (468 pages, one page missing,
in the Alderman Library; the last 56 pages are part of the
Texas collection). The differences from the manuscript in no
way affect the structure or the import of the novel.

· the corrected galleys (in the Texas collection).

· the salesman's dummy (issued by Harrison Smith, that is,
before the merger with Haas in March 1932), whose text probably
precedes that of the Virginia manuscript.[3]

Some or all of these documents (except the Oregon manuscript) have already been studied by Carl Ficken,[4] myself,[5]
and Regina Fadiman.[6] In the light of these documents and
studies and with the help of Joseph Blotner's biography of
Faulkner,[7] I will now draw the following tentative conclusions.

1. Before the inception of his seventh novel, Faulkner
was interested in a character, Gavin Blount, whose concern
with the past and his dead father clearly prefigures Gail
Hightower's obsessions and his vision in the dying fall of
the evening light. This character appears particularly in
"The Big Shot" (probably first written in the beginning of
1926, after Faulkner's return from Europe),[8] in "Dull Tale,"
first submitted to *The Saturday Evening Post* in November 1930,
and in "A Rose of Lebanon," later retitled "A Return," a
story also dating back to the end of 1930.[9] Faulkner's interest
in such a past-obsessed, idealistic, and ineffectual character
may account for the original title of the novel, "Dark House,"
a likely reference to the house of the ex-minister cut off
from outside life (high tower), and also to the house of
Joanna Burden, a dark abyss of femininity in the novel.

2. Faulkner apparently tried several openings for *Light
in August*: anyone familiar with the writing history of
Sanctuary will see here a recognizable Faulkner practice. The
uncertain evidence of the Oregon fragment may suggest that
in Faulkner's mind the Christmas material was originally
more important than Fadiman asserts in her book (a surmise
supported by a characteristic episode in "Dull Tale," when
Blount as a child crouches in a closet and later vomits[10]).
In a touch of genius, Faulkner brilliantly settled on the
spring scene for the opening of *Sanctuary*--a scene of fascination which shows the tetanizing force of evil and thus

already contains the whole novel; similarly, the first chapter of *Light in August* at once establishes, in the repetitive final remark of Lena Grove and in the urn motif, the circularity which informs the novel. Thus the curvilinear, round-bellied Lena, crossing Jefferson in her smooth travel on a rectilinear road, becomes the gauge of the other characters' movements and attitudes: the alpha and omega of the narrative, she fully justifies its title. However, this leaves unresolved the (minor) riddle concerning the time when Faulkner changed the title of his novel.[11] Suffice it here to say that Faulkner (how consciously?) confirmed with such change his recognition of the significance of his work.

3. The dates on the Virginia manuscript refer only to this document: with its 157 paste-on slips,[12] it is evidently a composite manuscript, incorporating certainly one, possibly two or even three (partial?) previous drafts. However, the examination of the shades of ink, of the cancelled page or chapter numbers, and of the numerous cancellations and additions in the text does not offer sufficient evidence for a complete reconstruction of the composition of the novel. It may be that Faulkner wrote first what corresponds to the narrative present, the ten days of the present action,[13] that is, almost the whole novel, minus the flashback into the past of Christmas (Chapters 6-12). Then, Christmas was not the tragic figure he would become, and no privileged access into his consciousness was obtained. The Christmas flashback appears to have been written separately, probably in three stages (childhood and adolescence, the Joanna Burden material, and the Bobbie Allen episode), and chronologically.[14]

In revising his material, it seems that Faulkner discarded a nonsignificant chronology in favor of an order relating symptomatic episodes, thereby giving the novel a thematic structure. For instance, all the episodes in Chapter 7 tend to exemplify Joe's hatred of Mrs. McEachern's femininity (which goes counter to the masculine, "white" values of his "fathers" and of the Southern community in which he lives): the episode of the bathing of his feet by Mrs. McEachern (the arrival scene) concluding the chapter can thus be recognized as the origin of Joe's present aversion and take up its primal significance. Similarly, the beginning of Chapter 8 (Joe's leaving at night the McEachern home for good, though he does not know it) is in this place perceived as the direct result of the arrival scene (concluding the previous chapter), and it renders necessary a return to the origin of the affair with Bobbie Allen, before reverting to that same night, at the beginning of Chapter 9. So Chapter 8 centers around this affair and Joe's loss of his idealism at the revelation of

the unacceptable reality of sex and of love. In this respect,
the episode of the sacrifice of the sheep is appropriately
juxtaposed to the scene in which Bobbie tells Joe the exact
nature of her "sickness."

Such chronological reordering does not aim at telling
the story of Joe's life so much as at revealing his belief,
albeit inarticulate, or even unconscious, that he has, from
the outset ("memory believes before knowing remembers"), been
warped by influences which cannot but result in the shattering
of his idealism and in his violent and uncompromising rejection of all that denies it, and which he will encounter again
in Joanna Burden. No longer following the order of chronology,
but that of memory, the events in Chapters 6-12 become the
emergence of Joe's past life into his consciousness, at the
precise moment he "decides" to kill Joanna, or rather feels
compelled to do it in the (not necessarily conscious) acknowledgment of his past ("Something is going to happen to
me"). Ordered differently, these episodes would not make up
such a powerful exposé of racism,[15] sexism, and puritanism
(in the narrow acceptance of the word), which is echoed by
the rest of the novel. Blacks, women, and the uncleanliness
of sex constitute a triple object of hatred, internalized
by Joe, and by the masculine and Southernized--in spite of
her ancestry--Joanna as well; it is the accepted creed of
the intruders, the pariahs in the novel (Doc Hines, Percy
Grimm, even Hightower), but also that of the community which
would reject them.[16] This is obviously a common ideology,
beyond the outward differences (of degree, rather than of
nature).

. . . .

Tentative though it may be, this overview of the genesis
of *Light in August* reveals alterations and hesitations in
Faulkner's design during the composition of the novel. The
genetic view, then, would not agree with the a posteriori
comment Faulkner made on the writing of this novel, in his
remarkable 1933 introduction to *The Sound and the Fury*:

> then I began Light in August, knowing no more about
> it than a young woman, pregnant, walking along a strange
> country road. I thought, I will recapture it [the
> ecstasy] now, since I know no more about this book
> than I did about The Sound and the Fury when I sat
> down before the first blank page.
>
> It did not return. The written pages grew in number.
> The story was going pretty well: I would sit down to
> it each morning without reluctance yet still without

that anticipation and that joy which alone ever made
writing pleasure to me. The book was almost finished
before I acquiesced to the fact that it would not recur,
since I was now aware before each word was written down
just what the people would do, since now I was deliberately choosing among possibilities and probabilities
of behavior and weighing and measuring each choice by
the scale of the Jameses and Conrads and Balzacs. I
knew that I had read too much, that I had reached that
stage which all young writers must pass through, in
which he believes that he has learned too much about
his trade. I received a copy of the printed book and I
found that I didn't even want to see what kind of jacket
Smith had put on it.[17]

Even though, at the outset, Faulkner knew nothing about the
"adventures" of Lena Grove, he knew who she was, and would
not be surprised by what she would do or become: that was
merely a matter of writing it down. One is struck here by
the confidence of the author in himself, in what he calls his
trade, and by what seems to have been a smooth, almost secure
writing process, as deliberate and undeviating as Lena's
road. Whereas *The Sound and the Fury* had remained ecstatically
unpredictable to its author, *Light in August* denied him the
joy of anticipation and discovery: in a manner of speaking,
under the supervision of the author in sure command of his
writing, the book took care of itself, growing according to
its own logic or principle, which Faulkner had now become
enough of a professional to recognize and control. It may
not be too much of an overreading to see in this statement
a remarkably modern (in 1933) awareness that a text, with
its motifs and metaphors, possesses an inner principle of
a sort, not to be confused with the author's explicit (or
unconscious) design, an order which makes it function and
prevents it from being fixed and exhausted in recognized,
acceptable, reassuring meanings or interpretations.

Searching for the unity of *Light in August* has certainly
been of use in illuminating the novel from all sides, but may
now appear an unsuitable approach to the possibility of
insight. Indeed, if the criticism of *Light in August* so far
seems somehow to have reached its limits, it may be precisely
because this novel, possibly more than any other in the
Faulkner canon, is about disunity and division.
The twentieth-century novelist is certainly obsessed by
the sense of fracture, disruption, discontinuity, and Faulkner
is no exception. In the first three sections of *The Sound and
the Fury* and in *As I Lay Dying*, the anonymous narrator com-

pletely disappears, and the narration is broken up and assigned
to several agencies, the latter novel carrying the process
almost to a limit. After these two novels, and after the
attempt at objective narration in *Sanctuary*, Faulkner reassumes
the narrative fatherhood, so to speak, and reclaims the position of the anonymous narrator in *Light in August*: he thus
gives this novel a narrative unity which *The Sound and the
Fury* and *As I Lay Dying* had not possessed, but the discontinuity
and division reassert their presence in the narrative breaks,
the chronological disruptions, the shifts in tenses between
present and past, and of course in the uncertainty as to who
the protagonist of the novel really is.

This narrative disunity appears to be the sign that the
fiction here is profoundly concerned with division, and the
reversal and reciprocity of values, making *Light in August*
an ironical novel.

Nearly all its characters can be paired as doubles of one
another, that is, as mirrors sending back reflections both
parallel and antithetical, or as masks (a major image in the
text), at once concealing and revealing the other.[18] On a
larger scale, this fundamental (dis)semblance in the novel
can be seen functioning in the ambiguous relationship between
the individual and the community, a relationship the better
illuminated here for its being unmediated. Among Faulkner's
novels, *Light in August* is indeed remarkable for the lack or
scarcity of intermediate family structures: the individuals
are seen as actual or "spiritual" bachelors, spinsters, child-
less couples, orphans—pariahs or intruders all, *excommuni-
cated* by their violence, fanaticism, perverse idealism, self-
exiled in the realm of the *imaginary* and thus cut off from
the possibility of access to the *symbolic*,[19] that is, a recognition of the Other, or of reality. The characters do not
really speak to each other: they are either silent, or engaged not so much in dialogues as in counterposed monologues,
the demented soliloquies of separate "I's" locked in what
Lacan calls the imaginary—a deadly relationship to one's
mirror-image, to sameness. But the community is no different
from them: it supports or condones the prejudices and the
violence of individuals who are in fact its apt representatives, even though they carry its ideology to a bursting
point, at once supporting and exposing it. And the same
ambiguity can be traced in the major motifs of the novel: in
the last analysis, all the values in *Light in August* finally
reveal their ambivalence.

So one is brought back to the image of the straight line
which can also turn back circularly upon itself (as Christmas
knows all too well), and of the circle represented by Lena,

truly the eponymous character, with her "luminosity older
than our Christian civilization," her "quality of being able
to assume everything"[20]--thus to include all the meanings of
the novel, similar and antithetical. On her circle (both
structure and motif), which is also that of Hightower's wheel
of thinking, identities and senses ceaselessly revolve in an
endless exchange of reflections and oppositions, resemblances
and dissemblances.

. . . .

   This reconsideration of *Light in August* has led me relatively to limit the number of what one might call "traditional"
essays, which are the vast majority, pertaining mostly to a
study of structure and themes--the first section in this
collection. I have retained two older articles, by Phyllis
Hirshleifer and Carl Benson, for the general, comprehensive,
still usable views they offer of the novel. With some fine
insights, Franklin G. Burroughs, Jr., renews the thematic
approach of the novel, and R.G. Collins analyzes its major
characters with a thorough, perceptive look (because of the
length of his essay, I have retained only two sections, in
my view the most useful to the reader). And although Donald
Kartiganer's book on Faulkner has been recently published
and is thus available, I have included part of his study of
Light in August for its "modern" approach, viewing the novel
as an attempt to fictionalize dualism and fragmentation--a
stance supporting the gist of this introduction.
   The second section (they are all organized chronologically)
includes a fair sample of symbolic and mythical approaches
to the novel, while the third emphasizes aspects of the novel
all too often neglected by critics more intent on carrying
on studies in the all but exhausted fields of structure,
themes, and symbols. I am convinced that a renewal of the
criticism of *Light in August* should concentrate on the problems of narration, voice, language--that is, the texture of
the novel, what Roland Barthes lovingly calls the "grain"
of the text.
   The appendix includes Stephen Meats's accurate and useful
chronology (an original essay for this collection). Finally,
if this collection is to be of any use to its reader, it
should incite him to carry on his own critical quest: hence,
the long bibliography, as complete as can be (one is never
exhaustive), generally both descriptive and evaluative, to
help him select his further reading.
   For convenience and clarity, all the references to the
text of *Light in August* are to the first edition (New York:

Harrison Smith & Robert Haas, October 1932) (the current, in-
expensive Modern Library College Edition of the novel, with
a sensible introduction by Cleanth Brooks, is a photographic
reproduction of that first printing). I have thus taken the
liberty, for some essays in this collection, of altering the
page references. Also, when I have excerpted parts of some
essays, I have renumbered the notes.

NOTES

1. The first close reader of Faulkner's papers is James B.
Meriwether. See his careful introduction to the section "The
Manuscripts" in his *The Literary Career of William Faulkner*
(Princeton, N.J.: Princeton University Library, 1961), pp.
59-63.

2. "*Light in August*: A Manuscript Fragment," ed. Deborah
Thompson, *Mississippi Quarterly*, 32 (Summer 1979), 477-80.
See the bibliography at the end of this volume.

3. See Carl Ficken, "The Opening Scene of William Faulkner's *Light in August*," *Proof*, 2 (1972), 175-84; François
Pitavy, *Faulkner's Light in August* (Bloomington and London:
Indiana University Press, 1973), pp. 9-10, 135-39. This document and the previous one are used in this collection, in my
essay "A Stylistic Approach to *Light in August*."

4. "A Critical and Textual Study of William Faulkner's
Light in August," dissertation, University of South Carolina,
1972 (University Microfilms 73-3597).

5. Op. cit. (see note 3).

6. *Faulkner's Light in August: A Description and Interpretation of the Revisions* (Charlottesville: University Press
of Virginia, 1975). See my essay-review of Fadiman's book in
Mississippi Quarterly, 29 (Summer 1979), 457-66.

7. *Faulkner: A Biography* (New York: Random House, 1974),
especially pp. 701-4, 760-66.

8. See Blotner, pp. 493-94, and Béatrice Lang, "An Un-
published Faulkner Story: 'The Big Shot,'" *Mississippi
Quarterly*, 26 (Summer 1973), 312-24.

9. These three stories are now available in *Uncollected
Stories of William Faulkner*, ed. Joseph Blotner (New York:
Random House, 1979). See Blotner's notes at the end of the
book.

10. *Uncollected Stories*, p. 531.

11. See my review of Fadiman in *Mississippi Quarterly*, pp. 460-61, and the anecdotes regarding the title in Blotner, p. 702.

12. Ficken (p. 268) has counted 160 paste-ons.

13. See Fadiman, pp. 30-66, and, in this collection, the "Chronology" of Stephen Meats.

14. See Fadiman, pp. 67-117.

15. It seems that at one time in the composition of *Light in August* Joe Christmas *had* black blood: by making Joe a "spiritual" mulatto, however, Faulkner did not alter his purpose, but emphasized it, rather, making racism not a matter of biology, but of reification in the look of the Other.

16. In his chapter on *Light in August* in *William Faulkner: The Yoknapatawpha Country* (New Haven and London: Yale University Press, 1963), called "The Community and the Pariah," Cleanth Brooks makes the community much more benevolent than it really is.

17. "An Introduction for *The Sound and the Fury*," ed. James B. Meriwether, *Southern Review*, 8 (October 1972), 705-10, quotation from pp. 709-10.

18. For a sample of such analogies, oppositions, and ambiguities, see Pitavy, pp. 42-47, 75-84.

19. The reader will have recognized here Lacan's categories.

20. *Faulkner in the University: Class Conferences at the University of Virginia, 1957-1958*, ed. Frederick L. Gwynn and Joseph L. Blotner (Charlottesville: University of Virginia Press, 1959), p. 199.

I. Structure and Themes

AS WHIRLWINDS IN THE SOUTH:
AN ANALYSIS OF *LIGHT IN AUGUST*

Phyllis Hirshleifer

I

Light in August differs rather strikingly from such novels
as *Absalom, Absalom!* or *The Sound and the Fury* in which a central family relationship provides a convenient and effective
dramatic focus. This sort of family framework is not merely
absent in *Light in August*; a positive effort has been made to
remove or obscure all suggestion of family ties, so that we
see the characters as conspicuously solitary individuals.
Even Lena, who is so much a symbol of family potentialities,
is first seen as a single figure on the road, distinct from
the society through which she is moving. Byron Bunch has lived
and worked in Jefferson for seven years, yet the town has
never discovered that he spends his Sundays leading the choir
in a country church, or that he visits Hightower. Through
Byron we encounter the baleful stranger Christmas, whose name
and complexion make him seem a foreigner, who deliberately
isolates himself in every way. Brown, the second stranger who
appears at the mill, is a man with an obviously false name,
of whom Byron thinks--

> ... there was no reason why he should have had or have
> needed any name at all. Nobody cared, just as Byron
> believed that no one (wearing pants, anyway) cared
> where he came from nor where he went nor how long he
> stayed. Because wherever he came from and wherever he
> had been, a man knew that he was just living on the
> country, like a locust. (p. 33)

Miss Burden, though a native of Jefferson, is a single,
lonely Northener living in her large empty house. The town
takes no interest in her until her death provides it with "an
emotional barbecue, a Roman holiday." Hightower, also a

Reprinted from Perspective, 2 (Summer 1949), 225-38.

resident of long standing, is a social outcast whose house no
one but Byron has entered in twenty-five years. Doc and Mrs.
Hines are strangers to Mottstown and, in large measure, to
each other. Percy Grimm, Christmas's "executioner," is at once
a leader of society and a personality estranged from it. He
can never forgive his parents for his having been born too
late to be in the war. His relation to the town is manipula-
tive, his dream something in which the townspeople become involved scarcely realizing its implications.

I wish to stress the isolated, or as Faulkner would put
it, "isolant" nature of the figures of *Light in August* because
it seems to me essential to Faulkner's purpose and because it
involves a narrative complexity and apparent lack of structural coordination which has troubled many readers. There has
been almost unanimous agreement among critics that *Light in
August* is one of the most beautifully written and strikingly
conceived of Faulkner's novels, but that it is structurally
defective. It seems to me, however, that thematic integration
is quite effective and that apparent flaws of the plot often
disappear entirely when the novel is approached in terms of
meaning.

The plot itself is, of course, complex and bulky. The
primary action, which takes place in and around Jefferson
during the week in August beginning with Miss Burden's death
and ending with Christmas's, takes on its full significance
only in terms of the background of the figures involved.
Because they are isolated figures, each with a distinct
history separately revealed, the sheer weight of the narrative is considerable. Time dislocations add to the complexity
of the plot, but serve to emphasize the continuity of past
and present by movement back and forth to related events
at different points of time. They also enable Faulkner to
juxtapose personalities and situations he wished to compare
or contrast.

Thus, as the first chapter closes we see Lena approaching
Jefferson. Chapter 2 opens with the stranger's arrival, but
the stranger is neither Lena nor Burch (for whom we might
reasonably have been prepared) but Christmas, who stands in
important symbolic contrast with Lena. The time of Christmas's
arrival is, of course, three years before Lena's. We are then
told briefly that Byron arrived seven years earlier--than
Lena, not Christmas. This brings together the comparable
personalities of Byron and Lena. Burch, arriving rapidly in
the narrative after his "master" Christmas, has actually
reached Jefferson two and a half years after Christmas, and
only six months before Lena.

These are only the first of a series of complex time
dislocations which seem to me to arise necessarily in a story

based on the interaction of strangers and, as almost all
Faulkner's novels are, on a gradually deepening perception
of the meaning of actions by repeated examination of them.
We are carried back into the past (and different points in
the past) in order to understand it and its influence on the
motivations of the present. And because the essential points
of similarity and contrast between the isolated figures of
Light in August might easily be obscured in direct chronological presentation, there is a unifying rather than a dis-
rupting effect in the juxtaposition of similar characters
and situations apart from the particular time involved.

This may not be what the critics find objectionable,
however. It is a technique characteristic of almost all
Faulkner's work, though the chunks of the past which interrupt
the main action of *Light in August* may seem particularly
lengthy and various. The failure of the two main characters,
Christmas and Lena, to meet at any point may be considered
a structural defect, but thematically it is utterly appropriate. They represent contrasted worlds, extremes of two
utterly opposed faiths, and their not meeting is significant
in a way in which no encounter could be. The symbolic value
of each is intensified by this apparent plot defect.

It is not, after all, the plot which is the center of
interest in a Faulkner novel, as Robert Penn Warren points
out, though the stories are so well told that they become
extremely engrossing in themselves. The structure of the
novel must surely be approached in regard to its theme or
meaning. This use of the term "theme" should, incidentally,
be distinguished from Malcolm Cowley's. In discussing the
structural defects of Faulkner's major novels, Cowley speci-
fies that there is a shift halfway through *Absalom, Absalom!*
"from the principal theme of Colonel Sutpen's ambition to
the secondary theme of incest and miscegenation" (*Viking
Portable*, p. 18). This seems to me misleading. "Incest and
miscegenation" represent the working out of Sutpen's doom
stemming from his ambition and do not constitute a separate
"theme" any more than violence, flight from women, consciousness of the negro world, are separate "themes" in *Light in
August*. They are various ways of looking at the central
theme of the plight of man cursed by the evil of the past
and his own alliance with that evil--a theme which is intensified rather than disorganized by the different areas
of symbolic reference which are associated with it.

Thematic integration is achieved by Faulkner in a variety
of ways. The recurrence of descriptive terms suggests that
certain figures are to be viewed in a similar light. Also,
though each story in the novel is different from the others,

there is a recurrence of such situations as that of a person
suffering savagely deliberate blows on the face. McEachern
abuses Christmas in this manner in connection with the sale
of the heifer, and the waitress's friends beat Joe in the
face after he has killed McEachern. Christmas himself repeatedly strikes Brown's face with ritualistic viciousness.
Doc Hines strikes his wife when she tries to stop him from
going after the circus man. There are related situations
involving injuries to the head. The savage fight between
Burch and Byron leaves the latter with a bloody head, Christmas's attack on Hightower leaves him with a bloody head, and
the decapitation of Miss Burden may be taken as the "type"
of such injuries.

The pattern of violence, of man's inhumanity to man, is
of course expressed in other ways as well, but the injuries
to head and face are important because they involve almost
every major personality of the book (and such minor ones as
Halliday, the man who captures Christmas in Mottstown and
quite unnecessarily hits him in the face several times). The
recurrence of the situation suggests recurrent human attitudes and a similarity of character and outlook among the
otherwise isolated figures of the novel.

The preoccupation with faces is of considerable symbolic
importance not only in the situations already mentioned, but
also as a recurrent image. Hightower sees his congregation,
and later the townsmen who mob Christmas, as "faces which
seem to glare with bodiless suspension as though from haloes."
His final vision is of a wheel in which all the faces he has
known are suspended peacefully at last. God, for Hightower,
is "the final and supreme Face Itself." The face is identified
with the whole being (or perhaps with the essence) and human
faces are seen in a "suspension" which suggests both crucifixion and the ascension through death into peace. The bodiless suspension of faces also indicates a cleavage between
mind and heart, conscious principle and human feeling, which
characterizes the crucified figures of the book, particularly
Christmas and Hightower himself. (This was first suggested
by Miss Ruth Lottridge of Radcliffe in a discussion of this
essay.)

Injuries to head and face, to the essential being, are
received and inflicted by almost all the major personalities
(except Lena who represents a contrasted way of life--indeed,
the way of life rather than death) and provide an important
link between them. *Light in August* is far less a novel about
distinct human beings with varied attitudes, compulsions,
hopes, and fears than it is a picture of man in a thousand
alternate situations which are critically alike, living out

a more or less inescapable pattern. It is not really inescapable, for Byron manages to ally himself with Lena, but the pattern is so nearly binding that the tragic figure of Christmas is the symbol of man. Hightower, when first told of the murder, says of Christmas--"Poor man, poor mankind," and the exclamation does not seem accidental. Christmas is, of course, a Christ figure, but he is so not as the Son of God, but as the Son of Man. He is Joe, son of Joe, as Doc Hines says, the figure of everyman driven by a violent past into a violent present, burdened by the curse of his ancestry, crucified as Hightower (and possibly Faulkner) sees every man crucified.

The isolated individuality of the personalities of the book, in view of the crucial similarities of their behavior and of the imagery by which they are depicted, suggests that almost any figures of the town--and the town is surely representative not only of the South but of human society in general--would exhibit similar tendencies. Faulkner has achieved a picture of the human family all the more striking in his having eliminated the immediate family background of his characters. Doc Hines is Christmas's grandfather, but primarily in the sense that man with his cruelties and evil is the progenitor of the next generation with its evil and despair. (If Christmas is a kind of Christ, Doc Hines may be considered an "old Adam.") Mrs. Hines's illusion that Lena's baby is "Joey," the son of Christmas, and Lena's own confusion at this, is of some significance. The baby is a kind of Christ child (to the circumstances of its birth may be added Hightower's impression of the child at Lena's breast as a face "which seems to hang suspended") and basically as much the heir of Christmas as Christmas is of "Grandad Hines." Christmas himself is as genuinely the son of McEachern, in spite of the accident of adoption, as Nathaniel is the son of Calvin Burden, who beats him as ruthlessly as McEachern beats Christmas. Miss Burden's corruption is the product of her grandfather's evil as surely as Christmas's savagery is his response to the code of brutality Hines and McEachern force upon him.

II

If *Light in August* is in a sense a novel about everyman, everyman is not without diverse potentialities and responses; and these are seen by Faulkner largely in terms of faith. Hightower is an ex-minister, Doc Hines is thought to be one. McEachern and Calvin Burden are religious fanatics. (The

names "Calvin" and the Scottish McEachern are pointedly suggestive.) If the avowed faith of these men is Christianity,
the actual one is a faith in violent self-assertion and almost
grateful acceptance of the violence of others. McEachern, that
righteous Christian, beats the boy to unconsciousness on a
Sunday, forgetting to go to church. His recollection of the
omission comes with the ironic description—

> McEachern began to pray. He prayed for a long time, his
> voice droning, soporific, monotonous. He asked that he
> be forgiven for trespass against the Sabbath and for
> lifting his hand against a child, an orphan, who was
> dear to God. He asked that the child's stubborn heart
> be softened and that the sin of disobedience be forgiven
> him also, through the advocacy of the man whom he had
> flouted and disobeyed, requesting that Almighty be as
> magnanimous as himself, and by and through and because
> of conscious grace. (p. 143)

McEachern, the advocate, is surely the most inverted Christ
of them all. His real religion is, of course, one of injure
and be injured. After Joe has fought with the boys McEachern
says, "I hope you left marks on them"; and he receives his
death at Joe's hands with "the furious and dream-like exaltation of a martyr." He is killed, it may be noted, by a blow
on the head, just as he is about to strike Christmas's face
as the representative of "the wrathful and retributive Throne."

Doc Hines, who also considers himself the instrument of
God's retribution against "bitchery and abomination," is an
ironic figure in the light of "He that is without sin among
you, let him first cast a stone at her." In a sense, Hines
and McEachern may indeed be God's instruments, but not as
they conceive it, as righteous men, but as the unrighteous
who originate and perpetuate the curse of evil which is on
all mankind. The faith of Joe Christmas, the man who professes
hatred of religion and who is taken for Satan by the negroes
whose church he breaks into—again to beat the minister about
the face—is in fact the same faith in violence as a return
for violence which the supposedly Christian Doc Hines holds.
(The latter also breaks into negro churches to preach hatred—
white supremacy!—instead of love.) In contrast with these
figures who do have a positive faith, however perverted, there
is the figure of Burch, who has no faith at all, not even the
merest pride in himself. When he has called the men at the
mill *bastards*, he is forced to retract in regard to each one
until there is no one left to whom the term can be applied
but himself. Burch's faithlessness is involved, of course,
not only in his flight from Lena, but also in his enactment

of the role of Judas to Joe Christmas. He is called a "disciple"
and described as betraying the man who befriended him for the
thousand dollar reward.

The central contrast of the book is, of course, between
the figures like Christmas who can respond to evil only with
further wrong and who cannot come to terms with the earth or
themselves except through martyrdom, and the figures of Lena
and Byron who have a faith which enables them to endure. Both
types of faith stem from the past. They represent a heritage
available to every man, but the choice must be made between
perpetuating the curse of the past by further violence or
enduring evil and holding on to what has been good in the
tradition, to human dignity, kindliness, and fidelity, which
to some extent mitigate the evil.

Lena's roots in the past are emphasized like Dilsey's.
The floor of her family's log house is also "worn smooth as
old silver by naked feet." She has faith and true humility
before God. She reckons the Lord will see to it that a family
will be together when a chap comes. She is not embittered or
even more than momentarily frightened by Burch's desertion;
for her faith gives her the strength to endure injury and,
in a way, to transmute evil to good. The society through which
Lena moves, the people who give her food, lodging, money, and
transportation because of her patient, undemanding modesty,
are, after all, the same people who crucify the Christmases
whose evil arouses their own.

Byron, in spite of Hightower's influence and his own
impulses to run away, is sufficiently secure in his faith,
even after his humiliation by Lena, to come back saying, "I
done come too far now. I be dog if I'm going to quit now."
The hillbillies, Byron and Lena, are, as Hightower recognizes,
"fine people," "the good stock peopling in tranquil obedience
to it the good earth." Their simple, unobtrusive faith in God
expresses itself in their kindly, courteous relations with
their fellow human beings. Byron offers his lunch pail to the
destitute Christmas "as reflex." He is as brave (in fighting
Burch) as he is generous, but his courage does not involve
a desire for either revenge or martyrdom; it represents only
the acceptance of a painful responsibility on behalf of Lena.

The sense of responsibility and of human dignity which
distinguishes Lena and Byron from the other figures of the
book is treated with some humor by Faulkner, but is nonethe-
less genuine. Lena, sucking the sardine oil from her fingers
as she remembers that she "et polite" at the Armstids, may
seem ludicrous, yet she really is a lady. She is unfailingly
courteous and thoughtful. She sweeps out the truck with a
gum branch (the branch itself is a symbol both of her relation

to God and her closeness to the earth) as responsibly as
any lady would set in order the family manor. For the earth
is Lena's home. However humorous her sense of the proprieties
by which one lives comfortably and considerately on it, the
sense is basic; she is in striking contrast with Burch who
is a locust on the land, a contemptibly humorous figure, and
with the tragic Christmas about whom

> there was something definitely rootless ... as though
> no town nor city was his, no street, no walls, no square
> of earth his home. (p. 27)

The humorous presentation of Lena and Byron, which at
least in part represents a consciously humorous view they take
of themselves ("Byron Bunch who weeded another man's laidby
crop..,," and Lena in climbing through the window to leave
home—"If it had been this hard to do before, I reckon I would
not be doing it now."), is of two-fold importance. Their
sense of humor, their lack of self-centered seriousness, is
perhaps part of the ability of these good, simple people to
endure. For the total effect of the novel, the humorous
handling of what are essentially the righteous figures makes
them far more agreeable than a serious treatment. Sympathy
is engaged for the tragic personalities while principle is
unobtrusively all on the side of Lena and Byron. Were they
self-righteous as well as right, the balance of the novel
would be destroyed. Faulkner's ironic view of the ideal (for
it is this that Lena largely represents in contrast with the
tragic reality of Joe Christmas) creates an element of surprise which he no doubt values, and also provides an essential
artistic balance.

The central contrast between the sincere, unpretentious
faith in God which characterizes Lena and Byron and the
fanatic faith in violence clothed in the language of Christianity which constitutes the religion of Doc Hines, McEachern,
Calvin Burden, is a contrast most strikingly exemplified in
Hightower's life. Hightower is Byron's friend and advisor,
assuming the role of a father confessor and conceiving of
his house almost as a church where Byron stumbles on the
first step whenever he enters, except when he enters in
pride. However, Hightower is not really Byron's guide in
relation to Lena, and Byron the good man, the sincere Christian, has little understanding of Hightower's character or
the meaning of his life. The bad odor of Hightower's "un-
washed flesh" is called by Byron in a moment of inspiration
"the odor of goodness," but in fact it relates the ex-minister
to Doc Hines who has a "quality of outworn violence like a
scent." (Bad smells are characteristically used by Faulkner

in this biblical sense as the outward sign of moral corruption. The romeo who by any other name would smell as sweet in "A Rose for Emily" and Charlotte's figurine named the Bad Smell in *The Wild Palms* are the most notable example of the device.) Byron is also mistaken in his interpretation of Hightower's passiveness. He thinks that Hightower has remained in Jefferson--

> ... because a fellow is more afraid of the trouble he might have than he ever is of the trouble he's already got. He'll cling to trouble he's used to before he'll risk a change. Yes. A man will talk about how he'd like to escape from living folks. But it's the dead folks that do him the damage. It's the dead ones that lay quiet in one place and dont try to hold him, that he cant escape from. (p. 69)

But this oddly distorted version of the "To be or not to be" soliloquy by no means explains Hightower's motives. He is indeed held in Jefferson by his dead grandfather, but far from wishing to escape this influence, he considers it the great satisfaction of his life--which makes the very worst ills not only bearable but positively welcome. It is not because he fears death, but because he has made the same covenant with it that Christmas has made, that Hightower refuses to leave Jefferson. The name "Hightower" itself may echo the threat in Isaiah that on the day of judgment "every high tower ... shall be bowed down, and the haughtiness of men shall be made low," and Hightower is assuredly one of those who have chosen the way of death. If Christmas's denial of life, of normal human responsibility, is expressed in his continuous irrational flight, Hightower's is no less explicit in the irrational refusal to flee. Both prefer a "voluptuous martyrdom" to the danger of involvement in ordinary human relationships.

Hightower is the most reflective figure of the book, and the next-to-last chapter, in which his background is finally revealed through his own despairing consciousness, is not anti-climactic after Christmas's death, but the vital philosophical counterpart of it. The moral alternatives are particularly clear in Hightower's life. His father and grandfather represent the two principles of man's heritage, indeed of his nature. The bluff heroic grandfather is identified with slavery and war, the father "was an abolitionist almost before the sentiment had become a word to percolate down from the North." He is a man of peace, yet when war comes, he takes part as a doctor (self-taught, for in peace he was a minister)--and is fully as heroic as the grandfather. Hightower's one feeling of admiration for this

father is that the blue patch on his coat may have meant that
he killed a Yankee, and this, of course, represents an utter
rejection of the whole meaning of the father's life. It is
not the heroism that Hightower values in his grandfather,
but the wanton self-destructiveness, as exemplified in the
moment of his death (breaking into a hencoop). It is this
principle with which the grandson allies himself, thinking,
"It is any man's privilege to destroy himself, so long as he
does not injure anyone else...." But the final horrifying
recognition is that Hightower has not only sacrificed his own
life in devotion to his grandfather but has driven his wife
to despair and death. And because Hightower had turned himself into the grandfather at that single instant of the latter's
career, the grandfather himself has destroyed the wife. The
grandfather has become a murderer through the effect of Hightower's worship of him, the dream itself corrupted by its
influence. This is perhaps the most complex statement of the
theme of sowing the wind and reaping the whirlwind, which
runs through the novel. Hightower's first name, Gail, which
he shares with his grandfather, suggests this theme, incidentally. He enters the church because it is "like a classic
and serene vase, where the spirit could be ... sheltered from
the harsh gale of living."

The rejection of his wife links Hightower with McEachern
and Doc Hines, both of whom reject and abuse their wives in
order to follow their false ideal, with Burch, whose rejection
of Lena and the child is the type of all denial of family love
and responsibility, and with Christmas, whose relationship
with Miss Burden (a grotesque survey of a whole lifetime of
sexual experience) demonstrates his utter unwillingness to
become involved in love. The religious significance of this
rejection of women is clear to Hightower. God created Woman,
he thinks, "to be not alone the recipient and the receptacle
of the seed of his body but of his spirit too." When Hightower
declines to make his wife the partner of his dream, the receptacle of his spirit, "the face of God turned away in very
shame." Hightower is doomed because on the stage of the church
he has offered the idol of his grandfather instead of "the
crucified shape of pity and love," because he has taken a
wife not for love--"not for My ends," the accusing Face of
God tells him--but for his own, namely to get to Jefferson.

It is perhaps worth noting that the conflict between the
"galloping hooves" of Hightower's dream and his wife has the
symbolic force of a contrast between normal and abnormal
sexuality. Horses are characteristically used by Faulkner in
reference to abnormal sexual experience in contrast with cows
which represent normal love and fecundity. (This is, of

course, most fully developed in *The Hamlet*.) Christmas's statement, "Why in hell do I want to smell horses?... It is because
they are not women. Even a mare horse is a kind of man,"
suggests the meaning of the horse symbol; and the relation of
Christmas to the rather masculine Miss Burden is in many ways
similar to the relationship between Jewel and his horse (the
obscenity, mingled caresses and blows) in *As I Lay Dying*.

The sexual aspects of Christmas's story have the symbolic
importance of a failure of love in the most general sense,
not only the love between man and woman, family affection,
and that between man and his fellows, but the love between
God and man which is expressed through human relationships.
Food, it may be noted, is a recurrent sexual symbol (Miss
Burden, the waitress, the dietitian all supply Christmas with
edibles, and the motif is concluded with his discovery shortly
before death that he no longer has to eat), but the rejection
of women's "muck" is the same when Miss Burden tries to entangle him as when Mrs. McEachern tries to mother the boy,
and both situations are comparable to the rejection of the
muck in Byron's lunch pail. Christmas systematically refuses
every form of personal tie. The only thing he consumes willing-
ly is the toothpaste, significantly enough called the "worm,"
and suggestive of the original falling off from God.

The imagery of *Light in August* stresses the dominating
religious motif. The Christ image, as seen primarily in Joe
Christmas, is a fundamental device of the book. The three
years Christmas spends with Miss Burden may be taken as an
enlarged three days of involvement in life (an ironic inversion of the three days in the tomb) from which he gains
release by the more explicit crucifixion which begins with
the arrest on Friday and ends with his death on Monday. This
is specifically described in terms which suggest resurrection--

> It [his blood] seemed to rush out of his pale body like
> the rush of sparks from a rising rocket; upon that black
> blast the man seemed to rise soaring into their memories
> forever and ever. (p. 440)

The three days in which Doc Hines removes Christmas from the
orphanage are perhaps a minor death for him which concludes
with his resurrection as Joe McEachern. Also, the three days
of waiting after Joe has watched the dietitian represent a
kind of martyrdom for her as well as for him. Hightower's
final vision comes as a kind of crucifixion for him and is
described in terms of ascension.

> Then it seems to him that some ultimate dammed flood
> within him breaks and rushes away. He seems to watch it,
> feeling himself losing contact with earth, lighter and
> lighter, emptying, floating. (p. 466)

"Ultimate dammed flood" indicates the nature of this and
the other crucifixions of the book.[1] If Faulkner constantly
draws the figure of Christ before us, the image is characteristically grotesque. Christmas's "slashed garments" after Grimm
has emasculated him may be a reminder of "They parted my
garments," but the scene involves monstrous irony. The whole
use of the Christ symbol is ironic. Christmas is identified
with hatred; he is the instrument of destruction (for McEachern, Miss Burden, Hightower, as well as himself).

There is the most striking recurrence of religious similes
and metaphors throughout *Light in August* which links similar
personalities and provides a sustaining atmosphere for the
Christ symbol. Grimm's voice is "clear and outraged like that
of a young priest." Max, the man in the restaurant, has "an
inscrutable and monklike face." The townsmen have "almost
the air of monks in a cloister." When McEachern is beating
him, Joe has "a rapt, calm expression like a monk," "save for
the surplice he might have been a Catholic choir boy." The
barn in which they stand is described almost as a church and
the snorts of the beasts bring to mind the manger in which
Christ was born. Incidentally, McEachern's statement, "You
would believe that a stable floor, the stamping place of
beasts, is the proper place for the word of God. But I'll
learn you that too," has special pointedness since a manger
was a suitable place for the Son of God. McEachern's feeling
that Christmas was a "heathenish name" involves similar irony.

Various images other than the religious ones are reiterated
with symbolic force. The "gale" suggested by Hightower's name
appears frequently in other connections as well. Christmas
feels the wind "dark and cool" as he goes to kill Miss Burden.
After her death, however, the pillar of smoke left by the
burnt house stands "tall and windless above the trees." When
the boys fight after Christmas has kicked the negro girl,
"it was as though a wind had blown among them, hard and clean."
Hightower's dream is, of course, a "cyclone"; his phantoms
come "like a long sighing of wind in trees." The wind is life,
the harsh life of crucified man and the harsh continuity with
the past. (Through it is not a religious image in the same
sense as the Christ symbol, the biblical suggestiveness of
the wind motif is clear.)

There is a consistent use of shadow imagery in connection
with Christmas and the figures like him. Hightower sees himself as a "shadowy figure among shadows," and, of course,
his past is seen in terms of phantoms. Between Miss Burden
and the town are "the phantoms of the old spilled blood and
the old horror of anger and fear." Christmas, as he goes
through the negro world of Freedman Town,

... contrived somehow to look more lonely than a lone
telephone pole in the middle of a desert. In the wide,
empty, shadowbrooded street he looked like a phantom,
a spirit, strayed out of its own world, and lost. (p.
106)

In the orphanage Christmas was "sober and quiet as a
shadow." He sneaks from McEachern's house "with the shadow-
like agility of a cat." When the waitress tells the outraged,
furious Christmas she is "sick," he flees, "the shape, the
shadow" fading down the road from her.

The image of the road and the pattern of flight and pursuit
are, of course, strikingly reiterated. Christmas is perpetually
in compulsive flight--from the waitress, McEachern, Jeffer-
son--essentially from himself. The hopelessly slow motion of
the horse he rides from the dance hall registers the futility
of all his frantic running. The street of Christmas's life
offers no escape except through death for, as Gavin Stevens
says, "there was too much running with him, stride for stride
with him. Not pursuers: but himself: years, acts, deeds omitted
and committed...." Like Christmas, Burch seems to be in constant motion throughout the novel, fleeing from Lena, running
with the dogs to capture Christmas, and finally fleeing from
Byron with a practiced agility in hopping trains. Lena's motion, in contrast with the frantic flight of the men, is, of
course, slow, measured, peaceful, "like a change of season."
She advances "like something moving forever and without
progress across an urn," for her life is "a peaceful corridor
paved with unflagging and tranquil faith." (There is, of
course, an ironic inversion of the "mad pursuit" and "struggle
to escape" of the figures on Keats's Grecian Urn in Faulkner's
use of the image.) Lena's slow motion reflects the assurance
of Isaiah that "he that believeth shall not make haste."

The title of the novel (like the symbolic names of so
many of the characters) emphasizes a number of important motifs.
Light in August may refer primarily to Lena, who is to give
birth, but also suggests the lightness of the ascension and
the Light of God and of religious insight. In addition to the
lightness of release which appears in connection with Christmas and Hightower (and surely the contrast between the lightness of Lena in bringing forth life and that which involves
passage into death is a crucial suggestion), there is a great
deal of emphasis on light and dark throughout the book. We
are shown houses that are dark, ones with one lamp or two--
and street lamps are specifically called "Augusttremulous
lights," so that comments on light and dark which might otherwise seem casual are caught up in the title. A chiaroscuro
pattern is a definite part of the artistic organization of

the book. (I think Richard Chase is quite right in this and
some of his other interpretations, though his notion that
Faulkner's technique is a poetry of physics seems a little
farfetched.)

The light-dark pattern is caught up with negro and sexual
symbolism in such a passage as:

> He [Joe] was standing still now, breathing quite
> hard, glaring this way and that. About him the cabins
> were shaped blackly out of blackness by the faint, sultry
> glow of kerosene lamps. On all sides, even within him,
> the bodiless fecundmellow voices of negro women mur-
> mured. It was as though he and all other manshaped life
> about him had been returned to the lightless hot wet
> primogenitive Female. He began to run, glaring, his
> teeth glaring, his inbreath cold on his dry teeth and
> lips, toward the next street lamp. (p. 107)

Joe's death, the soaring or lightness with which his
peace comes, is very basically an escape from the female
world which has tried to entangle him (in life itself) and
the negro world whose symbolic meaning is much the same. The
association of visual light and dark with male and female and
negro and white (Joe's light shoes coated with black mud
symbolize the negro and white aspects, as do his white shirt
and dark pants) draws together the implications of "light"
in regard to Christmas's plight, which is every man's. Faulkner's titles are always good, but seldom better than this, I
think.

Christmas's negro aspect, it is worth noting, is primarily
a matter of psychology. He does not know that he is a negro,
but finds it useful to believe. His negro blood is the symbolic source of his homelessness in the white world just as
his white blood would "make him look like a pea in a pan full
of coffee beans." He rejects the negro girl presumably to
reserve himself for the white world, but deliberately tells
the waitress he is a negro to avoid acceptance in her world.
The tragedy of Christmas's being both negro and white is
that not one but two worlds are open to him, in either of
which he could find a way to endure. But Christmas is utterly
a lost soul who has no place on earth and wishes none.

The negro in Christams is, of course, also the curse of
slavery (perhaps of human injustice in general) which the
white man must bear, the black cross on which Miss Burden
sees every white child crucified; but the curse is on black
and white alike. Nathaniel Burden says,

> The curse of the black race is God's curse. But the
> curse of the white race is the black man who will be

forever God's chosen own because He once cursed Him.
(p. 240)[2]

and Christmas is doomed both as a black man who has injured
and rejected his brothers and as a white--as man, in short.
I have seen him as everyman, but he might be called ultra man,
since his character and experience involve such concentrated
symbolism.

The central theme of *Light in August* is that of man's
inhumanity and the ruin it brings upon him. It is a theme
seen on several levels, historically, in terms of slavery
and the Civil War, on the personal level as violence between
man and his fellow man and the revulsion between man and
woman which is generally symbolic of the rejection of
divine love. The richness of symbolic reference and the
diversity of the personalities involved make for a complex,
but not, I think, for an uncoordinated novel. The isolated
figures of *Light in August* are drawn together by the most
striking parallels of imagery and situation, and the result
is a novel of great dramatic intensity. Christmas, Hightower, Miss Burden, McEachern, Grimm--the doomed general-
ity--stand together in contrast with Lena and Byron, the
faithful who are no more than a remnant, possibly only an
ideal.

NOTES

1. Interestingly, Hirshleifer had read here "damned"
instead of "dammed." I have restored Faulkner's text (editor's
note).

2. In both the manuscript and the typescript, Faulkner
wrote: "He once cursed him"--which invalidates any heretical
reading of this chapter (editor's note).

THEMATIC DESIGN IN
*LIGHT IN AUGUST**

Carl Benson

Of all the readers who have sought the thread which would
afford safe entrance into *Light in August*, a labyrinth of
tangled lives, creeds, fates, and destinies, Cleanth Brooks
seems to me to have come closest to comprehending the novel
in its totality. He says, "The community is everywhere in this
novel." And he says, "Unless the controlling purposes of the
individual are related in some fashion to those which other
men assume, the individual is indeed isolated, and is forced
to fall back on his own personal values with all the liability
to fanaticism and distortion." I subscribe fully to these
statements, but it seems to me that Mr. Brooks may be over-
simplifying and limiting *Light in August* when he says: "The
various characters who act and suffer in this novel are all
people outside the community, and whatever their special
psychological isolation, it is given objective reference and
dramatic meaning by their alienation from the community in
which they live or into which they have come."

*Read before the American Literature Section of the South
Atlantic Modern Language Association, November 1952. In addition to the critics of Faulkner cited in the text and many
others, I am indebted to Irving Howe for the Anderson parallel.
There are many points of agreement between my reading and the
essays of Robert D. Jacobs, "Faulkner's Tragedy of Isolation,"
and William Van O'Connor, "Protestantism in Yoknapatawpha
County," both available in *Southern Renascence*. Indeed, there
is general agreement as to the central moral issues in Faulkner's work; the problem is to relate the narrative structure
to the pervasive moral concerns.

Solidarity within the community is certainly the central
subject, but the characters are not all outside the community.
Furthermore, those who are outside are outside in different
degrees, and the book achieves its particular form because the
different degrees are so intermeshed as to constitute a narrative and dramatic presentation of an essentially thematic
structure. If we are to attain a Coleridgean ideal and account
for the work as a structural whole, we must account for the
presence in the novel of these "special psychological isola-
tions" and the battles which the characters fight, or refuse
to fight, or are unable because of important limitations to
fight; and we must so phrase a statement of theme as to account
for the presence and the relationships of these particular lives.

Light in August rises out of Faulkner's tragic vision of
man as inescapably dual in nature. In the psychological
dialectic sustaining it the thesis is: the world in which we
live is a chaos of mixed evil and good, a chaos which stems
from (1) limited or lip service to moral (community) orders
which are selfishly conceived and so corrupted, (2) human
incapacity to adopt any code without its ultimately becoming
rigid--humane conviction inevitably hardens into inhumane
convention. The antithesis: despite the moral anarchy arising
necessarily from this thesis, the individual realizes himself
only in terms of community values, and he must submit himself
to the larger good or perish.

The dramatically demonstrated impossibility of molding a
compassionate community of isolative and selfish motives and
ideals makes Light in August Faulkner's most pessimistic
novel. As the theme is worked out, we are made increasingly
aware of the ultimately insoluble ethic problem which is the
core of the tragedy: Man is not simply a moral being with
dual leanings towards self-realization and communal obliga-
tions; the two become in actual life (in the microcosm of
Jefferson in Light in August) so interwoven that one may
convince himself that his own private demands are, or should
be, those of the community; or he may seize upon certain
commonly esteemed values with such fervor that he cannot
allow his views to be questioned. We are reminded of Sherwood
Anderson's story of the old writer with his theory of how
truths become grotesque. "It was his notion," says Anderson,
"that the moment one of the people took one of the truths
to himself, called it his truth, and tried to live his life
by it, he became a grotesque and the truth he embraced became
a falsehood."

In Light in August Faulkner is dealing with a group of
such grotesques; but Faulkner cuts deeper than Anderson's
old writer, because Faulkner's grotesques, despite their

strangeness and despite the illusions which render them
grotesque, are all too human to allow us to conclude that
Faulkner is simply asserting the overriding importance of
community obligation. He is insisting that there are within
man and within the community itself forces that are inherently
divisive. He accomplishes his intent by exploring the rationale
of various types of alienation and illusion and by postulating
a graded scale of illusions and their effects upon their
possessors as communal beings. This graded scale constitutes
the complex of ethic judgment upon which the comprehension of
the novel as a whole depends.

What we have to deal with in *Light in August* is the
peculiar collocation in Jefferson, Mississippi, of various
lives whose stories cannot be accounted for on the basis of
narrative alone. If, however, we see that the thematic conflict is between rigid patterns of self-involvement on the one
hand and commitment to a solidarity that transcends self on
the other, we must see that the chief character, the moral
protagonist, because he alone can serve as an ethic sliderule
by means of which we can compute the relative failures and
successes of the other characters, is Gail Hightower, the old
unchurched minister who is, as we open the story, ironically
"Done Damned in Jefferson." It may be that at the end he is
still damned as far as Jefferson is concerned, but through
him the reader who inhabits a larger, though not dissimilar,
community is enabled to estimate the relative moral worth of
the other characters and the fixations which inhibit or limit
their participation in society.

Actually, it might reasonably be argued that Hightower
is also the central figure in a strict narrative sense and
that far too many readers have been misled by the seemingly
simple opposition of the violent Joe and the placid Lena.
After all, Byron brings to Hightower the problems of Lena
and Joe as well as his own. Joe's grandmother also comes to
the old minister for assistance. Indeed, a good part of the
action of the entire book seems designed to evoke the action
or the response of Hightower. But it is his function of moral
hero with which we are principally concerned. My argument
is that he is a Yoknapatawpha Heyst who, like Conrad's hero,
achieves a victory by traveling the moral distance from
selfish immunity to redemption by the conviction that immunity
cannot be bought. We have hints that his redemption is of
major importance almost from the beginning. As soon as Byron
Bunch brings him the problem of helping Lena, he breaks into
a sweat of fear of being drawn from the isolation he thinks
he had paid for. Thereafter, as Byron continues to ask his
aid, though he replies, "I won't," and "I have paid," his

compassionate nature gradually asserts its mastery; by the
end he is so involved with "poor mankind" that he has delivered
Lena's child and has tried to save Joe Christmas from Percy
Grimm.

If it be objected that Hightower is no fit candidate for
the role of moral hero, it may be said that Faulkner is aware
of this irony, because he made it. Indeed, Faulkner's profound
pessimism and his ultimate idealism both find witness in the
use of Hightower as moral standard: pessimism, because we are
given no better than Hightower as the sliderule for solidarity;
idealism, because Hightower rises from the most foolish and
inhumane illusion of all to tremendous heights by the abnegation of the illusion. He achieves moral stature in the only
way possible for him--by descending into the pit of himself
and ripping from his heart his dearest sin.

It is significant that Hightower's recognition of the true
nature of his cherished illusion should be saved for the magnificent penultimate chapter--a chapter which, despite its
strategic position and rhetorical splendor, has been generally
neglected. Faulkner has cunningly withheld the key piece of
his ethic jigsaw puzzle until the end so that the reader can
contemplate the finished lives of the characters with the
Hightower compassion in which the novel was conceived. The
very imagery of the chapter compels this reading.

We have seen Hightower earlier get on the road back to
the community. We have seen him first as the village "they"
describe him to Byron Bunch: the young preacher came to
Jefferson with a frustrated wife and a bewildering confusion
of God and a heroic grandfather. We have seen how the natural
outrage of his parishioners has deprived him of his church.
But we have also seen the sensitive though reluctant response
he made to Byron's overtures to interest him in action for
others. Shortly before this final chapter, his heart has been
so engaged by the need of others that he has delivered Lena's
baby and experienced a great satisfaction ("I showed them");
his sympathy has gone out to Joe's grandmother; he has even
tried, with an obvious lie, to save Joe. But all this is mere
prelude; and it is important to note that he has not yet seen
the rightness in Byron's love for Lena: he has not come from
his selfishness enough to do that, for it would imply a recognition of his own failure for his wife, a self-discovery re-
served for his last scene.

In this last scene we finally understand the childhood
obsession that formed the original cause of his desire for
immunity: the growing-up in a house populated by three
phantoms (the sick mother, the harshly rigorous yet tame
father, the old Negro woman) and a ghost, the heroic grand-

father about whom the Negro woman told him stories, who was
shot with a fowling piece while he was engaged in the very
unmilitary, and yet somehow grand, prank of robbing a chicken
coop. Brooding over this image of selfless, magnificent folly
has caused the young Gail Hightower to become convinced that
"I had already died one night twenty years before I saw light,"
and has compelled him to believe that "My only salvation must
be to return to the place to die where my life had already
ceased before it began." To this freakish illusion he has
subordinated his entire life. When, for instance, he receives
a call to the ministry, which should be a way to spiritual
life (a community), it is for him merely a shelter, wherein

> he could see his future, his life, intact and on all
> sides complete and inviolable, like a classic and serene
> vase, where the spirit could be born anew sheltered
> from the harsh gale of living and die so, peacefully,
> with only the far sound of the circumvented wind, with
> scarce even a handful of rotting dust to be disposed
> of. That was what the word seminary meant: quiet and
> safe walls within which the hampered and garmentworried
> spirit could learn anew serenity to contemplate without
> horror or alarm its own nakedness. (p. 453)

He uses the call to the ministry, the influences of the
seminary and of his wife, to "shun the harsh gale of living,"
to get the pastorship in Jefferson, where his grandfather
had died. Now, in his last revery as he sits dying, he perceives that by using the church to forward his own selfish
desire he has participated in the hardening of the church
into doctrinal inhumanity:

> ... that which is destroying the Church is not the
> outward groping of those within it nor the inward
> groping of those without, but the professionals who
> control it and who have removed the bells from its
> steeples.... He seems to see the churches of the world
> like a rampart, like one of those barricades of the
> middleages planted with dead and sharpened stakes,
> against truth and against that peace in which to sin
> and be forgiven which is the life of man. (p. 461)

Hightower is finally beginning to see the enormity of
his moral shortcomings, for he says, "I acquiesced. Nay, I
did worse: I served it. I served it by using it to forward
my own desire."
Here Faulkner introduces his effective turning-wheel
imagery. Hightower's awakened moral consciousness turns
slowly, like a wheel in heavy sand, as he unwillingly accepts

the implications of his misspent life. He sees that he has
been

> ... a charlatan preaching worse than heresy, in utter
> disregard of that whose very stage he preempted, offer-
> ing instead of the crucified shape of pity and love, a
> swaggering and unchastened bravo killed with a shotgun
> in a peaceful henhouse.... (p. 462)

He sees that in his search for immunity he has created a
humanly and religiously false martyrdom for himself; but he
still tries to find excuses:

> "But I was young then.... And after all, I have paid.
> I have bought my ghost, even though I did pay for it
> with my life.... It is any man's privilege to destroy
> himself, so long as he does not injure anyone else, so
> long as he lives to and of himself--" (p. 464)

And now the final horror, still in terms of the turning
wheel:

> He is aware of the sand now; with the realization of
> it he feels within himself a gathering as though for
> some tremendous effort. Progress now is still progress,
> yet it is now indistinguishable from the recent past
> like the already traversed inches of sand which cling
> to the turning wheel, raining back with a dry hiss that
> before this should have warned him: "... revealed to
> my wife my hunger, my ego ... instrument of her despair
> and shame ..." and without his having thought it at
> all, a sentence seems to stand fullsprung across his
> skull, behind his eyes: *I dont want to think this. I
> must not think this. I dare not think this* As he sits
> in the window, leaning forward above his motionless
> hands, sweat begins to pour from him, springing out
> like blood, and pouring. Out of the instant the sand-
> clutched wheel of thinking turns on with the slow
> implacability of a mediaeval torture instrument, beneath
> the wrenched and broken sockets of his spirit, his life:
> "Then, if this is so, if I am the instrument of her
> despair and death, then I am in turn instrument of some-
> one outside myself. And I know that for fifty years I
> have not even been clay: I have been a single instant
> of darkness in which a horse galloped and a gun crashed.
> And if I am my dead grandfather on the instant of his
> death, then my wife, his grandson's wife ... the de-
> baucher and murderer of my grandson's wife, since I
> could neither let my grandson live or die...." (pp. 464-
> 65)

Thus, in the moment of final recognition, Hightower sees
destroyed his cheating martyrdom, his justification for his
behavior to his wife and the church, his immunity, and the
cherished ghost itself.

In order to accentuate the significance of Hightower's
moral struggle and victory, resulting in the abnegation of
the illusion, Faulkner says, "The wheel, released, seems to
rush on with a long sighing sound.... It is going fast and
smooth now, because it is freed now of burden, of vehicle,
axle, all. In the lambent suspension of August [here perhaps
is the moral significance of the title] into which night is
about to fully come, it seems to engender and surround itself
with a faint glow like a halo." The function of the wheel
imagery shifts. The wheel is disengaged from the private
conscience of Hightower and spins before him carrying on its
circumference the faces of the people who have populated the
novel. It is as if the old minister, freed at last of his
morally debilitating illusion, has earned the right to pass
judgment on the people he has ignored, misunderstood, or
wronged. He sees all the chief figures of the novel and even
some individually insignificant members of his congregation.
And in the compassion he has attained by his acknowledgment
of the ubiquity of human responsibility, he perceives that
the faces of all suffering humanity are pretty much alike.

In summoning before himself for review and rejection his
past life, Hightower reveals the source of moral achievement:
he manifests the power of choice, of free will. Just as it
was within his power as moral agent to reject the community
for immunity, so also it is within his power to reject im-
munity--to earn his redemption, as Robert Penn Warren might
say, by being judge at his own trial before the bar of communal justice. In exercising the power of choice and in becoming the compassionate observer, Hightower seems to speak
for Faulkner and to be raised out of himself into a sort of
mediate figure between the community, including the readers,
and the more alienated figures of the novel. I think Warren
Beck has something like this in mind when, in speaking of
the "Compassionate troubled observers" of several of Faulkner's
works, he says, "It is no doubt significant of Faulkner's
own attitude that these compassionate observers so largely
provide the reflective point of view from which the story is
told and thereby determine its moral atmosphere."

If we reflect now on the story of Joe Christmas, we will
see that it is, in a sense, precisely antithetical to that
of Hightower. This Christmas story is of a man who has no
choice in any meaningful sense of the word. His responses are
entirely conditioned by exterior forces; though he tries to

attain selfhood as a moral agent, he is doomed to failure, because he cannot break out of the circle of conventional attitudes towards his being the son of a white mother and a mulatto father. The fact that he may have no Negro blood (Doc Hines is not exactly a reliable witness) only intensifies the moral nature of his struggle. He is convinced he has, and it is his consciousness of being a misfit between two worlds, of being unable to attain true human status in either, that is determining. He tries to live alternately as white with white, as black with black; but always, we are given to understand, the other side of his being, his other blood, rebels at not finding its realization.

But Faulkner is not content to explain the isolation of Christmas, his failure to find a community, in terms of conflicting blood strains alone. The isolation is reinforced by derivative and ancillary conflicts. Christmas is delivered as an infant to a mechanically administered orphanage, where, in the strict uniform of the wards of the community, he hears himself called "nigger" as early as he can understand the word. This psychic wound sets him apart from the other wards. Then, when we might expect at least some love from his foster parents, we discover that he has been adopted by a sadistic Calvinist, whose rigorous exactions of religious duties seem to Joe but a continuation, in slightly different terms, of the harsh treatment of the orphanage. He accepts the cruelty of his foster father, McEachern, rather than the love of Mrs. McEachern because of this continuity; the emotion of love or sympathy confuses him. In short, he reaches maturity in a world which has shown him so little compassion that he does not know how to deal with it. It is no wonder that his first love affair should be with the tough little prostitute, Bobbie Allen; and it is no wonder that Faulkner describes him, as he first appears in Jefferson, as having "something definitely rootless about him as though no town nor city was his, no street, no walls, no square of earth his home."

He is doomed to remain rootless, to find no home, but the point is that his failure to become integrated in a community derives from the fact that his world is deterministic; it denies choice, and it is deterministic because the conventionalized attitude others maintain towards him denies his individuality. Faulkner records this determinism and Christmas's pitiable attempt to become a human entity with sharpest distinction in a rather subtle passage. A week after his murder of Joanna Burden, Christmas is riding in a wagon towards Mottstown:

> "And yet I have been further in these seven days than in all the thirty years," he thinks. "But I have never

got outside that circle. I have never broken out of the
ring of what I have already done and cannot ever undo,"
he thinks quietly, sitting on the seat, with planted
on the dashboard before him the shoes, the black shoes
smelling of negro: that mark on his ankles the gauge
definite and ineradicable of the black tide creeping
up his legs, moving from his feet upward as death moves.
(p. 321)

Here Joe is attempting to assume responsibility for his own
acts (Faulkner always insists that responsibility is the
measure of the human condition), and it is in a way true that
in the seven days since the murder Joe has come closer than
ever before to attaining an independent being; at least society
has recognized him as an individual. But the circle was not,
as he would like to believe, constructed by his own acts; it
was, rather, composed of the loveless and mechanistic societal
patterns which surrounded all his years; and in the fine
rhetoric of the last sentence Faulkner has expanded the
synecdoche of the black shoes into a symbol which suggests
the true nature of the circle.

At one point Faulkner phrases the human-nonhuman limbo
in which Christmas lives even more pointedly. Just before the
murder of Miss Burden, Faulkner says of him, "He believed
with calm paradox that he was the volitionless servant of the
fatality in which he believed he did not believe." "Volitionless servant of fatality" is precisely the right phrase for
Joe Christmas, for the central contrast of the book between
Gail Hightower and Christmas is based upon an assumption which
reminds one forcibly of the distinction Yeats makes between
Fate and Destiny. Destiny is from within the very being of
the individual whereas Fate is imposed from without. In *Light
in August* the man of destiny, Hightower, shapes his own
destiny by acts of will, and he is, therefore, morally
accountable for his choices. Christmas, shaped by exterior
forces and attitudes, has no power over fate and can, therefore, never be responsible.

Some such distinction is what Faulkner has in mind when
he speaks through Joanna Burden and in his own voice as omniscient narrator of the black curse every white child bears
from birth and when he speaks of the Player who moves Percy
Grimm, as if Grimm is only the instrument of fate, implacably
into the pursuit, shooting, and emasculation of Christmas.
The Player, as opposed to the "crucified and suffering Christ"
who enters Hightower's last revery, is mentioned only in
this context; and I believe that the Player imagery and the
black curse mean that we have laid a curse upon ourselves
by depriving any man for whatever reason (black blood or

other) of his destiny. Such an intent would account for Faulkner's description of the effect of the death of Christmas upon
the representatives of the community who have joined in running
him to earth:

> For a long moment he looked up at them with peaceful
> and unfathomable and unbearable eyes. Then his face,
> body, all, seemed to collapse, to fall in upon itself,
> and from out the slashed garments about his hips and
> loins the pent black blood seemed to rush like a released
> breath. It seemed to rush out of his pale body like the
> rush of sparks from a rising rocket; upon that black
> blast the man seemed to rise soaring into their memories
> forever and ever. They are not to lose it, in whatever
> peaceful valleys, beside whatever placid and reassuring
> streams of old age, in the mirroring faces of whatever
> children they will contemplate old disasters and newer
> hopes. It will be there, musing, quiet, steadfast, not
> fading and not particularly threatful, but of itself
> alone serene, of itself alone triumphant. (pp. 439-40)

The "they" will remember because though Percy Grimm alone
committed the culturally sanctioned murder and atrocity, "they"
are implicitly involved; and they will never forget because
the symptomatic act in which they are involved is an act that
denies not only human justice, but also, as far as Joe Christmas is concerned, moral being. This interpretation, incidentally, is reinforced by the contrasting treatments of the
deaths of Hightower and Christmas. We are given the last
moments of Hightower and the rehabilitation of his moral consciousness in his own interior monologue; the death of Christmas, on the other hand, is handled steadily from without.

   Joe Christmas and Gail Hightower are the extreme poles
of morality between which all the other major and minor
characters fall. But, as I have pointed out, since Christmas
is blamelessly irresponsible, communally impotent, we have
to fall back on Hightower, who moves from selfish immunity
to compassion, as encompassing within the bounds of his single
being the range of communal morality. It is not Joe's tragedy,
because Joe is never truly an agent; he is always played upon;
despite his frenzied efforts to attain selfhood, his is a
fate he never made. Christmas and Hightower are in ethic
terms the most complex figures of the novel, and perhaps that
is the reason they have been commonly misunderstood, despite
the relatively much more elaborate treatment Faulkner has
given them. The other characters can be more quickly accounted
for.

   In terms of a graded scale of community participation,
Lena Grove is not communityless at all; in fact, wherever she

goes she relies on human fellowship; and it responds to her
trust by giving her what she needs--a night's rest with the
Armstids, Byron's room, a place to have her baby, and finally
even, we are led to believe, a decent man for a husband. She
always finds people "right kind" and sets out afoot to find
the man who seduced her, serene in her conviction that "a
family ought to all be together when a chap comes. Specially
the first one. I reckon the Lord will see to that." Many of
the good simple folk of Yoknapatawpha County are lucky enough
to possess such a feeling of thoughtless trust, and it is good
that such people should make happy communal adjustments; but
Lena's assurance does imply a high degree of moral unawareness, to which Faulkner calls attention by observing that she
possesses a "tranquil and calm unreason." It is aesthetically
fitting that her career should open and close the novel, for
she is the representative of the ordinary folk who possess so
easily the solidarity which is the focal point of the novel
and the goal, in some terms, of the more violent figures. But
to think of her as the moral standard of the novel is, it
seems to me, to ignore the careful elaboration of Hightower
and to create an ideal of uncritical simplicity. In truth,
she can no more break out of communal patterns of behavior
than Christmas can break into them; and it may be said that
she experiences no moral change or achievement.

At the opening of *Light in August* Byron Bunch is morally
neutral. He observes certain conventions faultlessly: for
instance, he rigorously minds his own five-minute rest periods
on Saturday mornings when there is no one around to check on
him, and he sings in a rural church every Sunday; but all he
does is done habitually, mechanically, without conviction;
and so, though he lives a life approved by community conventions, he may be said to be morally unawakened. When he falls
in love with Lena, however, he undergoes a transformation
and tries to become a part of the living community, not just
a clock-punching machine. To be sure, after years of noncom-
mitment, he finds that life comes haltingly hard; but by the
end Byron, as the salesman sees, is making progress toward
union with Lena, and, through Lena, with life itself. The end
of his achievement will be, on an absolute scale, higher than
that of Hightower; but Byron has not had as far to go, and
his moral victory is far less significant.

We must consider now those characters who remain alienated
from the community because their ideals, despite their origins
in genuinely human feelings, have become inhumane by being
codified into rigid patterns, and, persisting as codes, have
rendered their possessors incapable of true participation.
Joanna Burden, for example, because of a devotion to abolition

on the part of her forebears, continues in the abolitionist
tradition. But her adherence to the ideal of her grandfather
is, in her time, unreasonable, academic, and blighted by the
revenge motif which attends it from the beginning. She is like
Hightower in her devotion to the past, but unlike him in that
her moral enslavement to her Calvinist-abolitionist family is
so complete that the quintessential compassion, which finally
redeems Hightower, is absolutely lacking. She does not mesh her
life with that of Jefferson at all; and the town has set up
its own pattern of ignoring her, that is, until the residents
learn that she has been keeping house for a man of Negro blood,
whereupon, ironically, she fits into another pattern, this one
worthy of interest. In sum, her servitude to the codes of the
past has blotted out natural human affection (her unnatural-
ness Faulkner insists on by recurrent references to her masculinity); so that when life is offered to her in the form of
a passionate union with Joe Christmas, she responds unnaturally
and slips into a prolonged and aberrant sexual frenzy, which
she attempts to maintain by asserting falsely that she is
pregnant. That failing, she turns violently from the puritanical
hell in which she has been wallowing and attempts to bludgeon
Joe into praying with her, whereupon Joe kills her. So three
means of transcending self fail Joanna Burden--a great human
ideal, sex, and religion; and they fail her because she fails
them.

Two other characters have converted the object of worship
from "the crucified shape of pity and love," to use Hightower's
phrase, to vindictive demanding gods constructed in their own
image and compounded of bigotry and ignorance. Doc Hines, who
frequently "gets in touch with God," feels that he is in a
private league with an Almighty who is the supreme proponent
of white supremacy and the supreme opponent of "woman flesh,"
categorically assumed to be nothing more than "bitchery and
abomination." And Simon McEachern is so convinced of his own
stern righteousness that he cannot condone the slightest human
frailty. He is completely lacking in the pity that characterizes
Hightower and that led Hightower to perceive that the church,
as a McEachern would understand it, stands "against truth and
against that peace in which to sin and be forgiven ... is the
life of man." It should be said, at least parenthetically,
that there is a great deal about the failure of religion for
the modern world in *Light in August*. The recognition of this
failure is present most succinctly in the final revery of
Hightower, but it is dramatically handled, as I have suggested,
in the lives of McEachern, Joanna Burden, Doc Hines, and to
some extent in the congregation which ousted Hightower. I am
not certain as to just how far we may push the Christ-Christmas

parallel (which has often been recognized as a troublesome problem in the book), but it seems reasonably clear that the forces and conventions and people that prevent Joe from attaining the humanity he seeks and that ultimately "crucify" him are not spiritually responsive to "the crucified shape of pity and love." Perhaps it may be said that the use and abuse of religion as related to the maintenance of community solidarity constitutes a sort of leitmotif for the novel.

The illusion that separates Percy Grimm from the community is of an entirely different order. Born too late to achieve military glory in World War I, he becomes officious in the exercise of his National Guard captaincy. Of course, the pursuit of military honor has been at times the means of maintaining a social order, but not as Grimm conceives it, for he takes what he is pleased to call "law and order" into his own hands. When his desire to play the heroic soldier, which causes him to ignore the explicit orders of the shrewd and community-wise sheriff, combines with his irrational hatred of Negroes, he becomes less than human, just as bigoted in the certainty of his own rectitude as Hines (Faulkner says of him, ironically, "His face had that serene, unearthly luminousness of angels in church windows") and the fit instrument for the Player to use for the destruction of Christmas. The linkage of this pair by fate is emphasized by the fact that in Hightower's vision of suffering humanity as the figures of the novel turn before him on the wheel, only the faces of Christmas and Grimm are indistinct; they blur together before they come clear.

Lucas Burch is a representative of the Snopes class in the sense that O'Donnell defines that class. In the terms of this essay, the illusion which precludes his participation in the community is the inhuman conviction that money is the only worthwhile goal, a conviction grasped with such single-minded rigor that he has no interest in others except to exploit them. Byron Bunch recognizes Burch's lack of humanity by describing him in the imagery of a mechanical contrivance; Burch, he says, is like "one of these cars running along the street with a radio in it. You can't make out what it is saying and the car aint going anywhere in particular and when you look at it close you see that there aint even anybody in it." In terms of a graded scale of moral being, Burch is at the bottom. Hines, McEachern, and Grimm have so warped the once communal orders to suit themselves that *communal* is no longer a proper attributive, but at least the codes which their particular self-involvements render horrible travesties had their origin in the community. The materialism which motivates Burch, on the other hand, has always been nonmoral and consequently lacking in human ideals.

But what of the community itself, in which these versions
of humanity *manqué* move? What in it is worthy of devotion? It
must be said at once that Faulkner is too committed to bitter
reality and to the tragic view to make human solidarity an
obvious and unequivocal proper aim. As we have already seen,
the church, the spiritual community, has in Hightower's view
failed of its essential mission by being reduced to the doc-
trinaire tenets of some of its members; and simple human pity
can largely be abandoned if conventional attitudes towards
miscegenation and white supremacy are questioned. But Faulkner
is even more explicit about the hardening of convention; his
criticism gains a cutting edge when exploited by a sardonic
humor. For example, the composite "they," the voice of the
community, makes a judgment on "good" women:

> ... the town believed that good women dont forget things
> easily, good or bad, lest the taste and savor of forgive-
> ness die from the palate of conscience. Because the town
> believed that the ladies knew the truth, since it be-
> lieved that bad women can be fooled by badness, since
> they have to spend some of their time not being suspi-
> cious. But that no good woman can be fooled by it be-
> cause, by being good herself, she does not need to worry
> anymore about hers or anybody else's goodness; hence
> she has plenty of time to smell out sin. That was why,
> they believed, that good can fool her almost any time
> into believing that it is evil, but that evil itself
> can never fool her. (p. 61)

Again, the men of the town, when they were boys, followed Miss
Burden about, yelling "Nigger lover" at her, as their fathers
had before them; but at the time of the discovery of her dead
body, they want to catch and lynch the black son who murdered
and (they hope) ravished her. They shift thoughtlessly from
one conventionally inhumane attitude to another. Hightower's
congregation has always been shocked and amazed at his sermons, but does not move to oust him until the particular circumstances of the death of his wife bring notoriety to the
church; the members even have to be conventionally shocked.
Thereafter Hightower is unable to keep a Negro cook, for the
people of Jefferson, led by the Ku Klux Klan, having picked
up the habit of believing evil of the minister, insist on
believing that he is having "unnatural" relations with his
cook. In truth, as Byron says, "When anything gets to be a
habit, it also manages to get a right good distance away from
truth and fact."

The community, we may safely say, is not an unqualified
good. But in spite of its suspicions, bad habits, mixed good

and bad conventions, it is the arena in which moral battles
are to be fought. And the behavior of some of its citizens
offers some hope that the moral struggles will be recognized
for what they are: Martha Armstid gives her hard-earned money
to Lena; the sheriff, though he is willing to have a Negro
whipped to get information, is truly sympathetic towards Byron
when he thinks that Byron is having bad luck in love. Even
the most isolated characters, except Burch, are, in their own
minds, striving for good. The sin they have in common is a
failure in common kindness.

In attempting to abstract the moral significance of the
characters of *Light in August*, I have risked the accusation
of forgetting that Faulkner is a novelist and that his success
must finally be gauged in terms of fiction. But I hope I have
suggested also that the moral essence is caught and realized
by Faulkner in the bewilderingly complicated yet convincing
web of created lives so brilliantly, profoundly, and passion-
ately delineated. Yet the characters, while they live their
own lives, are the creations of a novelist of strong ethic
preconceptions; and only the complex of ethic judgments will
enable us to see why we have this assortment of lives and
just these treatments of the lives.

Faulkner is sometimes willing to voice his own moral convictions; this is true in the case of a bit of literary
criticism which appears in the midst of *Light in August*. When
Byron first tells Hightower that he has taken Lena to the
cabin on the Burden place and asks for Hightower's aid, the
old minister's desire for immunity still rules; when Byron
leaves, he tries to escape into Tennyson. Then Faulkner says:

> It does not take long. Soon the fine galloping language,
> the gutless swooning full of sapless trees and dehy-
> drated lusts begins to swim smooth and swift and peace-
> ful. It is better than praying without having to bother
> to think aloud. It is like listening in a cathedral to
> a eunuch chanting in a language which he does not even
> need to not understand. (p. 301)

I do not believe that this is willfully capricious deni-
gration. It is in keeping with Faulkner's conviction that a
relevant moral order must be applicable in a world of hardened
convention, of men and women of selfish desires, self-deception, and chicanery. Instead of a reaffirmation of new or
old community ideals, the best Faulkner can offer is a Hightower compassion, grounded on an understanding of the need
to recognize human weakness. As another of Faulkner's characters has phrased it elsewhere, all that God Himself asks of
man is that he "hold the earth mutual and intact in communal

anonymity of brotherhood, and all the fee he asked was pity
and humility and sufferance and endurance and the sweat of
his face for bread." So the moral power of Tennyson's never-
never land is meaningless, does not answer to man's nature and
needs as they are; it is significant that after delivering
Lena's baby, Hightower reads *Henry IV*, which Faulkner calls
"food for a man." By then Hightower's compassion is in the
ascendant, and it is capable of causing him to struggle to
transcend himself. In the final analysis it is the struggle
that is important, and perhaps its importance is emphasized
by the fact that it takes place within the unlikely breast of
Hightower. At any rate, through Hightower we see that even
moral splendor is relative and can be achieved by a man who
rises from the stench of selfish isolation to assert the
absolute value of pity. Of course, the proper understanding
comes too late for much social efficacy; and as Hightower
sits before his window awaiting death, the habitual thundering horses and flashing sabers tumble again into his revery.
But before that there has come his realization of his sins
and of his duty as communal man; and this realization for a
moment triumphs, though the one man dies.

GOD THE FATHER AND MOTHERLESS
CHILDREN: *LIGHT IN AUGUST*

Franklin G. Burroughs, Jr.

Sooner or later, explorations of *Light in August* come up
against the question of unity. Any reader perceives that the
novel is stitched together in a remarkable variety of ways,
and he may begin unravelling it by seizing on any of several
prominent strands. For those who like them, there are "image
clusters" including simple things like food, sex, and color,
as well as more arcane things like images of linear discreteness and the curve; there are recurrent motifs and situations,
characters (Joe Christmas, Lena Grove, Lucas Burch) crawling
in and out of windows in pursuit of love or in flight from
it, sacrilegious and obsessed preachers (Christmas, Hines,
Hightower, and, in a sense, Percy Grimm) outraging or terri-
fying their congregations; and there is a constant, but not
consistent, paralleling of events to the life of Christ.
Thematically, the novel especially concerns itself with the
crimes committed by collective, impersonal man against the
individual personality. Racial and sexual prejudice, sanctified by a Pharisaic, inhuman religion, denies Hightower,
Joanna Burden, and Joe Christmas the right, or even the
ability, to live in peace. A critic seeking themes, or patterns, or allusions, or other such familiar structural gadgets,
suffers only from an embarrassment of riches.[1]

But the problem of unity remains, because of the inescapable fact that the novel contains three plots. These
are the story of Joe Christmas and Joanna Burden, the story
of Byron Bunch and Lena Grove, and the story of Gail Hightower. To be sure, the stories touch in places: Byron Bunch
has a role to play in all three, and Hightower, the protagonist
of one, observes and comments upon the other two. And there
can be no doubt that Faulkner deliberately balanced and con-

From Twentieth Century Literature, *19 (July 1973), 189-202.*
Reprinted with permission.

trasted the plots. In the first half of the book, Joe Christmas and Lena Grove, harbingers of life and death, are clearly
conceived as antithetical portents converging on Joanna Burden's
barren and ruined acres. Joanna herself, the last inheritor
of an abolitionist crusade, is the mirror image of Hightower,
the passive custodian of futile Confederate heroism. The three
plots come to more or less simultaneous conclusion against the
backdrop of Jefferson, and the rituals and obsessions of the
community form a kind of definition of the human condition,
which each character may accept or resist, but not ignore.

Even so, the three plots preserve their distances. The
first three chapters introduce, respectively, the stories of
Lena, Christmas, and Hightower; the last three chapters conclude, respectively, the stories of Christmas, Hightower, and
Lena. Critics have generally assumed that the story of Joe
Christmas is the main plot, and that the other two are satel-
lites of it. Quantitatively, this is indisputable: Christmas's
story is told in much greater detail than that of any other
character. But Faulkner's own cryptic observation that the
novel "was mainly the story of Lena Grove," and that it was
written "out of my admiration for women, for the courage and
endurance of women," suggests that the center of gravity lies
elsewhere.[2] Clearly, the admiration for women does not express
itself in the usual narrative form; as has been often noted,
the women in *Light in August* are ignorant, weak, or depraved.
I would like to argue, however, that women do indeed become
the protagonists of the central thematic conflict of the novel,
and that a conception of their role will bring us closer to a
definition of the premise of which the various episodes of
the novel are ramifications.

                                    I

In the broadest sense, the theme of *Light in August* is
the theme of all of Faulkner's most impressive fiction--"the
human heart in conflict with itself"--and its purpose that of
all art--"to create out of the materials of the human spirit
something which did not exist before." Underlying these reso-
nant platitudes was Faulkner's conviction that the human
"spirit" or "heart" did not change in its ultimate potentiality; man was, as Isaac McCaslin understood, "shaped ... out of
the primal Absolute which contained all" and was therefore
"capable of anything any height or depth remembered in mazed
incomprehension out of heaven where hell was created too."[3]
Given this view of an unchanging potentiality in man, history
ultimately changes nothing; the historical circumstance both

reflects the human spirit that has created it and demands from that spirit a new manifestation of its resourcefulness. "Man's environment is the only thing that changes. He must change with it. He will cope with it. The problems he faces today are the same ones he faced when he came out of the mud and first stood on two legs."[4] The theology of such statements is essentially unchristian. It does not view history as a progression toward a Truth that lies beyond human experience; rather, it identifies Truth with the resources of the human spirit, which do not change. Man's nature is his only Providence.

When questioned about the Christian imagery of this and other novels, Faulkner resorted to his favorite analogy and insisted that the Christian myth was only one of the materials in his shop, and that he used it as the carpenter might use a corner brace, joist, or stud. Further, he held to something like a belief in archetypes: all fiction and indeed all human experience involved only a few plots, and the "same plot [is] repeated time after time with different people motivated by it or trying to cope with it." Thus, "sooner or later any writer is going to use something that has been used. And that Christ story is one of the best stories that man has invented, assuming that he did invent that story, and of course it will recur. Everyone that has had the story of Christ and the Passion as a part of his Christian background will in time draw from that."[5] Christianity is, then, a means rather than an end for the writer. It may help to illustrate the human heart in conflict with itself only because it has been generated by that conflict. Whether in its original version or its Yoknapatawpha recension, the Christ story deals with man's attempt to cope with change, and with the unchanging imperatives of his being.

Considered as one of the basic plots, the life of Christ ceases to be a unique event upon which all subsequent generations can base their hopes of redemption. Instead, it becomes a version of the widely spread story of the unprepossessing stranger who enters a community unheralded, and who seeks, or at least requires, food, shelter, and comfort. The stranger frequently turns out to be a god, as in the Baucis and Philemon myth, or of royal blood, as in the medieval romance of Havelok the Dane, or a commoner who will be exalted to nobility, like Cinderella or Richardson's Pamela. Typically, the stranger gains the power with which to repay his persecutors and benefactors; the revelation of his true identity may signal great social or political change, in which the humble and oppressed are exalted over the pitiless and proud.

Lena and Joe, intermittently identified with Mary and Christ, are such strange visitants to Jefferson, and the town

is judged by its reception of them. The judgment is not simple:
for Lena hungers and is given meat, thirsts and is given drink,
is a stranger and is taken in, while Joe, an equally hungry
and thirsty stranger, is beaten, abused, and finally killed.
It is not simply that each elicits a certain response from
the community; there is a very real way in which each insists
upon the response he gets. Lena, simply by waiting, seems to
demand charity, and Joe, from the time he tells Byron Bunch to
"keep your muck" until he finally allows Percy Grimm to shoot
him, embodies the denial he evokes. As she accepts food, shelter, transportation, and money without scruple, he dumps food
on the floor, hurls it against the wall, flees the shelter
offered him by Joanna Burden, rips off the garments that women
have given him, and refuses to accept money from his foster
mother. Unless we are willing to regard their visitations as
being only coincidentally simultaneous, we must see them as
somehow complementary in their significance.

                                    II

    Lena and Joe arrive in a town that is dominated by the
same religion as the one that has banished them from the households of their foster parents. In a sense, then, they are not
strangers at all, but only stepchildren who are not recognized
by their foster parents. The religion that fostered them and
that still governs the town is, in denomination, an indeter-
minate brand of Calvinistic protestantism; in practice, it is
Manicheism. The believer's world is a battleground between
the forces of light and the forces of darkness, and the forces
of darkness are so potent that the children of light can cope
with them only by assuming a perfect purity for themselves.
They must treat the least taint of depravity as being equivalent to total depravity, in their neighbors and themselves.
Thus Lena's brother reacts with inhuman outrage, ignoring her
years of service to his family, when he discovers that she
is pregnant. Thus the townspeople chastise Hightower not only
for his visible failings as a priest and husband, but also
find it necessary to assume that his fall from grace has been
followed by homosexual and heterosexual miscegenation. Similarly, they look on Joanna Burden's corpse with the conviction
that she has been ravished at least once before and once after
the murder. Ironically, Hightower himself is very reluctant
to say "just how far evil extends into the appearance of evil"
(p. 289).
    The Manicheism is important because it operates upon the
lives of all the major characters (with the possible exception of Lena) from within, as well as from without. None of

the major characters is whole. They are divided internally,
like Joe Christmas, who cannot come to terms with the mutually
exclusive racial stereotypes latent, as he imagines, in his
ancestry, and like Joanna Burden, who is dispassionate, orderly, sexless by day, and nymphomaniacal by night. Or they
are atrophied, like Hightower, who cultivates his own impotence, and like Byron Bunch, who, until the advent of Lena,
is an automaton driven by his fear of idleness and the "trouble" that it brings. Even the serene and steadfast Lena lacks
something. It is as though she has escaped frustration,
anxiety, and regret only by losing consciousness of herself
as an individual, and by becoming simply the agent of an all-
powerful maternal instinct, which has directed her from the
time her dying mother instructed her to "take care of paw,"
through her sojourn as keeper of her brother's children, to
her own pregnancy.

Late in his life, Freud, when asked what a normal person
ought to be able to do, reportedly answered: "lieben und
arbeiten"--love and work.[6] In a sense, the final union of
Byron and Lena fills this prescription neatly, making one
complete personality out of two heretofore incomplete ones.
In one way or another, the other characters (excepting, for
the moment, the ancestors of Joanna and Hightower) lack this
ideal capacity to combine discipline, necessary for significant accomplishment in their public lives, with the spon-
taneity necessary for emotionally adequate private life. In
Freudian terms, the religion of the town sets the divine
superego against the diabolic id. It exalts work and discipline above all other virtues; in McEachern's words to Joe:
"the two abominations are sloth and idle thinking, the two
virtues are work and the fear of God" (p. 135). Byron and
his fellow workers, however they may spend their weekends,
instinctively observe the "tenet that, no matter what a man
had done with his Sabbath, to come quiet and clean to work
on Monday morning was no more than seemly and right to do"
(p. 37).

As the theology of the region sanctifies work and discipline, so it mistrusts all manifestations of love--not only
eroticism, but also simple compassion and charity. Promul-
gated and enforced primarily by white males, it projects upon
the other race and sex all that it denies its adherents.
Negrophobia merges with misogyny as the public expression of
a pervasive private mistrust of feeling. Doc Hines, who
rants against "womansinning and bitchery," and who preaches
white supremacy in Negro churches, even at a time when he
"very nearly depended on the bounty and charity of negroes
for sustenance" (p. 325), typifies a contempt not only for

blackness and femininity, but also for charity, which is somehow an acknowledgment of inferiority.

Joe Christmas cannot avoid this demonology. In his sexual
initiation, he assaults the abstract and invisible "womanshenegro" in the shed; later, he feels obliged to assert his
blackness to every woman he encounters, as though in tacit
recognition of some mysterious alliance between it and femininity. The women emphasize the conspiratorial nature of the
relation by secret and subversive acts of charity: this begins
in the orphanage, where the dietitian offers Joe money which
he does not recognize as a bribe, and it continues with the
food Mrs. McEachern smuggles to him and the coffee Bobbie does
not allow him to pay for. It concludes with Joanna Burden, who
secretly feeds him in her kitchen, who insists that their
affair be conducted by hidden notes and letters and that he
enter her house furtively through windows, and who cries, while
in the throes of nymphomania, "Negro! Negro! Negro!" Passion
and compassion place even that most un-Byronic figure, Byron
Bunch, beyond the pale of orthodoxy, so that it seems perfectly
natural that his intercession on behalf of Lena, a girl in
trouble, should be followed by his intercession on behalf of
Joe, who is, as far as Byron knows, a Negro in trouble. When
Hightower belatedly and ineffectually attempts to protect Joe,
Percy Grimm immediately denounces him as a traitor to his sex
and his race: "'Jesus Christ!' Grimm cried, his young voice
clear and outraged like that of a young priest. 'Has every
preacher and old maid in Jefferson taken their pants down to
the yellowbellied son of a bitch?" (p. 439).

                                III

It does not seem to me very satisfactory to say that the
source of the individual neuroses and anxieties and of the
collective inhumanity is simply puritanism or institutional
Christianity. The religion of the town is rather itself an
expression of a human failure to cope with a historical change;
it represents the failure of man to find an image for himself
in a post-heroic society.

Our view of the earlier, heroic society comes indirectly,
through the meditations of Joanna Burden and Gail Hightower
upon their ancestors. The technique itself assures that we
will feel the powerful contrast between the descendants, whose
emotional inadequacies loom large, and the ancestors, whose
extraordinary vitality and heroic sense of purpose overshadow
the present.

Hightower's father, and Joanna's ancestors back to her
great-grandfather, were protestants of a decidedly puritanical

stripe. Their puritanism should not, however, be confused with
that of their descendants. What Erik Erikson has to say
about American puritanism has considerable relevance to the
generations of Hightowers and Burdens: "This much-maligned
puritanism, we should remember, was once a system of values
designed to check men and women of eruptive vitality, of strong
appetites, as well as of strong individuality." Erikson observes that only after a variety of historical developments
had put it on the defensive did this puritanism become rigid
and oppressive, with the result "that men were born who failed
to learn ... to love the goodness of sensuality before they
learned to hate its sinful uses. Instead of hating sin, they
learned to mistrust life. Many became puritans without faith
or zest."[7]

"Eruptive vitality" certainly characterizes the three
generations of Burdens. They are so exuberantly independent
that, beginning with Joanna's grandfather, each of them defies
his father, flees into wilderness and apostasy, and marries.
Only then, having demonstrated his ability to reject the family
faith if he so desires, does the son move, geographically and
theologically, closer to home, and signify his acceptance of
the family faith by naming his first son after his father.
Thus Calvin ran away from New Hampshire and the sermons of
his father Nathaniel. His rebellion reached its logical extreme in California, where he lived for a year in a monastery,
after which he married, named his first son Nathaniel, and
reared him in a faith that combined New England puritanism
with readings from a Spanish Bible. This Nathaniel in his turn
fled to the frontier, where he married a Catholic, produced
a son, named him Calvin, and then returned to join his father
in the crusade against "frog-eating slaveholders" and Demo-
crats. Each son takes advantage of the freedom offered by
the frontier to escape the iron discipline of his father;
ultimately, however, the escape serves to convince the son
that the father's strictness is necessary and right. Only
Joanna, the child of old age, accepts the "burden" of the
family faith passively, without having first acquired the
self-reliance which would enable her to bear it. The healthy
balance between freedom and control has been lost, and her
belated erotic awakening cannot restore it.

Hightower's case differs only superficially. His father
had rebelled against his grandfather, but these generations
of Hightowers, like their Burden counterparts, ultimately
fought for the same cause. Hightower's father chose a religion
which stood in direct contrast to the cheerful, undisciplined,
epicurean code of the grandfather. His Presbyterianism furnished
the "cold and uncompromising conviction" that allowed him to

find the right balance between "the puritan and the cavalier"
and to live usefully after the war which had destroyed his
father and the heedless, hell-for-leather world to which he
belonged (p. 449). But Gail Hightower, like Joanna Burden,
inherits the "cold and uncompromising conviction" passively,
and it stifles him. His professed faith and conduct reveal
him to be a puritan who, in Erikson's words, had "learned to
mistrust life." Only through a sentimental idolatry can he
touch the old, untrammeled vitality of the cavalier, which
has been transmitted to him as no more than a ghost and a
legend.

The Hightower and Burden family chronicles provide the
action of *Light in August* with a historical context, a specific
instance of the way in which man's environment changes, demanding that he change with it. The religion of the region,
whether Unitarian or Presbyterian in denomination, Yankee
or Confederate in politics, had necessarily been spartan and
militant in its teachings. It grew out of a civilization which
found itself beleaguered on all sides. It had to equip men
to deal with the external threats to life and property posed
by the frontier and by the continual feuding over the slavery
question, and it had at the same time to oppose the continual
temptation of the wilderness, with its promise of lawless
freedom from all civilized restraint. Under such circumstances,
the religion inevitably became a fighting faith, intent upon
bringing order out of the chaos that surrounded it. Like all
such faiths, it had some tendency to self-destruction (as
witnessed, for example, by the fierce filial conflicts within
the Burden family), but that tendency could be controlled
and directed as long as the faithful had their very tangible
external enemies to confront.

The old heroic religion did not provide any particular
role for women. As represented by Faulkner, it is entirely
patriarchal, descending from father to son with only the
absolute minimum of maternal participation. In the Burden
family, the mother plays no part in the curious love-hate
relation of successive fathers and sons. In the Hightower
family, Gail's grandmother is never mentioned at all, and
his mother, who died when he was young, and who was bedridden
long before she died, exists only as a biological necessity.
Gail was actually delivered by his father, and Joanna's
mother, sent for like an item out of a mail order catalogue,
provides her with no protection from the obsessions of her
father, or the memory of her brother and grandfather.

That wives and mothers figure so minimally in the Burden
and Hightower chronicles simply emphasizes the heroic character of the early civilization. In both genealogies, there is

something of the pervasively masculine atmosphere of the sagas or Homeric epic, or, for that matter, of much of the Old Testament. The stern discipline of the father was exalted because it was a necessity; maternal sympathy and encouragement were luxuries not to be indulged. Women themselves, and the domesticated stability of which they were the center, had no intrinsic dignity, no symbolic value, in the prevailing conception of life, or in the religion that embodied it. The warrior's virtues of fortitude, self-denial, and zeal prevented the recognition of other virtues, and pleasure and happiness were secondary, if not positively inimical, to them. Hightower's father, and Joanna's father and grandfather, were alike in their willingness to sacrifice domestic concord to the higher claims of principle. The father administered and defined the religion; his severity was that of the deity, and vice-versa.

IV

The men and women of the present live in circumstances very different from the past. Joanna and Hightower, attempting to preserve their ancestral legacies, find themselves out of touch with the old vitality, and imprisoned by the dead letter of the old creeds. Their fellow citizens, without being aware of it, suffer from a similar malaise. They welcome the murder and the fire as an "emotional barbecue, a Roman holiday almost" (p. 273), and they see in the flames, the corpse, and the sheriff a sudden possibility of drama and excitement, "a promise of something beyond the sluttishness of stuffed entrails and monotonous days" (p. 277). The men immediately begin looking for someone to crucify.

Fostered by the violence and hardship of the past, the old religion has survived to foster the savage frustrations of the present. The civilization has failed to make the transition to peace; it can express its fidelity to its heritage only through acts of violence. To relax the old heroic discipline would require greater courage and greater energy than to maintain it. It has become the new threat to life, causing a civilization which lacks external enemies to turn upon itself. Hightower, who accepts persecution and contempt in exchange for the "immunity" it gains him, and whose veneration for the old heroic discipline blinds him to the demands of the living, recognizes, in the distant music of the organ, a hostility toward life, of which he is both victim and example:

> Listening, he seems to hear within it the apotheosis of his own history, his own land, his own environed

blood: that people from which he sprang and among whom
he lives who can never take either pleasure or catastrophe or escape from either, without brawling over it.
Pleasure, ecstasy, they cannot seem to bear: their escape
from it is in violence, in drinking and fighting and
praying; catastrophe too, the violence identical and
apparently inescapable. *And so why should not their
religion drive them to crucifixion of themselves and
one another?* he thinks. (p. 347)

Examples of such crucifixion and self-crucifixion occur
throughout the novel. In characters like Lena's brother, Simon
McEachern, Percy Grimm, and Doc Hines, we witness the operation
of a creed that has turned malignant, attacking and denying the
will to live rather than nourishing and directing it. Their
convictions constrain these men to discover evil in a mortal
adversary, who may be scourged, banished, or destroyed. Out
of the instincts and longings of the human heart, they create
diabolic opponents against whom the most ruthless cruelty is
justified. The music Hightower hears has a "quality stern and
implacable, deliberate and without passion so much as immolation, pleading, asking, for not love, not life, forbidding it
to others, demanding in sonorous tones death as though death
were the boon, like all Protestant music" (p. 347).

It is natural that the great crises are precipitated by
copulation and by birth; the old dispensation is threatened
by each new life. Lena's brother is "a hard man. Softness and
gentleness and youth (he was just forty) and almost everything
else except a kind of stubborn and despairing fortitude and
the bleak heritage of his bloodpride had been sweated out of
him" (p. 4), and he banishes her from Doane's Mill, which is
soon to be a "stumppocked scene of profound and peaceful
desolation, unplowed, untilled, gutting slowly into red and
choked ravines beneath the long quiet rains of autumn and the
galloping fury of the vernal equinoxes" (pp. 2-3). Joe similarly emerges from a setting of man-made desolation; his grandfather assassinates his father and allows his mother to die.
He, like Lena's brother, sees the sinner as only the incarnation of sin, and the "womansinning and bitchery" by which Joe
is conceived enables him to regard his grandson as "the devil's
walking seed," the instrument of God's "purpose and vengeance"
(p. 362). God's purpose and vengeance devolve upon Doc himself,
who, at the chosen moment when he sees his prophecy fulfilled
in Mottstown, urges the crowd to lynch Joe.

Joe's foster father, like his grandfather, comes to see
the child as a diabolic antagonist, and himself as the divine
protagonist. His discovery of Joe's "lechery" is announced
with a sigh, "a sound almost luxurious, of satisfaction and

victory" (p. 154). It is with the same satisfaction that he
advances toward Joe across the dance floor, "with neither haste
nor anger while on all sides the sluttishness of weak human
men seethed in a long sigh of terror about the actual representative of the wrathful and retributive Throne," no longer
seeing the face of the "youth whom he had nurtured and sheltered
and clothed from a child," but instead the face of Satan (p.
191). It is with triumph, with the "dreamlike exaltation of a
martyr who has already been absolved," that he goes to his
death. He has succeeded in transforming the orphan into a fac-
simile of the great Adversary, born of woman and found in her
presence, upon whom his faith is postulated.

McEachern's appearance reflects a lifetime of self-denial:
"a thickish man with a close brown beard and hair cut close
though not recently. Hair and beard both had a hard, vigorous
quality, unsilvered, as though the pigmentation were imper-
vious to the forty and more years which the face revealed.
The eyes were lightcolored, cold. He wore a suit of hard,
decent black. On his knee rested a black hat held in a blunt
clean hand shut, even on the soft felt of the hat, into a
fist" (pp. 132-33). The fist clamped upon the unoffending felt
hat typifies an excess of forceful restraint, which McEachern
exercises upon himself and his family. Faulkner continually
describes him as though his rectitude had at last petrified
him: "cold, squat, big, shapeless, somehow rocklike" (p. 135),
"his clean, bearded face as firm as carved stone" (p. 141),
"a cheek jutting, granitelike, bearded to the caverned and
spectacled eyesocket" (p. 143), a head resembling "one of the
marble cannonballs on Civil War monuments" (p. 153). His
fastidiousness, an attempt to impose an immaculate standard
on all human conduct, leads him to an unconscious, but entirely
appropriate, disavowal of the Incarnation. When Joe unthink-
ingly puts the catechism on the barn floor, McEachern repri-
mands him: "You would believe that a stable floor, the stamping place of beasts, is the proper place for the word of God"
(p. 140). The living Word, Yeats's uncontrollable mystery on
the bestial floor, brings together all that McEachern's creed
keeps asunder; he can admit no reconciliation between the
perfection of the Word and the corruption of the flesh. His
idol is rather the heifer, a species of golden calf, which he
gives to Joe, "to teach you the responsibility of possessing,
owning, ownership. The responsibility of the owner to that
which he owns under God's sufferance. To teach you foresight
and aggrandisement" (p. 153).

Percy Grimm, Joe's ultimate adversary, resembles McEachern in his "cold ardor" (p. 431), and his "rocklike, calm"
face (p. 436). Like McEachern, he seeks a world of immaculate

and lifeless perfection, and it is the promise of such a world
that draws him into the National Guard: "He could now see his
life opening before him, uncomplex and inescapable as a barren
corridor, completely freed now of ever again having to think
or decide, the burden which he now assumed and carried as
bright and weightless and martial as his insignatory brass"
(p. 426). His violent reaction to what he imagines to be Joe's
sexual misdemeanors is parallel to that of Joe's foster father;
both men inhabit sterile worlds, which are defined against the
natural world, against which they must employ fist and knife.

Grimm, McEachern, and Hines all become, in their relation
to Joe, representatives of the "wrathful and retributive
Throne." In terms of the human heart in conflict with itself,
all three represent the enthronement of the superego, the
wrathful and retributive conscience bent on eradicating, rather
than governing, the unruly impulses of the heart. The community condones, or at least abides, their authority; it has
no other god except this archaic one who can be honored only
through rituals of sadism which are the degenerated vestiges
of the old rituals of heroic discipline. Doc Hines, sitting
of the top step with the shotgun while his daughter dies,
striking his wife with it when she tries to go for help, grant-
ing life to the child only because he is "the Lord God's
abomination, and I am the instrument of His will" (p. 360),
perverts the masculine role of guardian of the household.
Directing his energy against the life within, rather than
against any danger without, he is the emblem of the authority
under which Joe Christmas is born, lives, and dies.

                                 V

As avatars of a single deity, Hines, McEachern, and Grimm
determine the fate and character of Joe Christmas. At various
times in the novel, each of them demonstrates an uncanny certainty about what Joe will do, where he will turn; the closed
circle of his fate is their creation. But Joe, like Christ,
has a dual nature. If Hines, McEachern, and Grimm are all
avatars of the Father, whose will constitutes his Providence,
his mother, his grandmother, Mrs. McEachern, Bobbie, and
Joanna are all avatars of Eve, whose original transgression
descends to him and whose presence continually invites him
to transgress. The black blood which he imagines he inherited
from his mother's disobedience disqualifies him forever from
the world of his grandfather, foster father, and assassin.
In the orphanage of his childhood, the household of McEachern,
and the thousand savage and lonely streets of his maturity,
he has the opportunity to enter, like Grimm, a world "un-

complex and inescapable as a barren corridor." But, unlike
Grimm, he can never find peace in such a world; his blood
forces him into complicity with women, and inevitably brings
about his expulsion from every sanctuary that promises to
protect him against the duality of his own nature.

Joe's continual encounters with subversive feminine soli-
citude always end in frustration or betrayal. The grandmother
who cannot save him from the wrath of her husband at the
beginning of his life is no more able to do so at the end of
it, when she has finally found him again, and wishes only for
one day in which to pretend "like it hadn't happened yet. Like
the world never had anything against him yet" (p. 367). Mrs.
Hines's love is consistent from beginning to end. By steadily
ignoring all judgments against the infant and the man, it has
continued to hope all things and endure all things. Joe has
never benefited from it, or even known of its existence, and
yet (according to Gavin Stevens) when she tells him in jail
that Hightower's house will provide a sanctuary "inviolable
not only to officers and mobs, but to the very irrevocable
past" (p. 424), he instinctively believes her, and seeks
refuge there. This is but his last attempt to find in a woman
the embodiment of what Hightower calls "that peace in which
to sin and be forgiven which is the life of man" (p. 461).
He always fails, but the very persistence of his quest, despite
the pain it always entails, implies what is not so much a
Promethean defiance as an inability to controvert the fullness
of his own humanity.

His situation is beautifully revealed in an episode from
his childhood, after he has been whipped and sent to bed
supperless by McEachern for having refused to learn his
catechism. Mrs. McEachern, defying her husband, brings a tray
of food to his bedside. He gets up, takes the tray to the
corner of the room, and dumps its contents onto the floor.
"Then he returned to the bed, carrying the empty tray as though
it were a monstrance and he the bearer, his surplice the cutdown undergarment which had been bought for a man to wear."
The empty tray is a denial both of Joe's hunger and his foster
mother's love; it symbolizes, ironically, the very creed that
Joe has defied all day long. Denial has been his only way of
responding to all that has been denied to him; his foster
father's cutdown undergarment has become his surplice. And
yet, an hour after Mrs. McEachern has left the room, "he rose
from the bed and went and knelt in the corner as he had not
knelt on the rug, and above the outraged food kneeling, with
his hands ate, like a savage, like a dog" (pp. 145, 146). His
kneeling here is unconscious, not in obedience to any creed
advanced by his father, but in veneration for a hunger, which

neither Joe nor McEachern has succeeded in eradicating, that
cannot be satisfied by the empty monstrance. Against his will
and in secret, in the posture of a suppliant rather than the
surplice of an acolyte, he receives the true sacrament, which
has been adminstered to him, however furtively, by the woman
whom he wishes to despise.

Joe's public spurning of the food suggests the extent to
which the will of his foster father has established itself
as an internal monitor. Only in darkness and privacy can he
allow himself to satisfy his own deep craving, "like a savage,
like a dog." The grim drama of his birth, with the ruthless
and vindictive man thwarting the compassion of the woman and
pronouncing his curse upon the child, has become Joe's internal
drama. Doc Hines and McEachern reign within his consciousness
as within their own households, but in his consciousness, as
in the two households, there lurks a meek, intimidated, but
persistent opposition. The two women who nurse and nourish
Joe, and try to protect him against the severity of their
husbands, remain with him in spirit, or, to be more precise,
in body. His natural appetites periodically pull him away from
the disciplined, predictable world of men and expose him to
the uncertain world of women, where his conscious self-reliance
must yield to his unconscious need for love. His excursions
into this world in the end only provide an opportunity for
the wrathful Father to assert himself, in the avatar of McEachern, Grimm, or the suddenly unsexed Joanna Burden. When no
man is available to do it for him, Joe punishes himself, by
revealing his blackness to white prostitutes, or, when that
fails, by attacking the prostitute who ignores his color.

Joanna and Hightower, like Joe, are dominated by the
stern and inflexible image of a Father who is both human and
divine, and who cuts them off from life. Hightower can only
live vicariously, with his grandfather, in a past world of
exuberant masculine vitality; his father's religion, which
he inherits, stands as a barrier, preventing the transmission
of that vitality to him. Joanna's father and grandfather,
living in spirit although dead in fact, allow her femininity
only one desperate and furtive expression. When it is over,
the paternal creed reasserts itself, and she ceases to treat
Joe as a lover; instead he becomes an individual specimen of
the white man's burden. She demands that he join her in asking
pardon of the Father against whom they have both transgressed,
and seeks to kill him when he refuses.

Seen against this background, the affair of Lena, Byron,
and the new baby does seem to have overtones of something
larger than simply an individual act of unconventional courage.
While Doc Hines schemes and pretends to sleep, the baby is

born, and this time his wife seizes the child and holds it
aloft in triumph. The new life begins under the auspices of
the woman, who loves without judgment, rather than the man,
who judges without love. The old patriarchal religion, which
has transmitted a stern discipline from father to son, and
which has ended at last by pitting fathers and sons against
each other, and both against the life-bearing woman, approaches
its senility. In its stead, Hightower, "remembering the young
strong body from out whose travail even there shone something
tranquil and unafraid," foresees: *"More of them. Many more.
That will be her life, her destiny. The good stock peopling
in tranquil obedience to it the good earth; from these hearty
loins without hurry or haste descending mother and daughter.
But by Byron engendered next"* (p. 384).

Faulkner has the triumph of Mrs. Hines and Lena occur at
the scene of Joanna's defeat, on the day of Joe's murder, and
of Hightower's final submersion in the heroic twilight. Like
the almost simultaneous deaths of Lion, Old Ben, and Sam
Fathers in *Go Down, Moses*, these deaths formally signify the
passing of an era into history and legend. The image of Joe
Christmas's face rising above his mutilated body, "musing,
quiet, steadfast, not fading and not particularly threatful,
but of itself alone serene, of itself alone triumphant," is
the sum total of the "old disasters" from which the "newer
hopes" are born (p. 440). The unforgettable image itself becomes the judgment which the unprepossessing stranger has
delivered upon the community, whose creed has created and then
destroyed him. Lena, leaving town with Byron in tow, passes
out of the awareness of Jefferson unaltered and apparently
having altered nothing. But the child she has with her, secure
in the maternal devotion that has been denied to all of the
major characters, incarnates the "newer hopes," which exist
in the undefined potentiality of every new life.

From Faulkner's view of man it followed logically that
"nothing is extinct in any race, only dormant."[8] In *Light in
August*, we sense that every individual, regardless of the role
he plays, or the identity he has acquired through the interaction of his will and his environment, carries within him an
opposite self which, however vigorously suppressed, never
entirely vanishes. This may express itself in matrimony, the
man seeking in the woman an image of the opposite self. Byron
and Lena, of course, provide the supreme example of this;
the Hines and McEachern households, where the ruthless husband
is balanced by a compassionate wife, suggest a similar pattern.
The other characters often seem to labor under the curse of
Plato's myth, which has man and woman descended from a single
androgyne and doomed to a lifelong attempt to recover the

original wholeness. They never succeed in regaining what is
denied to them by their own anatomy; neither do they manage to
abandon "the desire and pursuit of the whole," which, in
Plato's parable, "is called love."[9]

In the society as a whole, women and Negroes must accept
the role of the opposite self. As such, they are subject to
scorn and persecution by the official self, the collective
superego as it is represented by men like McEachern, Hines,
and Grimm. The duality of the society is also the duality of
the individual, but while the society, through its courts and
churches, sanctifies the duality, the individual, because he
cannot do otherwise, seeks to overcome it. His efforts may,
as with Lena and Byron, be comic in their resolution, or they
may, as with Joanna, Joe, and Hightower, be tragically frustrated. Either resolution legitimately expresses the heart's
conflict with itself, and with the laws and creeds it has
fostered.

NOTES

1. *Light in August* has been so often and so variously interpreted that even the most perfunctory evaluation of existing studies would require an essay in itself. Richard Chase,
who found the novel an interplay of "images of linear discreteness ... and of the curve," initiated serious discussion
of the structural organization of the novel in "The Stone
and the Crucifixion: Faulkner's *Light in August*," *Kenyon Review*, 10 (Autumn 1948), 539-51. Alfred Kazin's celebrated
essay, "The Stillness of *Light in August*," reprinted in
Faulkner: A Collection of Critical Essays, ed. Robert Penn
Warren (Englewood Cliffs, N.J., 1966), pp. 147-62, correlates
theme and technique, finding in the oblique representation
of Joe Christmas "the stillness of a continual meditation,"
which underscores his aloneness and lack of a definable identity. C. Hugh Holman, in "The Unity of Faulkner's *Light in
August*," *PMLA*, 73 (March 1958), 155-66, believes the novel
to be held together by the "dim but discernible image of
Christ," which shines through several characters. Olga W.
Vickery's skillful treatment of the novel in terms of the
interpenetration of public and private realities (*The Novels
of William Faulkner*, Baton Rouge, 1964, pp. 66-83) invites
comparison with that of Cleanth Brooks (*William Faulkner:
The Yoknapatawpha Country*, New Haven and London, 1963, pp.
47-74) whose interpretation of public and private realities
in terms of a "community" containing a variety of "pariahs"
leads him to see the novel as being ultimately comic in mode.

2. *Faulkner in the University*, ed. Frederick L. Gwynn and Joseph L. Blotner (Charlottesville, 1959), p. 74.

3. *Go Down, Moses* (New York, 1942), p. 282.

4. *Lion in the Garden: Interviews with William Faulkner*, ed. James B. Meriwether and Michael Millgate (New York, 1968), p. 221.

5. *Faulkner in the University*, p. 117.

6. Quoted in Erik H. Erikson, *Childhood and Society* (New York, 1963), p. 265.

7. Erikson, pp. 292-93.

8. *Lion in the Garden*, p. 264.

9. "The Symposium," the Jowett translation, in *The Philosophy of Plato*, ed. Irwin Edman (New York, 1956), p. 357.

THE OTHER COMPETITORS FOR THE CROSS:
JOANNA BURDEN AND GAIL HIGHTOWER

R.G. Collins

II. Joanna Burden: Competing for the Cross

Poor old Joanna Burden has found little sympathy and less understanding in the body of criticism devoted to *Light in August*. Her murder is not simply the more or less just deserts of an aging nymphomaniac, but a token act that gains its significance through her particular personality and the nature of the relationship between herself and Joe Christmas.
First of all, Joanna Burden is decidedly *not* what Faulkner seems to have originally conceived of her as being (a concept that must have antedated any actual writing of her story)—a representative of the North in the racial conflict of the South. One critic, and a good one at that, has defined this novel as the story of the South moving against "its antitheses ... The Negro, the Yankee, the Apostate,"[1] as represented by Joe Christmas, Joanna Burden, and Gail Hightower. Nonsense. The characteristics of the major figures are not antithetical to, but representative of, the South, if we may continue to take Faulkner's conception of his area as a useful one, illustrative in significant ways of the entire human arena. So far as that goes, there *is* no force of society, abstract or otherwise, except that which is revealed in the characters. In the case of Joanna Burden, certainly we have no picture at all of the North, but we do have a picture of

Excerpted from R.G. Collins, "Light in August: Faulkner's Stained Glass Triptych." *This article originally appeared in* "The Novels of William Faulkner," *a special issue of* MOSAIC: A Journal for the Comparative Study of Literature and Ideas (University of Manitoba), 7, 1 (Fall 1973), 97-157, to whom *acknowledgment is herewith made. The new title for Sections II and III (reprinted here) was proposed by the author. The notes have been renumbered.*

the South in the same stratum as that exemplified in the
character of Joe Christmas. They are, in fact, very much alike,
if we can conceive of similar characters sometimes taking a
reverse form. Faulkner himself gave a measure of support to
this view in speaking of Joanna Burden:

> Maybe she had begun to assume the attitude of so many
> Southern people that it [slavery] couldn't be changed
> and altered because the Negro would be incapable of
> change, and she must have hated herself for going against
> the tradition, the beliefs of her father.[2]

Faulkner ended that discussion by admitting that he did not
remember the book too well, and in part of his answer--the
reference to the father--I shall have to agree. Joanna Burden
does not abandon the beliefs of her father at all, because
her father was no more a Northern puritan than was Doc Hines
(or William Faulkner, to establish, perhaps, the ultimate
limitation). In the most significant experience of Joanna
Burden's life, one that colors her entire future, the father
solemnly invests her with "the curse of the white race" which
is "the black man." Early Yankee black-birders notwithstanding,
the curse of the Negro simply is not part of the individual
New England psychological heritage, religious or otherwise.
The average New Englander did not live with that curse as
part of daily life. On the other hand, as Faulkner himself
constantly demonstrates, it is very much part of the heritage
of the South ... indeed, is not that exactly what the bulk
of Faulkner's novels seek to establish? In other words, the
curse of the Negro is significant to the Burdens to the degree
that they themselves accept and represent the communal identity
of the South, not the North.

In fact, so far as the details go, Faulkner makes only
one minor effort to establish a decisive New England background for Joanna Burden: he has her frontier father send to
New Hampshire for a second wife after his first--a Mexican
woman--dies. However, the lady from New Hampshire is the most
anonymous figure in the novel; after the original reference
to her existence and another identifying her as Joanna's
mother, she is never mentioned again. She is not even named,
Joanna receiving her name from the first, Mexican, wife
(Joanna--Juana; Joe--"son of Joe"). Certainly the anonymous
actual mother has no influence whatsoever on Joanna Burden.

Her grandfather, father, and half brother are alleged to
be New Englanders, but the allegation is no more than that.
The grandfather has far less resemblance to the characteristic native of New Hampshire than he does to his mirror-
image, fanatic old Doc Hines. In fact, turn Doc Hines's ob-

session around, and you have in the grandfather of Joe
Christmas a perfect picture of the elder Calvin Burden, caper-
ing and howling his gospel of guilt. Is not a racially obsessed grandfather one more item in a string of resemblances
between Joanna and Joe Christmas? Certainly, as is the case
with Hines, religion is made a rationale for race obsession;
and, as with Hines, it is a religion that has little to do
with any recognizable form of Christianity. Its relationship
to Calvinism--the critical view of William Van O'Connor notwithstanding[3]--is tenuous, at best. Calvin Burden, according
to the novel itself, invents a compound religion, composed
allegedly of a mixture of native Unitarianism (never a major
sect in New Hampshire as it was in Massachusetts. In any
event, he left New Hampshire at the age of twelve, so we may
if we choose excuse his forgetting the rationalistic founda-
tion of Unitarianism), Spanish mystic Catholicism picked up
from missionary priests in California (he was a Catholic for
ten years while in passage), and a natural fundamentalism
that smells more of shouting Baptist than anything else.
Actually, the compound religion, even, is a red herring.
Calvin Burden's religion is simpler than that: Hell and the
slaveholders are equivalent, and from there on he agrees
wholeheartedly with Hines that the Negro is the original ac-
cursed of God and therefore represents the white man's guilt.

The claim of the North on his son, Joanna's father, is
still more equivocal. Born in frontier Missouri, Nathaniel
Burden has as mother a French Huguenot (newly from Carolina
via Kentucky, the route of the original settlers of Jefferson).
The younger Burden, we are told, is a small, dark man from
this infusion of exotic blood. "'Another damn black Burden,'"
says his father when he sees Joanna's half brother for the
first time. "'Folks will think I bred to a damn slaver. And
now he's got to breed to one, too'" (p. 234). Whether or not
this was unconscious correlation on Faulkner's part, it
evokes a parallel to Joe Christmas. The parallel is still
more precise when we hear that Nathaniel Burden marries a
Mexican woman, who exactly resembles his Huguenot mother,
and that this dead Mexican woman is a sort of spiritual mother
to Joanna. Later, of course, we discover that Joe's father
was allegedly Mexican (a good logical choice, since the racist
in the South and Southwest today still refers to Mexicans
as "niggers").

In short, Nathaniel Burden's tie with New England manifests itself in nothing more than the mail-order request for
the second wife--an unexplained act that I suspect was due
to Faulkner's sudden realization that New Hampshire had all
too little connection with the Burdens by this time. In

temperament and personality, Nathaniel Burden differs from
his racially obsessed father only to the degree that he is
pictured in his youth, during which time he is conceived as
a frontier hell-raiser very much like those found in Long-
street's *Georgia Scenes*. Generally, Faulkner's conception of
New England seems to be restricted to that of antislavery,
with a dash of Connecticut's apostate son, John Brown, tossed
in, perhaps. After which Faulkner promptly invests the Burdens
with all the attributes of the Southerner.

Joanna Burden's most intimate family association, after
her father, is her half brother Calvin Burden, who in fact
died, some dozen years *before* her birth. Calvin is obviously
the one with whom she feels the strongest psychological tie,
for she refers to him at several critical points. This half-
Mexican youth, shot at the age of twenty by Colonel Sartoris,
we know very little about except that he dies over "a question
of negro voting." The word martyr may be a little excessive,
but it is not completely inappropriate in view of Joanna's
father's pronouncement over the graves of the boy and his
grandfather:

> Your grandfather and brother are lying there, murdered
> not by one white man but by the curse which God put on
> a whole race before your grandfather or your brother
> or me or you were even thought of. A race doomed and
> cursed to be forever and ever a part of the white race's
> doom and curse for its sins. (p. 239)

The curse borne by Joanna Burden is the same one, we know,
that claims Joe Christmas as a sacrifice. While Joe's death
is much more symbolic, the death of the half-Mexican youth
long before seems a definite foreshadowing, creating a pe-
culiarly fateful bond between Joanna Burden and Joe. Clearly,
then, those readers who dismiss Joanna Burden as a simple
representation of the North in a Southern culture miss much
of what she contributes to the novel.

The link between Joe and Joanna includes, also, such
things as their ambivalence and duality. The dark blood referred to earlier as being part of her heritage is less,
supposedly, than that of Joe, but her communal status is
equally that of physical alien. In fact, recognition of her
status in the town is one of the reasons Joe originally
decides to stay--"Then I won't be bothered here." Moreover,
while Joe's fate is that of combining both races, Joanna is
repeatedly presented as being sexually ambivalent; in her
conjoin both male and female--one might say McEachern and
Bobbie Allen. Joe demonstrates duality of the blood; Joanna,
the duality of sex, the corruption of the woman combined with
the hard clean honesty of the male.

For the first year, she is "hard," "almost manlike."
During this phase, she seems to represent two things: (1) a
refutation of his concept that the essentially corrupt woman
can only be dealt with by offering her violence; (2) and the
inaccessible white society that he has tried both to violate
and merge with:

> ... it was as though he entered by stealth to despoil
> her virginity each time anew. It was as though each
> turn of dark saw him faced again with the necessity to
> despoil again that which he had already despoiled--or
> never had and never would. (p. 221)

This sexual conflict seems to be deliberately presented
by Faulkner as an allegory of integration in the complete
sense. Faulkner's, or Joe's, comment is implicit and fore-
shadows the ultimate result of the affair: "It was as if he
struggled physically with another man for an object of no
value to either, and for which they struggled on principle
alone" (p. 222).

This duality in Joanna is brought to the surface by Joe
Christmas and reminds us of the opposition of male and female
attributes--in his mind--as they have earlier been identified:

> A dual personality: the one the woman at first sight
> of whom in the lifted candle ... there had opened before
> him, instantaneous as a landscape in a lightningflash,
> a horizon of physical security and adultery if not
> pleasure; the other the mantrained muscles and the man-
> trained habit of thinking born of heritage and environ-
> ment with which he had to fight up to the final instant.
> (pp. 221-22)

By now, it should be apparent that the three-year affair
with Joanna Burden, equally divided in three parts, was a
miniature view of Joe Christmas's struggle (and that of the
Negro, to an extent) throughout his life, as he conceives it.
The first year is the rigid rejection of white society; the
second, the corruption and succumbing of white society through
the point of vulnerability, female lust, by the Negro; the
third, the need for expiating the guilt, the final rejection
of the Negro by white society, as the basis of corruption,
sex, fails. The white society, again "male," decrees or re-
affirms the Negro's apartness. The successive stages, of
course, are restricted to the night, recalling Joe Christmas's
identification of *Negro-sex-womanhood* with darkness and
establishing the outlaw nature of the entire experiment.
During the daytime, Joanna Burden always appears as hard and
masculine, even during the wild lust of the second year.

Faulkner describes the transition between the first and
second phase in language clearly suggestive of its symbolic
nature: "that surrender terrific and hard, like the breaking
down of a spiritual skeleton the very sound of whose snapping
fibers could be heard almost by the physical ear" (p. 242).
But, as he puts it:

> The sewer ran only by night. The days were the same as
> they had ever been.... he knew that she was in the house
> and that the coming of dark within the old walls was
> breaking down something and leaving it corrupt with
> waiting. (pp. 242-43)

The corruption of darkness is not only that of evening, but,
in the symbolization of Joe's thoughts, the coming of the
Negro himself.

It also becomes clear now, I think, why Joanna Burden
was given to us as a Northern woman when she has so little
Northern heritage. The experiment in the merging of races,
conceived as based upon corruptibility, guilt, and life-re-
jection, has to be abstracted somehow away from direct relation to the Southern community. Joanna Burden really is a
Southern woman, superficially disguised as a Northerner, used
much as an animal might be used in a dangerous experiment in
place of the human that it resembles. There is no way of
proving it, and no need to prove it, but I am inclined to
think that Joanna Burden is a Northerner solely because of
Faulkner's own emotional refusal to use a "native" white.
Temple Drake of *Sanctuary* could be depraved, but not with a
Negro, not even an equivocal one. But such is fruitless
speculation finally, and I offer it only because the thematic
structure of the episode seems to substantiate it, and because
it explains an otherwise curious flaw.

As a very small child, Joanna had been taken by her
father to a cedar grove, the one where her grandfather and
half brother were buried, to be invested with the curse. In
telling Joe Christmas about the episode, she explains:

> But after that I seemed to see [Negroes] for the first
> time not as people, but as a thing, a shadow in which
> I lived, we lived, all white people, all other people.
> I thought of all the children coming forever and ever
> into the world, white, with the black shadow already
> falling upon them before they drew breath. And I seemed
> to see the black shadow in the shape of a cross. And
> it seemed like the white babies were struggling, even
> before they drew breath, to escape from the shadow that
> was not only upon them but beneath them too, flung out
> like their arms were flung out, as if they were nailed
> to the cross. (p. 239)

The dark shadow of the Negro here is clearly offered as the equivalent for original sin, falling upon life as a curse at the moment of birth. Faulkner seems to be suggesting that the sin of Cain, not the sin of the Garden, is the generic one; that the Negro is the white man's sin upon which the white man is crucified. The conception is related to that mythic one which puts the object of sin as a burden upon the sinner. One might also recall here the Christian interpretation which says that the cross upon which Christ was crucified was the sins of mankind.

In any event, Joanna's vision is nothing new for Joe Christmas, who has lived it as orthodoxy all his life. It is a slightly different phrasing of Doc Hines's fanatic belief, and represents one more link between Joanna Burden and Joe Christmas. There is in it no vestige of love for the Negro, just as, curiously, Joanna Burden never reveals love for the black people to whom she has devoted her life, and because of whom she is an outcast. The implication is that her "devotion" to the Negro is an obligation, the bearing of a cross not dissimilar to, and scarcely more voluntarily assumed than, the cross Joe Christmas bears. As she explains her view in greater detail, one realizes that she herself sees her task as a futile one.

> What I wanted to tell him [her father] was that I must escape, get away from under the shadow, or I would die. "You cannot," he said. "You must struggle, rise. But in order to rise, you must raise the shadow with you. But you can never lift it to your level. I see that now, which I did not see until I came down here. But escape it you cannot...." (pp. 239-40)

The failure of the relationship between Joanna and Joe is foreshadowed, even made inevitable here. In effect, in the crumbling of the "spiritual skeleton" as Faulkner calls her succumbing to lust in the second phase of the relationship, the "shadow" has pulled her down. She revels in *sex-guilt-the Negro*; she is, in the darkness, *totally* the corrupt female--so much so that even Joe Christmas is awed by her. She embraces not only "sin but filth. She had an avidity for the forbidden wordsymbols; an insatiable appetite for the sound of them on his tongue and on her own" (p. 244). She develops an incredible interest in the intricacies of sexual performance, the "interest of a surgeon." Knowing Faulkner's--or Joe Christmas's--equation of guilt, we can conclude that Joanna is wallowing in the deepest part of that "original abyss." Naked in the darkness, lying beneath the shrubs "in the wild throes of nymphomania," writhing in erotic intoxication--"in the close, breathing halfdark without

walls.... 'Negro! Negro! Negro!'" (p. 245) she chants as a
litany to the symbol of lust and guilt.

Within six months, we are told, she was "completely
corrupted." However, it is not Joe as a person who corrupts
her. It is what he represents *to her*. It is necessary, always,
to remember Joe's dual nature: that when he lies with her,
an apparent Negro, he regards the act as a white man, with a
certain measure of revulsion. At no time is there delight in
the relationship for him. In the darkness she now represents
the equation of guilt, foul and corrupt, one of the "cracked
urns" of his youthful vision. He begins to be afraid of her,
much as he was horrified in the Negro town by the "hot wet
primogenitive Female" that seemed to engulf "all manshaped
life." Now, with his white consciousness, he feels as though
she is beginning to corrupt and taint him; he sees himself
"like a man being sucked down into a bottomless morass"
(another image that represents obvious material for a Freudian
critic). The corruption she seems "to gather from the air
itself," that is, from the Negro as abstract; the echo is
Joe's experience in Freedman Town once again--Negro bodies
and voices "fluid ... with the now ponderable night inseparable and one." His impulse is to escape; but he, who for that
first year had to violate her anew each night, now is himself
the victim. The affair goes on, "submerging him more and more
by the imperious and overriding fury of those nights. Perhaps he realised that he could not escape" (p. 246).

The Negro part of him had been the catalyst of corruption,
but the white part of him is now violated, along with her.
Joanna stands as the symbol of what happens when the *Negro-
guilt* half of the equation succeeds in merging with the *sex-
female* half. This, for Joe, is the final meaning of the
crucifixion of guilt, the image of crucifixion given by Joanna's father. The shadow pulls down the white. Appropriately
enough, Joanna herself draws that parallel. Believing that
she is pregnant, she muses bitterly: "A full measure. Even
to a bastard negro child. I would like to see father's and
Calvin's faces" (p. 251). It is, significantly, not Joe
himself that she regards as having brought her to this, but
the father who has invested her with the curse of her existence. Like Joe, she has now come to the point where she
perceives all life as tainted. The Negro--sex--is guilt; it
poisons life and brings death. Certainly this is a far cry
from the "nigger-loving" Northerner.

The pregnancy is an illusion, and the relationship now
enters its third phase: that of the bitter, sterile consequence. Images of death and futility begin to pervade her
thoughts. Their wild nights "were as dead now as the hollow

fencepost"; "that was all dead: the faultlessly played scenes."
"'It's over now,' she thought quietly, 'finished.'" Faulkner
even employs nature to provide a contrast to the lust of
summer: "A frost had come, and some of the leaves were beginning to turn" (p. 252). Joe himself is gripped by the hollow-
ness of the aftermath; he found himself "in the middle of a
plain where there was no house, not even snow, not even wind"
(p. 255).

It is now that Joanna Burden becomes a sort of Hines-
figure--"cold, remote, fanatic." One must publicly expiate,
and expiation is what she urges on Joe. The form of sackcloth
and ashes, the expiation, is to declare himself as a Negro.
He must, in effect, admit himself to be guilty of vileness.
The attempt to lift the shadow, to make it equal, to bring
together the irreconcilable division of race has failed, as
her father had long ago forecast. She knows it emotionally;
Joe, of course, has always known it, because he combines both
sides within himself; and the white revulsion for the Negro
has never abated. He has never believed differently because
he has never believed in the possibility of any other result
than that which inevitably occurs. For him the affair has been
from the beginning an affirmation of the corruption of existence, the only doubtful element being her daylight maleness.
He is therefore unwilling to accept her demand; although he
believes firmly enough in guilt, he will not expiate, just
as earlier he would not allow himself to think about marrying
her because he had built his entire life on acceptance of
the guilt equation. "'No'" he had said, thinking of the possibility of marriage, "'If I give in now, I will deny all the
thirty years that I have lived to make me what I chose to be'"
(p. 250-51). That was before she had asked him to declare
himself as Negro; "giving in" at *that* time meant to him passing finally as white. His choice has been ambiguity, dis-
engagement from both races as the only means of salvation.
Just as he would not bring a tainted body into the white
race, he cannot accept the horror of declaring a Negro identity. Can we still believe those critics who see Joe as trying to force an identity out of society?

Joanna Burden's religious obsession now assumes the same
form of racist belief as that of Hines, without of course the
public hostility of the old man's. Sex has led to guilt,
and she wants Joe to become Negro publicly to expiate both
himself and her. She will stand by the side of the public
manifestation of guilt--the Negro--and share in it. She even
conceives of a period of formal preparation for the expiation: he will go to a Negro school and then read law in the
office of a Negro lawyer. The distinction between white and

Negro must be reestablished, because it is the nature of God's
judgment, and that nature has been violated.

The two are, on the surface, poles apart at this moment;
but in fact, the milder form of Hines's gospel that she is
preaching is the one to which Joe himself basically subscribes.
Yet, he is white in consciousness always, and it is that which
makes him strike out at her. The gospel is truth; but since
it is his corruption that it asserts, he cannot accept it even
though he believes it. As Joanna lies there bleeding from the
force of his blow--the customary purgation--she utters the
words that bring them back to a fatal point of common belief,
although he is not yet ready to admit it. "'Maybe it would
be better if we both were dead,' she said" (p. 263). This is
the final meaning of the guilt equation carried to its extreme
implications. If life is foul, death is the only answer for
those who read in the gospel of Hines as true believers, the
inevitable result of that corruption that life itself is seen
as being. She then prays over him, after which their strange
compact is made.

> After a time she said quietly:
>   "Then there's just one other thing to do."
>   "There's just one other thing to do," he
> said. (p. 265)

They have reached the end of things; each now sees the final
answer to be the slaying of the other. She, consciously accepting the experience as a more final thing--though with no more
complete belief in guilt than his own--is ready to kill herself, also. Joe moves more quickly during that crucial moment
in the bedroom when she raises the old double-barrelled re-
volver (appropriately, a Civil War relic), and so has to find
his answer, a somewhat different one, a week later.

As with the lynch-law of the community at large, Joanna
Burden and Joe Christmas see in murder the only opportunity
for self-vindication. It proves for them, finally, the truth
of the *Negro-guilt-sex* equation; paradoxically, it also proves
their need for self-crucifixion. A culture that sees life as
tainted inevitably reaches a point first of murder and then
of suicide. Psychologically, Joe Christmas is not alien to
the community but a symbolic expression of their most fundamental concern; psychologically, Joanna Burden is not a rootless stranger but a person who affirms the community belief
and becomes a ritual sacrifice to establish the inevitability
of the result. Doc Hines is not simply the madman of Mottstown,
but the oracle, the high priest of communal faith (so complete
is Hines's conviction that he preaches the doctrine of white
superiority not to the white--who already knows it--but to
the Negro, who symbolically provides sustenance for him). The

death of Joanna is nourishment for the communal belief; it is
not the dead who are served by the vengeance of lynch mobs
but the society in its periodic blood-lust. That unhappy woman
had, Faulkner says, "died three years ago and had just now
begun to live again"; her death is affirmation "of an attained
bourne beyond the hurt and harm of man" (p. 273). So, too,
with Joe Christmas, ten days later.

However, the peace of death is not *answer* but *release*;
their sacrificial roles have been played out. When Joe accepts
his Negro nature he does not affirm final truth but communal
"truth," the pathetic faith by which he has lived and the
only one that he knows. In a society where inhumanity is
doctrine, he finds it is better to be a victim than a master.

The larger-than-life figures of Joe Christmas and his
grandfather, and Joanna Burden and her family, stand as epic
representations of the racist South of actuality, cursed by
its own guilt. It is, then, beyond them that one must look
for any ultimate answer.

III. Gail Hightower:
The Enchanted Soul of the South

Richard Chase, surprisingly, perhaps, for an early critic,
regarded Gail Hightower as "one of Faulkner's best characters."[4] In contrast, Alfred Kazin says of the retired Presbyterian minister that he:

> by general consent, is one of the failures of the book:
> he is too vague, too drooping, too formless, in a word
> too much the creature of defeat and obsession, to com-
> pel our interest or our belief.[5]

Well, Hightower is not easy to know; he is, even more than
Joe Christmas, a complex figure, and we get much less complete
a view of him in action. But then inaction is his nature.
Perhaps more than anyone else in the novel, he emerges a
richer character with each additional reading. While I think
Faulkner fails in one respect with him, it is not in any of
the ways cited by Kazin. Rather, a contrary one; it is when
Hightower operates as a "real" person--in that dialogue devoted to distinct action in which he is involved--that he
is least convincing. In his stream of thought, his musings,
memories, visions, he becomes one of Faulkner's best creations. Kazin's objections to him as vague, drooping, the
creature of defeat and obsession, are precisely those things
which he represents with greatest significance for the novel.
Hightower is, for most of the story, the impotent force of
tradition in the South, that defrocked minister of a traditional belief, who has failed his people.

Just as Joe Christmas's abstract features represent the
ambiguous nature of his mixed blood, and Doc Hines's dirty
stubbled face with the clear, mad eyes is the South of fanatical racism, the ruined dignity of Hightower is an index of
his function. Byron Bunch, coming in and finding him asleep,
studies him for a few moments before waking him. Hightower's
hands are folded on a book:

> ... peaceful, benignant, almost pontifical. The shirt
> is made after an old fashion, with a pleated though
> carelessly ironed bosom, and he wears no collar. His
> mouth is open, the loose and flabby flesh sagging away
> from the round orifice in which the stained lower teeth
> show, and from the still fine nose which alone age,
> the defeat of sheer years, has not changed. [It seems] ...
> as though the whole man were fleeing away from the nose
> which holds invincibly to something yet of pride and
> courage above the sluttishness of vanquishment like a
> forgotten flag above a ruined fortress. (p. 343)

The hands folded on the book echo one of the associations
made several times in connection with Hightower; he is an intellectual to the degree that books, the world of illusion
("the gutless swooning" and "dehydrated lust" of Tennyson),
are his refuge. The folded hands recall, too, the popular
metaphor for inactivity. His pleated shirt is in the fashion
of his grandfather's day--the Civil War--rather than 1930;
and its shabby condition is appropriate to the man. "The loose
and flabby flesh" is that of stagnating life, the "defeat of
sheer years." But Hightower is a man just past fifty, close
to what Faulkner elsewhere speaks of as the prime of life.
However, he has from youth removed himself from all active
participation in the community. Yet--there is that nose, in-
vincible, with "something yet of pride and courage above the
sluttishness of vanquishment like a forgotten flag above a
ruined fortress." The nose, of course, is Roman, the distinct
feature of a classical visage; and it stands here for that
spirit of the past--the "pride and courage"--which for a brief
moment in history was the greatest achievement of the South.
Now, it is nothing more than a symbol, discarded by the community that is not even aware of its need of it, discarded
not merely because of the perversity of the community but
through its own default.

That Hightower is the stagnant tradition of the Southern
past is something that he himself subconsciously perceives.
The community, the South, has need of him and what he represents, the glory and force of its own tradition; and the
default of that force has created the present debasement of

the community. Note, for example, Hightower speaking of the townspeople at a point before the crucial week of Joanna Burden's death:

> They are good people. They must believe what they must believe, especially as it was I who was at one time both master and servant of their believing. (p. 69)

If, as I have suggested, *Light in August* represents a break in the progressive view of the South with which the novels of the Yoknapatawpha saga are concerned, Hightower encapsules beautifully in himself the decay of the entire Sutpen-Sartoris-Compson tradition. The meaning of this aspect of the saga is summarized in him without, I think, any real loss. Certainly his stagnant body ("unfastidious sedentation," "static overflesh"), his chair "evocative of disuse and supineness and shabby remoteness from the world," stand as symbolic parallels to the decadent reality of the great plantation tradition--to the point, perhaps, where he is a personified cliché.

Hightower's failure is twofold, the second being the most obvious. Afraid of life, he has resigned from society and will not allow himself to become involved with it. "'I am not in life anymore,' he thinks. 'That's why there is no use in even trying to meddle, interfere'" (p. 284). As with Joe Christmas, it is not simply that society has rejected him. He has *chosen* this role of noninvolvement and tries to protect it desperately when his isolation is threatened. When he hears that Joe Christmas has been captured, he feels an intense shock. He finds himself emotionally brought in, despite his urge to avoid responsibility for life. The counter of the store in which he is standing seems to move against him--"it was more like the earth itself were rocking faintly, preparing to move." And he thinks, without even accounting for the thought--"I wont! I wont! I have bought immunity. I have paid. I have paid" (p. 292). The last two thoughts here are contradictory, although Hightower does not realize this until much later. To buy immunity is to buy something of personal choice, while the implications of "I have paid" suggest that he has discharged the debt which society holds against him.

The simple fact, of course, is that Hightower prefers the sanctuary that his name implies; at most he will accept the role of sounding board, a confessional priest, for the apparently innocuous Byron Bunch--who, eventually, is the person who succeeds in shaking his world. For instance, when Byron Bunch comes to tell him of the arrangements made for Lena Grove, Hightower anticipates that Byron has taken a step: "'And he didn't offer to tell me,' he thinks. 'I would

have listened, let him think aloud to me'" (p. 294). The
phrasing here is significant.

Twice in the novel Hightower is described as resembling
"an eastern idol."[6] In addition to the implication of denying
the life of the body, this image also suggests Hightower as
the oracle of fatalism, the figure who may have ultimate
knowledge, perhaps, but is trapped in his own remoteness.
As Byron becomes entangled in his love for Lena Grove, Hightower offers advice several times. It is always the same:
"'Go away, Byron. Go away. Now. At once.'" This solution,
escape, is that which he has applied to his own life; and,
therefore, it is clearly wrong, particularly for Byron Bunch,
the one figure in the novel who squarely faces his responsibility in all the business of life. Our initial view of Hightower is that of a man who knows a great deal and is intellec-
tually compassionate. That he really represents religion is,
of course, untrue, just as it is in the case of Joanna Burden
or Doc Hines. The supposed sect with which he is involved
is again one that is not common in the South--Presbyterianism--
and again one may assume that is because his belief has
nothing, really, to do with orthodox Christianity. Just as
the fanatic racist shakes out religion in order to pour his
hatred into the container, Hightower transforms his obsession
into a faith to live by. That aspect of the South that he
represents deifies its own saints and enthrones its own god;
its golden age is the Civil War. Certainly the word "faith"
has an ironic suitability in Hightower's case. Further, while
he is compassionate in thought (the overquoted passage "'Poor
man. Poor mankind'" occurs very early in the novel), he himself instinctively reacts to the guilt equation that governs
the communal belief as represented by Joe Christmas and Hines.
In fact, one of the ways in which we may measure his change
in the novel is by his shifting attitude towards womanhood.

There is something approaching poetic justice in the fact
that Joanna Burden, bearing all her life "the curse of the
black man," devotes her fortune to Negro charities. There
seems to be a similar irony in Hightower's situation, in
that, deceived by his wife, he helps thereafter to maintain
a home for delinquent girls. Again, just as Faulkner shows
Doc Hines's obsession to be one that makes him incapable of
engaging in worthwhile labor, he makes Hightower's obsession
with the glorious manhood of the past a thing that destroys
his own manhood. His wife became adulterous, simply enough,
because Hightower--as local legend has it--"couldn't or
wouldn't satisfy her himself." One has the impression that
this is what Faulkner believes the Hightower aspect of the
South has done to its women, denying them a healthy life of

the body because it does not live in the present but in the fleshless dream of the past. In keeping blind and absolute faith with the dead, it denies life in a way different from, but not more true than, the life denial of a Hines. Hightower's impotence is explained as directly due to the obsession; it is--

> ... as though the seed which his grandfather had trans-
> mitted to him had been on the horse too that night and
> had been killed too and time had stopped there and then
> for the seed and nothing had happened in time since,
> not even him. (p. 59)

Hightower's offense against his wife is greater than hers against him, for in denying the realities of the flesh, he denies her function as woman to her. His feeling towards her for twenty-five years is not one of hatred but of rejection of all attitude. He will not think about it. He never speaks of her, and until that final vision he seems to have been successful in expunging the thought. Yet, he sees womanhood as fundamentally destructive to the male. He warns Byron Bunch to flee from Lena Grove, and Byron answers that he did not expect Hightower to turn "'against a woman wronged and betrayed--.'" Hightower says:

> No woman who has a child is ever betrayed; the husband
> of a mother, whether he be the father or not, is already
> a cuckold. Give yourself at least the one chance in ten,
> Byron. If you must marry, there are single women, girls,
> virgins. It's not fair that you should sacrifice your-
> self to a woman who has chosen once and now wishes to
> renege that choice. It's not right. It's not just. God
> didn't intend it so when He made marriage. Made it?
> Women made marriage. (pp. 298-99)

The adultery of Hightower's wife explains the appeal made on the surface here, that of the sanctity of marriage.

Underneath that, and much more meaningful, however, is Hightower's attack on motherhood. His own wife had not been a mother, so the cuckold father reference does not function in his own direct experience. What he is saying here is that Byron should ally himself with a virgin, not so that he may have her virginity but so that he may *protect* it; that mar-riage is simply a woman's way of using a man as an instrument to create life, that *this* process is the real cuckolding of man. Hightower here reveals a pale, mental reflection of what manifests itself as violence in Joe Christmas: a con-ception of woman as the source of evil in her function as child-bearer. He then goes on to say: "'There have been good

women who were martyrs to brutes, in their cups and such.
But what woman, good or bad, has ever suffered from any
brute as men have suffered from good women?'" (p. 299). Again,
this is not the personal experience of Gail Hightower speaking, but his mental conception of life itself as a thing of
horror. It is also worth noting that immediately after this
conversation in the novel, we are given a significant passage
in which Faulkner describes Hightower's attitude towards
"darkness." When a very young man, he had loved to walk in
the night.

> Then the ground, the bark of trees, became actual,
> savage, filled with, evocative of, strange and baleful
> half delights and half terrors. He was afraid of it.
> He feared; he loved in being afraid. Then one day while
> at the seminary he realised that he was no longer afraid.
> It was as though a door had shut somewhere. He was no
> longer afraid of darkness. He just hated it; he would
> flee from it, to walls, to artificial light. (p. 300-
> 301)

There is no reference here to the Flesh, but it is almost unnecessary. The "strange and baleful half delights" certainly
echo the wild nights of corruption of Joanna Burden and Joe
Christmas, and Hightower's hatred of darkness is not far
removed from Joe's feeling towards the palpitating "Female"
darkness of the Negro town. Hightower's solution is to flee,
as he does after the conversation with Byron, to Tennyson,
described appropriately in a sexual--or antisexual--reference:
"sapless trees and dehydrated lusts ... like listening in a
cathedral to a eunuch chanting ..." (p. 301).
    Hightower's life is not to be lost in quite the same
sense as that of Joe Christmas, however. The means of his
salvation, such as it is, is twice presented through Byron
Bunch, the first time unsuccessfully. It is, of course, human
responsibility, which Byron himself represents all through
the story. The final symbol of it will be Lena Grove, the
avatar of life and goddess of birth. Before he is finished,
Hightower will reverse himself completely; but at first he
makes one more desperate attempt to avoid involvement. As
Byron becomes more enmeshed with Lena, Hightower begins to
accuse him of coming between "husband and wife," although he
thinks at the very same time that Byron "could never do anything that would be very evil."
    Actually, his own involvement with Byron, hitherto the
innocuous one of being a sounding board, has slowly involved
him with mankind once again. Almost hysterical, his voice
shaking "a little, high and thin," he sneers at Byron for the

very qualities that make Byron worthwhile: "'Byron Bunch,
the guardian of public weal and morality.'" Then he begins to
cry and says: "'I dont mean that. You know I dont. But it is
not right to bother me, to worry me ... That this should come
to me'" (p. 344). Then Byron, apologetic though he has not
yet asked anything of Hightower, confronts him with the awful
(for Hightower) words: "'But you are a man of God. You cant
dodge that.'"

It is a direct assertion of Hightower's responsibility,
and the older man promptly rejects it, placing the blame not
on himself but on "'them like you and like her and like him
in the jail'" that he has been defrocked and is "'no longer
a man of God.'" Byron, the simple country laborer, then states
the truth that Hightower has evaded for twenty-five years:

> "I know that.... You made your choice before that....
> You were given your choice before I was born, and you
> took it before I or her or him either was born. That
> was your choice. And I reckon them that are good must
> suffer for it the same as them that are bad...." (p. 345)

Byron is the catalyst of truth, and Hightower's instinc-
tive rejection of what is about to happen to him has valid
grounds. When Byron leaves, Hightower for a few moments has
his thoughts to himself. It is Sunday evening, one of the
two nights a week when the services in his former church
bring the strains of organ music floating through the twilight. It is on these nights that Hightower evokes the memory
of that frozen moment of time--the Civil War raid when the
blast of a gun caught his grandfather in the saddle--which
has been his lifelong obsession. The music comes, bringing
"something of that peace which is the promise and the end
of the Church." It is now that Hightower's particular religion blends decisively with the central theme of the novel,
for the music conveys to him "that quality of abjectness
and sublimation, as if the freed voices themselves were
assuming the shapes and attitudes of crucifixions, ecstatic,
solemn, and profound ..." (p. 347). The peace "which is the
promise and the end of the Church" thus ties with the release
of death. Now, the music brings to him the first of the two
visions in which the meaning of his life and that of his
culture become manifest:

> ... the music has still a quality stern and implacable,
> deliberate and without passion so much as immolation,
> pleading, asking, for not love, not life, forbidding
> it to others, demanding in sonorous tones death as
> though death were the boon.... Listening, he seems to
> hear within it the apotheosis of his own history, his

own land, his own environed blood: that people from
which he sprang and among whom he lives who can never
take either pleasure or catastrophe or escape from
either, without brawling over it.... *And so why should
not their religion drive them to crucifixion of themselves and one another?* he thinks. It seems to him that
he can hear within the music the declaration and dedication of that which they know that on the morrow they
will have to do. It seems to him that the past week has
rushed like a torrent and that the week to come, which
will begin tomorrow, is the abyss, and that now on the
brink of cataract the stream has raised a single blended
and sonorous and austere cry, not for justification but
as a dying salute before its own plunge, and not to any
god but to the doomed man in the barred cell ... in whose
crucifixion they too will raise a cross. (pp. 347-48)

Hightower has perceived the nature of Joe Christmas's sacrifice: that his death is part of the eternal crucifixion, of
the eternal expiation of mankind believing itself guilty. Joe
Christmas is the sacrificial lamb of the culture in which
Hightower exists; his death is part of the constant process
of laying the ghost of their own guilt, which constantly rises
anew. The sagging figure lying inert in the August twilight
perceives the tragedy, but he is not yet ready to accept his
own role in it.

     Byron's first attempt to make him do so occurs now as,
returning with the old Hines couple, he has the woman gradually
reveal what she wants of Hightower. On the level of reality,
the request is slightly ridiculous, and if granted, would
probably be futile. However, that is beside the point. What
they want Hightower to do is to say that Joe Christmas was
with him the night of the murder, and every other night that
Brown said he went up to the Burden house. On the symbolic
level, they are asking Hightower, the "avatar" of the traditional South, the spirit of the tarnished glory that once
was, *to declare himself*. He is to take the side of the Negro,
to stand up and confute the betrayer Brown. He is, in short,
to recognize the link of humanity that binds Negro and white
together, to accept it and to accord his protection to the
Negro. This is what the natural leader of the communal South--
in body, the minister as "master and servant of their believing," in mind, the heir of those phantom horsemen whose glory
still crashes on the silent air--this is what he *can* do.
This is the redemption that could have been. But the tradition
is an inert one, frozen at the moment of its climax, not re-
deeming the present age but poisoning it.

The scene brings Hightower, for the first time, into a position where the answer is incipient. But he is incapable as yet of accepting it. His involvement in mankind is a prospect that horrifies him, although he instinctively perceives its truth even as he vehemently rejects it. This scene, following his dream vision, explains that moment of unwitting perception still further. The community rising to the moment when it will sacrifice Joe Christmas was visualized as a stream about to plunge over a cataract to its own death, giving a wailing "dying salute" to "the doomed man in the barred cell ... in whose crucifixion they too will raise a cross." Together with his thought of a moment before, that of the community driven "to crucifixion of themselves and one another," the death of the community in the figure of the crucified murderer is verification of the interlocking identity of mankind. Because the white holds the life of the Negro in contempt and destroys it, he cannot free his own life of the very same poison. He hates life because he hates life in the Negro; he is cursed because he has cursed the Negro. Only when he cherishes all life can his own life become something of value. Only when he looks beyond hatred can love begin. It is this that Hightower is asked to do; it is, symbolically, this that the South needs of its past.

This recognition of one's obligation to humanity seems to show in Hightower's tortured face as he sits there. Byron, looking at him, thinks: "*It's right funny. You'd think they had done got swapped somewhere. Like it was him that had a nigger grandson waiting to be hung*" (p. 367). The one thing needed, the projection of the self outside the self, is the one thing of which Hightower is incapable; the moral leadership of the South is paralyzed. "'What is it you want me to do? Shall I go plead guilty to the murder? Is that it?'" he cries bitterly (p. 368). In a sense, this is only slight exaggeration, as he himself has already realized in his conception of the common guilt of mankind. He shouts his refusal, insisting that he will not do it, not because he "'dont dare to ... because I wont! I wont! do you hear!'" (p. 370). Driving them from the room, he falls across the desk, covering his face, having denied his link with humanity.

Byron's first attempt to rejuvenate Hightower thus fails. The reason is that Hightower cannot himself be a redemptive force without first himself being redeemed. It is, I think, significant that Hightower, representing that element of the South—potential moral leadership—of which the community has such great need, should be called upon by Byron Bunch. Byron, frequently overlooked as a serious figure because of the comic implications of the last chapter of the novel, is

the "good element" of the folk, just as Brown is that element
which betrays. Hightower has allowed the Browns--in the robes
of the Klan--to violate him, in order to secure immunity from
a moral obligation to the community (just as the "old aristoc-
racy" of the South, according to Faulkner, by default has
allowed the Klan to take over social control and so destroy
the moral fiber of the community). Byron is a simple man, a
hard-working Christian who sees a moral obligation in every
man's need. It is this element of the South that calls upon,
and stimulates, a return to those qualities of value which
the Southern mind revealed for a brief valiant moment during
the Civil War.

   At this moment, Hightower has reached bottom; he can only
come up. He does so, early the next morning, and again it is
Byron Bunch who establishes the opportunity. Lena has begun
labor. Coming to Hightower's house, Byron finds the older man
asleep:

> There was a quality of profound and complete surrender
> in it. Not of exhaustion, but surrender, as though he
> had given over and relinquished completely that grip
> upon that blending of pride and hope and vanity and
> fear, that strength to cling to either defeat or victory,
> which is the I-Am, and the relinquishment of which is
> usually death. (p. 372)

"*A poor thing. A poor thing*" thinks Byron looking down
at him, and he wishes that he did not have to wake him. "'But
it aint me that's waiting,'" he answers himself. The person
who is waiting is Lena Grove, the avatar of basic and enduring
life. This time Byron does not make his mistake of the evening
before; he simply tells Hightower that a doctor has not yet
been called, that Hightower must go to the cabin and attend
to the girl. Before the man can object, Byron is gone, and
the startled minister finds himself with not the choice but
the necessity for involvement. Byron knows that once, years
before, Hightower had successfully delivered a Negro child
when a dilatory doctor had failed to come on time. Now, Byron,
leaving the house to search for a doctor, ponders:

> Yet it was not exactly the solicitude of an incipient
> father. There was something else behind it, which he
> was not to recognise until later. It was as though
> there lurked in his mind, still obscured by the need
> for haste, something which was about to spring full
> clawed upon him. But what he was thinking was 'I got
> to decide quick. He delivered that nigger baby all
> right, they said....' (p. 374)

His decision is made a moment later. He goes to the "same

doctor who had arrived too late" for the delivery of the
Negro child at which Hightower had officiated years before.
When they finally arrive back at the cabin, history has
repeated itself; this time Byron Bunch has successfully involved Hightower. In the past twenty-five years, Hightower
has done only two things for the community: delivered a Negro
child, and now a white one. Through Byron, he has been brought
to attend to the need of the life force, and the experience
rejuvenates him.

Returning home, Hightower fixes himself a huge breakfast,
thinking that he should feel badly and surprised to find that
he does not. Then, "there goes through him a glow, a wave,
a surge of something almost hot, almost triumphant" (p. 382).
After eating he gets a book, not Tennyson this time, but
"food for a man"--Shakespeare's *Henry IV*. Sitting down in
the chair, he decides that he will not sleep "because Byron
will be in soon to wake me. But to learn just what else he can
think of to want me to do, will be almost worth the waking"
(p. 383). He has, one assumes for the first time in his life,
discovered a sense of value outside his dream illusion.
Falling asleep immediately, his face "innocent, peaceful,
and assured" in contrast to the look of "profound surrender"
that he had worn when Byron came to wake him before dawn,
he finally awakes six hours later with the impression that
someone had called him. "'Yes?' he says 'Yes? What is it?'"
There is no one there, but "for a moment longer he looks about,
seeming to listen and to wait, with that air forceful and
assured. And the glow is not gone either" (pp. 383-84). He
obviously now thinks of himself as a man for whom there is
a "use"; he feels "purpose and pride."

His twenty-five-year sleep has ended, and he is again--
or finally--a member of society. Gone, too, is his sneering
rejection of Byron's relationship with Lena, his condemnation
of her and womanhood in general. He has for the first time a
desire to be perpetuated, for he now thinks of life not as
valueless but as a mystery, as beauty. Almost afraid to allow
the thought to occur, he then rubs his hands in delight and
muses on the possibility of Lena's naming the new child after
him. "*I have no namesake*." His thoughts become almost maudlin
sentimentality, but he is a man unaccustomed to human sentiment so we need not judge him (or Faulkner) too harshly:

> *She will have to have others, more* remembering the
> young strong body from out whose travail even there
> shone something tranquil and unafraid. *More of them.*
> *Many more. That will be her life, her destiny. The good*
> *stock peopling in tranquil obedience to it the good*
> *earth; from these hearty loins without hurry or haste*

> *descending mother and daughter. But by Byron engendered*
> *next. Poor boy. Even though he did let me walk back*
> *home* (p. 384)

He now accepts sex, he accepts womanhood ("descending mother
and daughter"), he accepts "the good stock" obediently bringing forth life in response to the nature of "the good earth."
The switch is a complete one for Hightower, releasing him
from his passive imprisonment in the same communal attitude
that makes a sacrifice of Joe Christmas. Hightower now moves
out of the twilight element that has characterized him all
through the novel; he walks forth in the sunlight, delight-
ing in the "fecund odor of the earth, the woods." Passing
by the charred remains of Joanna Burden's house, he thinks
with compassion: "'Poor, barren woman. To have not lived only
a week longer, until luck returned to this place'" (p. 385).
The luck, of course, is the new life of Lena Grove's child,
which has rejuvenated him and a denial of which he instinctively associates with the tragedy of Joanna Burden, with
all tragedy. As contrast to the death of the "poor, barren
woman" (as well as in unconscious contrast to the thoughts
of Joe Christmas in Freedman Town), Hightower now conceives
of birth as redemption and links it decisively not only to
Lena but to the Negro. He imagines the earlier life of the
Burden house (forgetting that they were abolitionists or
perhaps not concerned about petty consistency):

> ... he can see, feel, about him the ghosts of rich
> fields, and of the rich fecund black life of the
> quarters, the mellow shouts, the presence of fecund
> women, the prolific naked children in the dust before
> the doors.... (p. 385)

For the first time in the novel, "fecund" does not mean
"corrupt." Negro life is elemental, not cursed. The horrifying imagery of the black pool of corruption is washed away
in the reality of life and sunlight; the darkness of despair
is a perversion of the mind, engendered by the communal
hatred of race. Like a chuckling grandfather, "hearty,"
"gentle, beaming, and triumphant," Hightower goes to call
on Lena and the child.

In the following scene, Hightower is faced with the
realization that his rejuvenation is a limited, personal
thing. The Joe Christmas theme now reappears in the persons
of the elderly Hines couple, who had been staying in Joe
Christmas's cabin with Lena (more "moral obligation" on
the part of Byron Bunch) and so had been present at the
birth. Lena tells Hightower about Mrs. Hines's confusion of
identities, the old woman believing that Lena's baby is the

infant Joe stolen from her thirty years before. Actually, of
course, the confusion of identities is a fusion of identities:
just as Hightower had conceived of Joanna Burden's death as
mitigated in a rebirth concept (with the imagined Negro fecundity at the site of the ruined house), so the death of Joe
is to be mitigated by the new life brought forth on his abandoned cot. The fusion of identities is pushed quite hard by
Faulkner here, to the point where he has Lena herself, who
has never seen Christmas, say: "'I get mixed up and it's like
sometimes I cant--like I am mixed up too and I think that his
pa is that Mr--Mr Christmas too--'" (p. 388). It is offered
symbolically and we might as well take it that way. In the
sense that Joe Christmas dies as sacrificial figure, his death
is that of mankind--a point conceived earlier by Hightower;
while the new realization of Hightower, the involvement of
all men in the destinies of one another, gives some substance
to the idea of Lena's child as a successor of sorts to Joe
Christmas. (The confusion of identities, it seems to me, would
have more meaning if it had occurred to Hightower; coming from
Lena, it is less effective.)

For a moment, Hightower's doubts return, and he attempts
to persuade Lena to send Byron Bunch away. Then the eternally
serene Lena loses her placidity for the first and only time
in the novel; she tells of Byron Bunch's earlier departure,
indicates a belief that she will never see him again, and
begins to weep. Dumbfounded at the realization that Lena loves
his friend, Hightower thinks: *"Thank God, God help me. Thank
God, God help me.*" He leaves, then, in search of Byron. His
euphoria returns; he looks around the planing mill with "exul-
tant interest," for he is seeing the town for the first time
(the bookkeeper speaks in deprecation of these "hillbillies,"
and Hightower nods--"fine people ... fine men and women").
In the "good stock," the hard-working common folk of the South,
too involved with the fundamental concerns of life to hate
or deny, the rejuvenation of the decadent tradition can be
accomplished. Thinking of the absent Byron, Hightower confesses
his enormous debt: "'After all he has done for me. Fetched
to me. Ay; given, restored to me'" (p. 392). Although he does
not yet know it, he is about to receive once again the opportunity to commit himself for another's life, to redeem Joe
Christmas. Having failed the occasion earlier, he will accept
it this time--but he has slept away his life one day too long.

The next time we see Hightower, it is in the death scene
of Joe Christmas. This entire section is governed by the conception of Joe Christmas as communal "immolation." Percy Grimm
is society's high priest wielding the sacrificial knife; Joe
Christmas is the pagan deity of darkness run to earth; High-

tower is the sleeping guardian of the sanctuary who keeps the
door locked just a little too long.

Once restored, Hightower seems to have become a figure of
redemption himself. We are told that Mrs. Hines is supposed
to have precipitated the escape by telling Joe that Hightower
was going to "save him." He is once again described as a minister, although none of the characters--not even Byron--has
so referred to him up to this point in the novel. It seems
apparent to me that in Mrs. Hines's statement Faulkner is once
again linking Hightower to that elusive tradition of the past,
the aspect of the South that he had represented so effectively
in passivity and which symbolizes a form of moral leadership
that could be vital and would be redemptive if it were only
to become operative. Notice, for example, the nature of the
thought that Mrs. Hines is described as having expressed to
her grandson:

> ... somewhere, somehow, in the shape or presence or
> whatever of that old outcast minister was a sanctuary
> which would be inviolable not only to officers and mobs,
> but to the very irrevocable past; to whatever crimes
> had molded and shaped him and left him at last high
> and dry in a barred cell with the shape of an incipient
> executioner everywhere he looked. (p. 424)

In short, she wishes to turn back time, to go back and cancel
out that moment when guilt began.

When Joe Christmas, pursued by Percy Grimm, bursts in on
Hightower and strikes him down with a lightning motion, he
has come we are told because of his white blood "which rising
in him for the last and final time, sent him against all
reason and all reality, into the embrace of a chimera ..."
(pp. 424-25). Hightower, his own blood running symbolically
down his own bald head and "big pale face," seeks now to
assert Joe's innocence by saying that he had been there the
night of the murder. He has come to see, too late, life as
a value in itself which must be preserved (which, of course,
is the only justification, or even reason, for his telling
the lie). Joe dies a ritual death, which brings about the
final vision of the stricken Hightower. Before analyzing
this climactic revelation, however, I believe it necessary
to take a good look at Percy Grimm in pursuit of his quarry.

The break, and final flight, of Joe Christmas are scenes
in which Joe does not have any personal character at all. It
is deliberately abstracted by Faulkner, merged into the
ritual which Joe acts out almost as obligation to the community. I do not think that he escapes because of faith in
Hightower, of whom he has no personal knowledge and from whom

he really expects nothing, since he has on the preceding
Friday accepted his sacrificial role and subsequently delivered
himself into the hands of the mob at Mottstown. What faith
is placed in Hightower is that of Mrs. Hines. Joe escapes in
order to carry out his sacrificial role; he must die by the
communal code which has lynching as its method of execution.
And paradoxically, as we shall see in a moment, if he did
not escape, the one man who would have prevented his lynching
would have been Percy Grimm.[7]

Joe is described, really, only once during the chase,
when he appears before Hightower. As I have mentioned, he
appears then as a pagan deity, hunted by the young "priest."
In this sense, he is indicative both of the cold-blooded in-
tolerance of the new faith (much, say, as Heinrich Heine considers the displacement of the Greek deities by Christianity)
and of a judgment directed against Hightower for his own sin:

> ... Christmas, running up the hall, his raised and armed
> and manacled hands full of glare and glitter like light-
> ning bolts, so that he resembled a vengeful and furious
> god pronouncing a doom.... (p. 438)

Percy Grimm, on the other hand, is a strange form of
Christian saint, whose peculiar sense of "purity" is expressed
in the castration of the dark god. A standard critical cliché
is that which identifies Grimm as a Nazi-style Storm Trooper,
but that really explains nothing. Even in the community Grimm
is not representative; rather, he is regarded with awe by the
townspeople because of his absolute belief in and dedication
to certain principles. He is, contrary to some views, not a
representative of mob law. He is, rather, a pillar of communal
law, his effectiveness based upon a complete faith in the
community. What the community faith is has already been discussed. Percy Grimm sanctifies and preserves the law by which
Joe Christmas dies, as the high priest of Joe's immolation.
His role as such is made possible only because Joe acts out
his part in the ritual by escaping. Had he remained in custody,
Grimm's task would have been to protect him and he would have
done so. In doing so, however, Grimm would have been merely
carrying out a task, he would not have been "fulfilled."

In order to complete the scene, Faulkner provides Grimm
with an entourage of attendant priests. Grimm himself is at
first "indefatigable, restrained yet forceful," "irresistible
and prophetlike" (p. 428). As he communicates his attitude
to his men, they become marked off from the crowd by "a profound and bleak gravity ... grave, austere, detached, looking
with blank, bleak eyes" (p. 433). When the break comes, Grimm
moves in pursuit with the inevitability of a reflex action,

as though his cue has been given and he is carrying out his
carefully memorized part. In him there is "a fierce and con-
strained joy." He makes his moves "fast too, silent, with the
delicate swiftness of an apparition, the implacable undevia-
tion of Juggernaut or Fate" (p. 435). His expression "was
rocklike, calm, still bright with that expression of fulfillment, of grave and reckless joy" (p. 436). Joe Christmas now
appears like a demon figure hunted by the young priest--"with
an effect as of magic, his manacled hands ... glinting as if
they were on fire." Still animated by that "quiet joy," Grimm
stops abruptly for a moment: "Above the blunt, cold rake of
the automatic his face had that serene, unearthly luminousness
of angels in church windows" (p. 437). Moving without thought,
accurately, as though a "Player moved him on the Board," he
carries out the steps of the ritual in an almost dream-like
way. The sacrificial figure runs into Hightower's house, and
Grimm is just behind him followed by three of his attendant
priests:

> ... bringing with them into *its stale and cloistral*
> *dimness* something of the savage summer sunlight which
> they had just left.
>   *It was upon them, of them: its shameless savageness.*
> *Out of it their faces seemed to glare with bodiless*
> *suspension as though from haloes* as they stooped and
> raised Hightower.... (p. 438; italics added)

A moment later, in answer to Hightower's stammering attempt
to shield Joe Christmas, Grimm cries out, "'Jesus Christ!' ...
his young voice clear and outraged like that of a young priest."
     A moment later he wields the knife in ritual castration.[8]
It is, of course, a blood rite in which the ancient enemy--
the Negro--the force of darkness, is robbed of his power, his
ability to taint the white destroyed beyond the grave. There
is in it a clear implication of the ghost returning, of the
superstitious desire to nail the dead man through the heart
in a sexual sense. It is, of course, in that sense that he
really exists as *the Enemy*.
     My interest in pulling together the above quotations is
to show that while Grimm may be vaguely explained by referring
to him as a Mississippi fascist, the figure that Faulkner
actually draws is a mixture of a Spanish Jesuit and a primitive priest of a blood cult. The reason that I think this is
important is that Percy Grimm does *not* disappear from the
novel at this point; he blends with the figure of Joe Christmas in the final dream vision of Hightower.
     The long penultimate chapter of *Light in August*, during
which Gail Hightower sits mutely thinking over his past, has

been criticized as anticlimactic and unnecessary. After the magnificent paragraph devoted to Joe Christmas's death, it is difficult not to concede that dramatic anticlimax *does* exist here. However, murders notwithstanding, this novel, as such, is *not* primarily dramatic. The chapter, then, is by no means unnecessary, for the thematic climax of Hightower's story--as well as the final meaning of Joe Christmas's--is developed in it. In the chapter, Gail Hightower has both a personal and a generic vision, in which his own sin--the sin of the South of tradition--and the tragedy of his people are crystallized.

Hightower has through Byron Bunch and Lena Grove been "restored," but he has not been *redeemed*, for his acceptance of life came too late. In our last encounter with him, he is back in the twilight setting of the earlier scenes, although he is not the same man as he was then. The reverie begins with thoughts of the wife whose memory he has kept from his consciousness for so many years. He thinks of her as she must have been, standing "with division and regret and then despair" somewhere in the shadows behind him in those early days while he sat enraptured by his obsession. He had not spoken with her of his thoughts then, in those days when the "isolation of the seminary" had seemed to him a fine and proper way of life. He knows now that that was his first sin, that he should have done so:

> Not even to her, to woman. *The* woman. Woman (not the seminary, as he had once believed): the Passive and Anonymous whom God had created to be not alone the recipient and receptacle of the seed of his body but of his spirit too, which is truth or as near truth as he dare approach. (pp. 441-42)

This is the answer that Lena Grove has revealed to him by the simple actuality of her existence. Woman, the bearer of life, is the means by which man can keep faith. Not only his body but his spirit must be relinquished to the force of life.

As though to search back for the origin of his failure, Hightower's thoughts go back to his childhood, to his family and the grandfather whose ghost had poisoned his existence. For the first time he realizes that the truth had been before him even in childhood, in the person of his father whom he had denied in favor of the grandfather. The father was himself a minister in his youth, an educated Byron Bunch of sorts, who like Byron rode "sixteen miles each Sunday" back in the hills to preach in a small Presbyterian chapel. A quiet man, the father had lived by principles of absolute morality, keeping no slaves and going to the Civil War only as a chaplain. "He fired no musket and wore instead of uniform

the somber frock coat which he had purchased to be married
in and ... used to preach in" (p. 443). Twenty-five years
later, this coat becomes a symbol to the young man, who finding it in an attic chest sees on it a patch from a Union Army
uniform. The coat to him represents only one thing, that
patch, together with the overwhelming desire to know--"with
that horrified triumph and sick joy"--if his father had killed
the man that had worn the blue coat. For the actuality of
the father, his dedication to principle, is something from
which the boy is completely removed. Between them "there was
so much of distance in time that not even the decades of years
could measure, that there was not even any physical resemblance" (p. 444). Thinking back on his father now, Hightower
sees him as a figure living by his own truth, a man whose
nature had harmonized with that of the earth--"a sheer fortitude that did not offer, in his lifetime anyway, physical
ease for reward" (p. 448). The father had known that only
by the work of days are the days worth having.

Unlike that aspect of the South that Hightower himself
became, his father "lived by his principles in peace [the
humanitarianism that made him opposed to slavery], and when
war came he carried them into war and lived by them there ..."
(p. 448). Except for these principles, he lived "without
other equipment save his strength and courage" and when

> the war was lost and the other men returned home with
> their eyes stubbornly reverted toward what they refused
> to believe was dead, he looked forward and made what
> he could of defeat by making practical use of that
> which he had learned in it. He turned doctor. (pp.
> 448-49)

It is this shift in his life that most clearly distinguishes
him from his son, who later turns to the seminary as a refuge
from reality. The father becomes a healer, not only through
the words of religion (which Faulkner suggests must always
be inadequate since they can be twisted to any use), but as
a minister of the body as well.

> The father who had been a minister without a church
> and a soldier without an enemy, and who in defeat had
> combined the two and become a doctor, a surgeon. It
> was as though the very cold and uncompromising convic-
> tion which propped him upright, as it were, between
> puritan and cavalier, had become not defeated and not
> discouraged, but wiser. As though it had seen in the
> smoke of cannon as in a vision that the layingon of
> hands meant literally that. As if he came suddenly to
> believe that Christ had meant that him whose spirit

alone required healing, was not worth the having, the
saving. (p. 449)

Now Hightower realizes that out of the war his father had
learned the value of life itself, of his responsibility towards
humanity in a total sense. We are told that his wife, Hightower's mother, was a chronic invalid who became the father's
first patient, that he probably kept her alive, that "he
enabled her to produce life." His father, in short, had learned
what the war might have taught, should have taught the intelligent South if it had not kept its eyes "stubbornly re-
verted toward what they refused to believe was dead." Yet,
Hightower had never accepted his father's truth. The reasons
are three: his mother, his grandfather, and the Negro woman
who was a former slave of the grandfather and who had tutored
the boy in that glorious, static moment of the South's past.
All of them are alienated from reality, and all of them are
more real to him than his father had been.

His mother is clearly a symbol of life rejection in the
classic sense. She is frustrated, immobilized:

> ... he thought of her as without legs, feet; as being
> only that thin face and the two eyes which seemed daily
> to grow bigger and bigger, as though about to embrace
> all seeing, all life, with one last terrible glare of
> frustration and suffering and foreknowledge.... Already,
> before she died, he could feel them through all walls.
> They were the house: he dwelled within them, within
> their dark and all-embracing and patient aftermath of
> physical betrayal. He and she both lived in them like
> two small, weak beasts in a den, a cavern, into which
> now and then the father entered ... a stranger ... a
> foreigner, almost a threat.... He was more than a stran-
> ger: he was an enemy. He smelled differently from them....
> the child could feel the man fill the room with rude
> health and unconscious contempt, he too as helpless
> and frustrated as they. (pp. 449-50)

The mother thus creates in the boy a feeling of hatred
towards life; perhaps, also, a sense of sex as violation,
certainly a sense of the nonreality of the woman's body. He
shrinks from physical life and substitutes for it a world
of imagination. That world is the one of his grandfather,
the first Gail Hightower, who had died in the Civil War, but
is kept alive for the grandson by the half-mad Negro woman,
Cinthy. Although his father's natural health is something
from which he retreats, the boy finds no terror in the knowledge that his grandfather had killed men "by the hundreds";
there is "no horror here because they were just ghosts, never
seen in the flesh, heroic, simple, warm" (p. 452).

As he gets it, filtered through the Negro woman's words
of "savage sorrow and pride," Hightower comes to know the
grandfather as a classic figure of the period immediately before the war: hard-drinking, sexually aggressive, a glorious
shadow figure whose courage and pride were monumental, a mythic
hero, a Sutpen figure, in short, who looked on his preacher
son with good-natured contempt. The grandfather had participated with his men in a raid on Grant's storage depot in
Jefferson. After firing the stores, he and his men had paused
to raid a chickenhouse, and the grandfather was cut down by
a blast from an anonymous shotgun, probably in fact fired by
an irate housewife. The reason for the death is lost on the
boy; it is only the death itself, coming as a glorious climax
to the raid, that seizes his imagination:

> ... they were boys riding the sheer tremendous tidal
> wave of desperate living. Boys. Because this. This is
> beautiful. Listen. Try to see it. Here is that fine
> shape of eternal youth and virginal desire which makes
> heroes. That makes the doings of heroes border so close
> upon the unbelievable that it is no wonder that their
> doings must emerge now and then like gunflashes in the
> smoke, and that their very physical passing becomes rumor
> with a thousand faces before breath is out of them, lest
> paradoxical truth outrage itself. (p. 458)

The reality of that past moment might be anything. Hightower knows that, but he does not accept it, does not even
care what the reality was. Even if it were invented, it makes
no difference, for "even fact cannot stand with it." The
moment supplies the symbol for what he wishes to believe;
the father as realist who had learned actuality from the war
is contradicted in his son by the myth of his own father,
the grandfather of the young Gail Hightower resurrected in
the boy as one of those looking back "toward what they will
not believe is dead" ... if it had ever lived. The wish become
myth "lest paradoxical truth outrage itself" is the curtain
over the reality--the death of the "hero" as chickenthief,
a symbol of the ignoble truth of that materialistic cause for
which they fought, the retaining of human property, slavery,
the curse upon life. What Hightower believes in is not the
moral principle of the Civil War, for in any *ultimate* sense
there was none for the South. He is gripped by and succumbs
to "the shouts, the shots, the shouting of triumph and terror,
the drumming hooves, ... that red glare ... the jagged edge
of the exploding and ultimate earth ... the troops galloping
past toward the rallying bugles" (pp. 458-59). He was in love
with the moment of death, dealt out and received. His identity

has always been that of the long-dead Civil War hero who was
not even a hero but a "swaggering and unchastened bravo killed
with a shotgun in a peaceful henhouse, in a temporary hiatus
of his own avocation of killing" (p. 462). Looking back, Hightower sees now that he has not even been inert, "not even
been clay," but a creature possessed by death: "I have been
a single instant of darkness in which a horse galloped and
a gun crashed" (p. 465).

It was, then, not simply that he was obsessed by glory
but that he was obsessed by gesture rather than a truth of
principles. This is the failure of the South, of mankind,
looking back always at its own tradition. It is gripped by
what it sees as glorious death, while in plain fact the grandfather died as a "bravo," a boy on a lark as a result of which
death descended on the land and holds it still in its grip.
(On the other hand, I do not think that Faulkner intends to
deny the meaning of valor here, for he carefully establishes
his situation so that the raid on the town is distinguished
from, even ruined by, the "lark" in which the grandfather
dies.) We have, as a clear marker, the meaning of principle
emerging from the war, acquired by the father turned healer
of *both* body and spirit. This hard truth, however, is not
the one which the development of myth recognized.

Hightower's vision shifts once more to his wife and the
dim faces of his congregation of twenty-five years ago. The
thought provides an occasion for Faulkner's use of time fusion.
The moment is one of impending realization, of something near
mystical realization, "two instants about to touch": that past
single moment which is "the sum of his life"--the frozen
instant of his grandfather's death--together with "the suspended instant" of the present, in which "the *soon*" is already unfolding. The congregation, the community (and this
includes even the robed figures who had flogged him years
ago, he now realizes), were not really the guilty ones. True
enough, they had been creatures "of frustration and doubt,"
but that was their part. They had played it, while he had
not. "I was the one who failed, who infringed. Perhaps that
is the greatest social sin of all; ay, perhaps moral sin."
The church that he had accepted and represented was that
which had "removed the bells from its steeples," which fails
man because it fails to heal his doubt and frustration, and
so give him peace in life. The church that Hightower made
his own was that of the isolate ego: "empty, symbolical,
bleak, skypointed not with ecstasy or passion but in adjura-
tion, threat, and doom ... against truth and against that
peace in which to sin and be forgiven which is the life of
man" (p. 461). A high tower, "empty, symbolical...."

He had made his ministry that of the death obsession upon
which his childhood was founded. The congregation had come to
him, extending him the sacred trust of their destiny, and he
had not seen that their hands were "raised in supplication."

At this point his entire failure becomes centered in his
lack of faith with womanhood, the symbol of life, as represented in his wife, the acceptance of which by any man is
"the first trust of man." His obsession had destroyed not
only himself but her:

> And if that was all I did for her, what could I have
> expected ... save disgrace and despair and the face
> of God turned away in very shame? Perhaps in the moment
> when I revealed to her not only the depth of my hunger
> but the fact that never and never would she have any
> part in the assuaging of it; perhaps at that moment I
> became her seducer and her murderer, author and instru-
> ment of her shame and death. After all, there must be
> some things for which God cannot be accused by man and
> held responsible. There must be. (p. 462)

"Her seducer and her murderer," thinks Hightower, and while
a few more minutes will be required before the link with Joe
Christmas is accomplished, his thought is a clear echo of
his earlier cry of outraged denial to Byron--"Shall I go
plead guilty to the murder?" Hightower sees himself as
responsible not only for man's welfare but for his guilt as
well. He is a man who had accepted "that one calling" the
very nature of which is responsibility for the dignity and
peace of one's fellowman; he had accepted that calling and
had failed it, totally. Around him now in his vision he seems
to see a mass of faces; "the faces seem to be mirrors in
which he watches himself.... a figure antic as a showman, ...
a charlatan preaching worse than heresy, in utter disregard
of that whose very stage he preempted, offering instead of
the crucified shape of pity and love" what?--his grandfather's
image, that "swaggering bravo" shot down on a casual holiday
from his customary "avocation of killing." The illusion of
honor has been perverted to, and preached as, a dogma of
ego; this is what the guardian of tradition has offered to
his people. This is the failure of the mind of the South.

For a moment, Hightower, caught up in the swell of faces
accusing him, attempts to escape by retreating to the fact
of his own violation, the moment when he had been dragged
from his bed and beaten, and then deposited in the shabby
exile of his house on what "had once been the main street."
Another voice tells him, however, that he had simply indulged
"that patient and voluptuous ego of the martyr" for his own

gratification, for the isolation which he in fact cherishes.
Defiantly, he makes his last attempt to escape the consequence
of complete truth:

> I have bought my ghost, even though I did pay for it
> with my life.... It is any man's privilege to destroy
> himself, so long as he does not injure anyone else, so
> long as he lives to and of himself-- (p. 464)

He stops suddenly, trapped by the very thought by which he
had hoped to escape. It is not only his life with which he
has bought his ghost, but that of his wife ... and that of
the man who died the day before.

Now "the wheel" of vision spins faster, "sweat begins to
pour from him, springing out like blood" in an obvious parallel
to the vision of sin in Gethsemane. The involvement of man
in mankind is inescapable. Avatar of living death, the grandfather in him had debauched his wife, had been his own murderer. The blur of vision clears; the great tragedy of his
people and himself manifests itself, but simultaneously the
interrelationship, the common identity of that brotherhood
of man, is seen. It is this which represents the divinity,
the "apotheosis" of mankind,

> the lambent suspension of August ... like a halo. The
> halo is full of faces ... not shaped with suffering ...
> not horror, pain, not even reproach. They are peaceful
> as though they have escaped into an apotheosis; his own
> is among them. In fact, they all look a little alike,
> composite of all the faces which he has ever seen. (p.
> 465)

This moment of vision, then, is the real meaning of the
title--*Light in August*.[9] The halo of the apotheosis is that
of the mutuality of mankind sanctified. Just a moment later
Hightower will realize what it is that sanctifies life in
this sense. Now, for the first time it seems to me, the
complete significance of the religious associations of Percy
Grimm and Joe Christmas in the death chase becomes apparent.
Now, too, the curious references to serenity and triumph in
the death of Joe Christmas are explained. As Joe dies, standing over him are Grimm, Hightower, and the three others described as surrounded "by haloes" of savage sunlight:

> For a long moment he looked up at them with peaceful
> and unfathomable and unbearable eyes. Then his face,
> body, all, seemed to collapse, to fall in upon itself,
> and from out the slashed garments about his hips and
> loins the pent black blood seemed to rush like a re-
> leased breath. It seemed to rush out of his pale body

like the rush of sparks from a rising rocket; upon that
black blast the man seemed to rise soaring into their
memories forever and ever. They are not to lose it, in
whatever peaceful valleys, beside whatever placid and
reassuring streams of old age, in the mirroring faces
of whatever children they will contemplate old disasters
and newer hopes. It will be there, musing, quiet, steadfast, not fading and not particularly threatful, but
of itself alone serene, of itself alone triumphant.
(pp. 439-40)

It is obvious that Joe's death is release from the agony that
his life had been, but that kind of release in itself is not
enough to justify "triumph." What Faulkner establishes here
is Joe Christmas as not simply social martyr in the pathetic
sense, but as a sacrifice that sanctifies life. Because of
the common identity of mankind, that man who dies as the
victim of society throws into symbolic relief the life and
death relationship of mankind. It is, indeed, death which
gives life its meaning and value.

With this vision, Faulkner joins the ranks of those rare
artists who are able to take an intense immediate situation
and use it as a magnifying glass to look at the universe.
Thomas Mann found it necessary to use even more allegorical
elements--although, again, with a dream vision for the mystic
revelation--to establish the same truth. The parallel is an
interesting one, and worth a brief glance. It occurs in *The
Magic Mountain*, in the chapter "Snow" which Mann himself
identified as the key to the novel. The protagonist, Hans
Castorp, is lost in a blizzard. Benumbed, he dreams of a
fair land, peopled by handsome, graceful, generous citizens,
who in the course of their daily activity pass with a gesture
of veneration a beautiful mother, who is nursing a child.
Behind this idyllic scene, however, Hans Castorp sees a temple
of ancient appearance. Entering, he finds two foul old hags
tearing apart a live child and consuming it, the warm blood
dripping from their withered lips. When he awakes, Castorp
thinks:

I have dreamed of man's state, of his courteous and
enlightened social state; behind which, in the temple,
the horrible blood-sacrifice was consummated. Were
they, those children of the sun, so sweetly courteous
to each other, in silent recognition of that horror?
It would be a fine and right conclusion they drew. I
will hold to them, in my soul.... I have made a dream
poem of humanity. I will cling to it. I will be good.
I will let death have no mastery over my thoughts. For

therein lies goodness and love of humankind, and in nothing
else.... Love stands opposed to death. It is love, not
reason, that is stronger than death. Only love, not
reason, gives sweet thoughts. And from love and sweet-
ness alone can form come: form and civilization, friendly,
enlightened, beautiful human intercourse--always in
silent recognition of the blood-sacrifice.... I will keep
faith with death in my heart, yet will remember that
faith with death and the devil is evil, is hostile to
humankind, so soon as we give it power over thought
and action. *For the sake of goodness and love, man shall
let death have no sovereignty over his thoughts.*[10]

Hightower has committed the error of sin against mankind: he
has allowed death to have control over his thoughts and actions.
Death, too, as life hatred had poisoned the existence of Joe
Christmas. The death of Joe, however, as a symbol now fully
understood by Hightower in the fading light of his vision, is
that which proclaims the dearness of all life.

In the blur of faces, all resembling each other, he begins
to distinguish different features: those of Byron Bunch, his
own wife, Lena Grove. Among them, he realizes, is that of
Joe Christmas, but of them Joe's features alone remain unclear:

It is confused more than any other, as though in the now
peaceful throes of a more recent, a more inextricable,
compositeness. Then he can see that it is two faces
which seem to strive (but not of themselves striving
or desiring it ...) in turn to free themselves one
from the other, then fade and blend again. But he has
seen now, the other face, the one that is not Christmas....
"Why, it's that ... boy.... The one who killed ...
fired.... (pp. 465-66)

The other face is that of Percy Grimm: in his vision Hightower has perceived the common identity of the murderer and
the murdered, that Grimm destroys himself in Joe and that Joe
redeems even the priest who destroys him. Grimm the priest
is identical with Christmas the sacrifice. Now, too, it becomes clear why Faulkner conceived of a murderer as a Christ
figure; he has taken the traditional Christ story and extended
and enriched it to a myth more nearly representative of his
particular thematic concern. Christmas has accepted the guilt
of mankind by committing the murder and delivering himself
up: Grimm has tied himself forever to his victim by wielding
the knife. There remains one thing, and that is for Hightower,
who has alone perhaps realized the truth of the sacrifice,
to receive the touch of grace. It comes, in a description that
parallels that of the ascending of Joe Christmas's spirit.

> Then it seems to him that some ultimate dammed flood
> within him breaks and rushes away. He seems to watch it,
> feeling himself losing contact with earth, lighter and
> lighter, emptying, floating ... that final flood which
> had rushed out of him, leaving his body empty and lighter
> than a forgotten leaf and even more trivial than flotsam
> lying spent and still upon that window ledge which has
> no solidity beneath hands that have no weight; so that
> it can be now Now (p. 466)

Hightower has realized the truth of humanity, the denial of
which had poisoned him, the South, mankind. The sacrifice of
Joe Christmas has been for him; in the expiation of Joe, Hightower's own guilt has now been lifted. Believing, in the rush
of experience, that he is dying (Faulkner subsequently claimed
that Hightower did not die in the novel, but the point is of
no interest here), Hightower thinks: "I should pray." He does
not do so, for he knows now that that is not where redemption
lies: "all air, all heaven, filled with the lost and unheeded
crying ... among the cold and terrible stars" (p. 466). There
is something left for Hightower, however, and it comes now
"as though they had merely waited until he could find something ... to be reaffirmed in triumph and desire with, with
this last left of honor and pride and life" (p. 466).

Now, closing the scene, come the phantom horsemen of his
grandfather's troop, exploding in a wild confusion of dust
and brandished arms. The minister has been freed from his
lifelong covenant with death; and Faulkner seems to suggest
he can now look at the obsesssion "with something found to
be reaffirmed with." Perhaps, in that novel that always extends beyond the last page, he can even use the past in the
service of life.

For all practical purposes, Faulkner ends the novel at
this point. Joe Christmas's story has been the epic struggle
of the modern South, its life twisted and tortured by racial
guilt. Hightower's epic has been that of the mind of the
South paralyzed by inability to perceive its human obligation,
trapped in the phantom smoke of a brutal defeat cherished
as noble, finally passing into the universal search of the
soul. It is there that the two stories merge. There remains
only that of Lena Grove and Byron Bunch to make the three-
part tale complete.

NOTES

1. Olga Vickery, *The Novels of William Faulkner*, revised
edition (Baton Rouge: Louisiana State University Press, 1964),
p. 75.

2. *Faulkner in the University*, ed. Joseph L. Blotner and Frederick L. Gwynn (Charlottesville: University of Virginia Press, 1959), p. 112.

3. O'Connor takes the references to Calvinism at face value and treats the novel as largely dealing with Puritan righteousness, in order to draw comparisons with Hawthorne (a pairing that has attracted many subsequent critics).

4. Richard Chase, *The American Novel and Its Tradition* (New York, 1957), p. 215.

5. Alfred Kazin, "The Stillness of *Light in August*." In *Interpretations in American Literature*, ed. Charles Feidelson, Jr., and Paul Brodtkorb, Jr. (New York, 1959), p. 359.

6. Beach Langston, "The Meaning of Lena Grove and Gail Hightower in *Light in August*," *Boston University Studies in English*, 5 (Spring 1961), 46-63, makes extensive correlation between Hightower and Oriental mysticism in more formal patterns than seem required to accept the analogy for what it is.

7. That view of the flight of Joe to Hightower is expressed in the novel by Gavin Stevens. In 1957, Faulkner repudiated it in these words: "... an assumption, a rationalization that Stevens made. That is, the people that destroyed him made rationalizations about what he was." *Faulkner in the University*, p. 72.

8. A common misconception is that "lynching" involves hanging by a mob; in fact, it is any punishment--though generally conceived of as death--administered without the formal authorization of law. That the shooting of Joe and his final castration is punishment rather than simply the deterring of a fugitive is fully established in the context of the study.

9. Most critics who have dealt with *Light in August* seem to have been excessively beguiled by the amusing implications of the country phrase "to go light" as a figure of speech for a domestic animal giving birth--i.e., Lena Grove. It almost certainly does have that additional meaning with regard to her, but it is a strained association to begin with, peripheral in value, and, according to Faulkner himself, unintentional.

10. Thomas Mann, *The Magic Mountain*, trans. H.T. Lowe-Porter (New York, 1952), pp. 495ff.

LIGHT IN AUGUST

Donald M. Kartiganer

I

Light in August is the strangest, the most difficult of
Faulkner's novels, a succession of isolated, brilliantly etched
characters and scenes that revolve around, finally blur into,
an impenetrable center--the character Christmas. As remote
from us and his author as he is from the society around him,
Christmas withholds some ultimate knowledge of himself, some
glimpse into the recesses of being which we feel necessary
to understanding. Yet just as obvious as his distance is the
fact that he epitomizes every character and movement in the
book. Whatever is in Light in August is here archetypally in
this figure whose very name begins his mystery: Joe Christmas.
He is, as Alfred Kazin has observed, "compelling rather than
believable," a character who "remains as he is born, an abstraction."[1] Like an art image that has never had the privilege of being human, he is never to be merely "believed";
yet at the last he is to "rise soaring into their memories
forever and ever. They are not to lose it...."
The mystery of Christmas, which doubtless for Faulkner
begins, prior to the novel's turning it to account, with the
opacity of the mulatto and an uneasiness concerning miscegenation, would appear at first to be the weakness of the novel.
Yet this mystery is the meaning of Light in August, for the
impenetrability of Christmas becomes the only way Faulkner
can articulate a truly inhuman, or larger-than-human, wholeness of being of which the others--Lena, Hightower, Byron,
Joanna, Hines, Grimm--are the human shadows. For us, they are
the recognizable figures for which we read novels; they ex-

From Chapter 3 (Sections I and II) of The Fragile Thread:
The Meaning of Form in Faulkner's Novels, by Donald M. Kartiganer (Amherst: The University of Massachusetts Press, 1979),
copyright © 1979 by The University of Massachusetts Press.

plain Christmas in their freedom from his special agony of
seeming not quite born. In reality it is he who explains them,
these "characters" who solidify into crisp, static shapes
only because they are less than he. Dimly aware of the pursuit of self that ensures Christmas's isolation, they assume
the roles that guarantee their place at least on the edge of
society, and those roles, as well, of the comprehensible
figures of fiction. They are not only the visible, partial
reflections of the wholeness which is Christmas's suffering,
but what Faulkner himself returns to at last: the people he
must portray as the bright fragments of the mystery in his
book that is necessarily beyond him.

Although *Light in August* is not told as a series of
voices, its structure retains the fragmentariness of Faulkner's
earlier novels. Through a narrative that juxtaposes blocks
of seemingly unrelated material, *Light in August* creates a
quality of incoherent mosaic. Despite the fragmentation,
however, *Light in August* moves toward a resolution of the
problems of *The Sound and the Fury* and *As I Lay Dying*: the
broken form, the incompatibility of twin commitments to flux
and design, process and product. *Light in August* is dominated
by the imagery of dualism: whiteness and blackness; hardness
and softness; the "cold hard air of white people" and the
"fecundmellow voices of negro women"; "the far bright rampart
of the town" and "the black pit ... the original quarry,
abyss itself": all the patterns in which people confine their
lives and the violence that threatens and finally breaks
loose.[2] This dualism, however, transforms itself into a
dynamic in the figure of Joe Christmas.

At the center of *Light in August* is the mulatto--more
important, the *imagined* mulatto. This is the role that Christmas, never being sure of what his origins are, has chosen.
Able to "pass," to choose a single identity, Christmas chooses
instead his doubleness. The only identity that will satisfy
him is the one which, in Faulkner's South, is no identity
at all, but rather an image of disorder. As a black worker
at the orphanage to which Christmas is sent as a child says
to him: "'You dont know what you are. And more than that,
you wont never know. You'll live and you'll die and you wont
never know'" (p. 363).[3]

Missing from Christmas is the kind of stable and consistent meaning that fictional characterization and the context of the novel insist on: a stability based, as we shall
see, on repression and commitment to a fixed pattern. Being
neither black nor white, Christmas is doomed to indefinite-
ness. And yet he is more than a blankness. On the one hand
he *is* a life, a structure, a single character--difficult yet

visible, lacking the clarity of Hightower and Lena and Joanna,
yet capable of being summoned up in our minds by the words
"Joe Christmas." On the other hand, he is the disorder that
lives always at or near the surface of *Light in August*, the
chaos of mixed bloods that brings forth from the life of
Jefferson an inevitable violence. The mulatto is the Faulknerian symbol of what is beyond comprehension or art; Joe Christmas is the expansion of that symbol into a precarious yet
memorable design that both confronts, and is made of, its
own disorder.

In other words, Faulkner begins to move toward a more
complex idea of fictional meaning, of a way in which a human
life and a fictional creation can unveil a vacancy that yet
projects a signifying form, a form that is more than a vacancy.
The fragmentariness of *The Sound and the Fury* is echoed in
the uneven development of *Light in August*--the juxtaposed
but incongruous incidents, the major characters (Lena and
Joe) who never meet--but these fragments now begin to cohere
in a tragic dialogue, a modern form in which design emerges
as the voice of a chaos that is signified by and subverts
that design.

This modern form is epitomized for us in the figure of
Christmas, in the process of his fictional existence. His
possible black-white division suggests a reality of perpetual
making: a reality of forces whose individual identity is
problematic and whose projected meeting is an outrage. The
stable dialectic of the rest of the novel encounters in
Christmas a dynamic that it finds intolerable. The society
of Jefferson and the novel *Light in August* are equally
threatened by the meaning of Christmas, for the mode of his
being and his characterization are equally destructive to
society and to fiction. This opposition of town and text to
their own center is an irony underlying the whole novel, for
Christmas as a character is as inaccessible to the community
of Jefferson as he is to *Light in August*, even as he generates
the most profound meanings of both. "This face alone," Hightower thinks, "is not clear" (p. 465). He represents an
interaction of forces that the novel and Jefferson can only
compartmentalize. Black and white, and all they imply, are
distinct sectors, carved in stone, except in the example of
Christmas.

The book is about this difference between itself and
Christmas, its failure to be equal to his story, to live its
life in the same struggle between oppositions as he lives
his. Failing to portray Christmas according to traditional
criteria of characterization, Faulkner yet suggests to us
the struggle of which Christmas is made, and thus makes clear

the inadequacy of the portrayal. We are given the general
shape of Christmas's contradictory actions, but we are never
provided full insight into his inner drama.

Faulkner compels his novel to revolve around a shadowy
figure, in whom a strange union of forces represents the
impossibility of his existence in verbal form. Yet the *fact*
of that impossibility is alive in the novel as a palpable
guilt: the awareness of a failure to grasp no more surely than
society the truth of the man who becomes its victim; the
failure to recognize who Joe Christmas really is.

This may sound more complex than it is, for in certain
ways we are on familiar modern ground: the articulation in
language of the difficulties of language, in this case the
creation of a fictional being, the failure of whose portrayal
is something like a strategy. The novelist implies the further
range of meaning that both undermines the creation yet com-
pounds the significance.

F.R. Leavis, dealing with Conrad's *Heart of Darkness* (an
author and work similar to the Faulkner I am trying to describe) and its attempt to suggest levels of horror beyond
articulation, makes what is still a forceful argument against
this sort of thing: "He is intent on making a virtue out of
not knowing what he means. The vague and unrealizable, he
asserts with a strained impressiveness, is the profoundly
and tremendously significant."[4] The answer to such an argument can only be that an art form (the opposite of incoherence)
can describe the struggle toward, and even the qualified
failure of, art forms. In *Light in August* the failure of the
writer to give his central figure a complete fictional life
is mirrored by a situation in which society fails to include
this figure in its own structure, yet is deeply marked by his
life and death. The man who can have no part in the community,
who is in fact cast out of it, finally has a most important
part. So too, the figure who is never "realized" in the novel
comes to dominate it, casting over its strikingly peopled
surface an unearthly light that alters everything.

II

Christmas then is clearly the key: in one sense insuffi-
ciently developed as a character, he supplies the rest of the
novel with significance. For most readers he is a victim who
never frees himself from the circle of his crossed blood
(real or imagined), and who is killed by a society enraged
at his flaunting of the mixture. But Christmas is more than
this, more than his victimization. The conflict driving him
toward a violent death is also the conflict he in part creates.

This death and the form it takes are what he chooses: his
own version of "It is finished."

Readers have always been aware of the parallels between
Christmas and Christ, yet have rarely known what to do with
them. The tendency among Faulkner's best critics has been to
avoid clear-cut identification between the two; there seems
little enough in common between the personality of the Christ
of the Gospels and the central figure in *Light in August*. Yet
it appears to me that the daring of Faulkner's creation here
is that Christmas *is* a Christ in the novel, a figure whose
form--the antithesis in which his personality is rooted, the
struggle for a wholeness of identity unknown to human beings--
repeats the structure of the life of Christ.

Joe believes that he may be part black, part white. Blackness is for him what it is for the South in which he lives:
an unpredictability, an abyss where life is perpetual flow;
passive, yet faintly hostile, and never quite understood.
Whiteness is the essence of design: cold, hard, man-like,
as predictable as behavior in the context of Simon McEachern's
iron laws of good and evil, or the cool and lonely street
that stretches before Christmas.

Light in August is permeated with the idea of division,
but Christmas is unique among the characters in that he is
the only one who insists on unifying the forces rather than
accepting, indeed depending upon, their separation. Not, as
in Lena's case, by having sufficient faith to do away with
the duality or, as in Joanna's, by living that duality one
element at a time. Rather he searches for a wholeness that
serves alike the dual sides of himself.

This quest for wholeness is to some extent a *given* one
for Joe: as he is the model of the division known to all, he
is also the most extreme example of the novel's pervading
fatalism. Of all the characters' lives his seems the most
arbitrarily determined, as if he were invented by minds prior
to the maturity of his own. Referring to the circumstances
surrounding Joe's birth--Milly's affair with a man possibly
part Negro, Hines's assumption of the role of witness to
God's inevitable vengeance--Olga Vickery writes that "Joe is
born into a myth created for him by others."[5]

This myth that precedes Joe into existence involves more
than the mad assumptions of Hines that he is part Negro, the
anti-Christ, the incarnation of sin and corruption. It is
also formed by the dietitian and McEachern. From the dietitian
Joe learns a relationship blending women, sex, unpredictability, and secrecy; for the five-year-old boy she is an
image of disorder, completely unfathomable behavior that
explains itself only by shouting "'You nigger bastard!'" (p.

117). From McEachern, however, he learns the example of rigid
definition, the opposite of what he has learned from the
dietitian. Joe's foster father provides him with a powerful
image of predictability, rooted in the belief in a design
fashioned by God of the destined elect and the destined damned.
This Calvinistic sense of a preordained order results in an
absolutist belief that there are distinct roles prepared for
each man and in an insistence, as if a duty to the God who
has created those roles, to fulfill them.

To the black-white division, created by Hines and complicated by the dietitian, McEachern's Calvinism adds a commitment to self-knowledge and self-fulfillment. This evolves into
the need for Joe to complete his given identity, whatever
its nature.

It is in the combination of these influences on Joe's
development that we can begin to see the strange dilemma that
has been prepared for him. On the one hand he has been informed that his nature is divided between what he will eventually realize are the opposite poles of existence: the black
and the white, the fearfully free and the coldly, permanently
ordered. On the other hand he has learned a commitment to being
what he is, and a hatred of that hypocrisy and cant that
would allow him the peace of accepting less. Christmas is
committed, then, to a design rooted in contradiction, a narrative whose completion is impossible according to the terms
of the world into which he has been born. His quest for order
is fatally bound to an endless process, the hopeless reconciliation of black and white.

In one sense he is the inheritor of an externally conceived plot, yet we must note the difference between the
situation here and that of *As I Lay Dying*. Addie Bundren's
imposed funeral journey, despite the Bundrens' private motives,
has much more of the structural priority common to narrative
than does the identity Christmas receives from his various
inventors. It is not Hines or the dietitian but Joe himself
who supplies weight to that possible identity, giving it most
of whatever strength it comes to possess. The "given" of
Joe's blackness, unlike Addie's journey, does not function
as an arbitrary pattern to limit consciousness; and the
behavior of Christmas is different from the Bundrens' willingness to honor publicly and dismiss privately the given
plot. Joe transforms this pattern into something larger than
its origins. He at once obeys and enlarges its outlines,
making it responsive to his own emerging identity, completing
the narrative of the anti-Christ even as he lifts it to its
sublime opposite. Plot in this novel is not the "determinate
poetic form" controlling character energy but the unfounded

fable that Christmas reinvents and transforms through a continuing act of consciousness.

Christmas is comprised of what Nietzsche called the
Dionysian and the Apollonian, the will to destruction and the
will to order. Nietzsche's understanding of those concepts
and his insistence on the dynamic relationship between them
captures the dynamic of Christmas's character and the tragic
conflict he epitomizes. Christmas is both the Dionysian force
and its verbalization by an Apollonian force, that difficult
fusion that Nietzsche said was the focus of every Greek
tragedy: "the one true Dionysos appears in a multiplicity of
characters, in the mask of warrior hero, and enmeshed in the
web of individual will. The god ascends the stage in the
likeness of a striving and suffering individual. That he can
appear at all with this clarity and precision is due to ...
Apollo."[6]

In Faulkner's terms, this hero is the black man in the
appearance of a white, the god in the guise of a human being.
He is the meeting ground of the elements that form him: a
commitment to a stable design that the chaos of content is
forced to deny. Joe Christmas well knows, as does Faulkner,
that there is no language, no action, no available myth or
version of reality, that will allow him to live the entirety
of his contradictory being. His life is spent in the quest
for such a possibility, but not in the north or south of his
universe does there exist a name for his wholeness. If there
is a wholeness available to him at all, it can lie only in
the process of his life, a life gathering itself from the
polarities of white and black, design and motion: visible,
if still beyond discourse or reason, only as the crossed
sticks of his conflict and crucifixion.

Yet he drives incessantly toward identity, fiercely
defying all attempts to define him by reduction to less than
his awareness of himself. To say "toward identity," however,
is to suggest possibility of a kind that doesn't really exist
in the novel. By the time Joe has arrived in Jefferson, he
knows there can be no conclusion to his particular quest;
for it is not a quest to achieve, to win, to bring back, but
a quest simply to *be*. Design as an unchanging order that
seals its identity forever, like Hightower's adolescent
memory of daring boys in wartime he can review again and
again, always the flames of burning stores in Jefferson,
always the same sound of the shotgun concluding a romantic
tale--there can be no such design for Christmas because he
can never accept the conclusion of a tale. The whole meaning
of his life is that it has no such conclusion. Christmas must
create his black-whiteness in every action, destroying each

action in the next, the white of the black man's prison, the
black of the white man's desire. He can conclude nowhere, for
the wholeness he embodies is superior to language, conception,
society, art, to all the articulations of action; he can only
be the perpetual process of himself. Each motion is no more
than a momentary definition, a fragment, a lie, but each
joins the *succession* of motions that is the identity of
Christmas. His life is always living, never has it *been lived*;
he exists in persistent change, and pattern is nowhere but
in the act of his becoming.

If there is ever a time when Christmas believes that the
unity he desires is something he can know within the contexts
society and people provide, it is during his relationship
with the waitress-prostitute Bobbie Allen. Prior to that
relationship Joe is convinced not only that black and white
are separate, for there is no question yet of reconciliation,
but that he can prevent the invasion of certain forms of
that blackness into his own life (despite the fact that he
is aware of his own possible blood division). Blackness in
this case is the menstruation of women which Joe, influenced
by the dietitian, easily connects with unpredictability and
chaos: the "periodical filth" that fatally mars "the smooth
and superior shape" (p. 173) of women. Despite what is told
him of menstruation, Joe is still adolescent enough to be
able to think, "*All right. It is so, then. But not to me.
Not in my life and my love*" (p. 174).

But on the first of his evening meetings with Bobbie,
Joe discovers she is having her period and he responds by
striking Bobbie and fleeing to the woods, there to find the
trees, "hard trunks ... hardfeeling, hardsmelling" (p. 177),
like the hardness of McEachern's ruthless design but now
imperfect. The trees are like "suavely shaped urns in moonlight.... And not one was perfect. Each one was cracked and
from each crack there issued something liquid, deathcolored,
and foul" (pp. 177-78). But unlike Hightower, who also
worships the possibility of a pure life, "complete and inviolable, like a classic and serene vase" (p. 453), Christmas
gives up this particular version of what order and design
mean. He becomes involved with Bobbie despite his initial
disgust; more than that he reveals his suspicions about his
black blood, not as a weapon as in subsequent encounters,
but simply as a part of his identity: the blackness he dis-
closes to her even as he has received and accepted hers.

He even dares to accept favors from Bobbie (or what he
assumes to be such), the "mercy," associated with the dietitian, which he has come to associate with all women as a
part of chaos. Since mercy is a redemption from design, a

reprieve from that order of things every fact points toward,
Christmas sees it as the enemy of order, creating dependencies
difficult to honor because one's expected role has been changed.
The meaning of mercy to Christmas corresponds to the meaning
of his own blackness; faced with an undeserved favor, Christmas usually resists as doggedly as if he were contesting the
triumph of the blackness within himself. In part this is because he associates the *need* for mercy with the degraded
condition of the Negro; the food Joanna Burden prepares for
him is *"Set out for the nigger. For the nigger"* (p. 224). To
accept such mercy becomes then a retreat from his insistence
on living the whole of his identity, the whiteness as well as
the blackness of his being. It is therefore remarkable that
he *is* prepared to accept favors from Bobbie Allen, even as
he is prepared to accept the menstruation symbolizing her
female imperfection, or to share with her the suspected truth
of his blood division. And so when Joe begins to visit Bobbie
in her room, "he did not know at first that anyone else had
ever done that. Perhaps he believed that some peculiar dispensation had been made in his favor, for his sake" (p. 185).

The Joe discovers that Bobbie is a prostitute, but he is still
prepared at the last to marry her, as if his notions of black
and white could actually coexist, cancel each other out in the
love of a man and a woman. It is this belief of Joe's that
gives the episode with Bobbie a curiously idyllic quality,
as if his commitment to identity were somehow not hopelessly
complicated by his inner division, as if he could actually
be, on earth, the black-white man who is loved and accepted
as such, and who can find in that acceptance the necessary
language with which to know and accept himself. Bobbie,
however, faced with the embarrassment of McEachern's attack
at the dance hall and with the deeper problem of Joe's possible
murder of his foster father, must revert to the categorizations of her society: she must free herself of the relationship with Joe and return him to his unacceptable divisions:
"'Bastard! Son of a bitch! Getting me into a jam, that always
treated you like you were a white man'" (p. 204).

The fifteen-year street of Joe's quest for identity begins
here, an identity that depends on his refusal to accept all
possible versions of it. His life--the one he insists he has
chosen--becomes the series of alternating roles that seem to
divide him, but that are really the difficult terms of his
wholeness.

The actions of Christmas from that time on are extremely
complex, never allowing the kind of simplistic definition
society requires. Invariably these actions combine white and
black aspects, subtly bringing together opposing character-

istics that allow Joe to remain distinct from white and black,
even as he includes the wills of each. This is not simply
a matter of challenging whites with his blackness, blacks
with his whiteness, but with his capacity, his need, for
deliberate reversals, to make of contradictory actions a
single seam of personality.

Upon his appearance at the sawmill in Jefferson, in the
second chapter of the novel, we find him carrying his name
like "an augur of what he will do," yet no one can interpret
it: "'Is he a foreigner?' 'Did you ever hear of a white man
named Christmas?' ... 'I never heard of nobody a-tall named
it'" (p. 29). Apparently a white man--allowing himself to be
thought that anyway--he takes a "negro's job at the mill"
(p. 31) as if in subversion of that whiteness. Yet he counters
the effect of a menial job with a contemptuous look that is
at odds with it. And while no one understands the meaning of
these reversals, everyone senses their strangeness.

The climax of his life is the murder of Joanna and his
subsequent behavior as he endures his own Passion Week, his
every action appearing to contradict the previous one, yet
the whole a sequence of man moving in a tortured harmony.
The murder is a blend of determinism and deliberateness.
Completed in Joe's mind before he performs the act--"*I had
to do it. She said so herself*" (p. 264)--it is still an act
of self-assertion as well as self-imprisonment. As he remarks
earlier, musing over the ease and security of marriage to
Joanna: "'No. If I give in now, I will deny all the thirty
years that I have lived to make me what I chose to be'" (pp.
250-51).

In hiding from his pursuers, in his capture and his subsequent escape, Christmas reveals his commitment to dual
forces. In choosing to stay in the area, he demonstrates,
according to some, his blackness: "'show he is a nigger, even
if nothing else'" (p. 292). But though he refuses to leave
the county, he has little trouble avoiding his pursuers,
and so his believed ignorance becomes his arrogance, the two
combining to make clear categorizations of Joe impossible.
Putting on the black brogans for which he has traded his
city shoes, Christmas "could see himself being hunted by
white men at last into the black abyss which had been waiting, trying, for thirty years to drown him and into which
now and at last he had actually entered" (p. 313). But as
he senses himself moving toward that primal abyss, which is
chaos to him--and toward which he has partially moved all
his life--he also tries to maintain an *order*, to keep intact
an "orderly parade of named and numbered days like fence
pickets" (p. 314). Such, of course, is his conception of

whiteness, the dry, firm design that closes off a space,
marking the boundaries between the understood and the unknown.
He inquires about the day of the week, and it becomes evident
that in the wildness of his behavior since the murder--fleeing
without really trying to escape, pausing to curse God in a
Negro church--he is also carrying out the required actions
of some ritual in his own mind, completing some design. This
design will strike the reader as in some ways similar to the
life of Christ (driving the money-changers out of the temple,
for instance), but its prime importance, it seems to me, is
simply the fact of design itself: Christmas is trying to time
his capture according to some idea in his own consciousness,
according to some pattern that exists prior to the act and
that must be fulfilled. Whatever the precise reason--and there
is no way of telling what it is--it is important to Christmas
that his arrest take place on a certain day, and he chooses
the day like a man whose primary concern is not to give himself up on Friday or Wednesday because it is that day, but
who is creating an illusion of life *as the fulfillment of an
order*. This is a gesture entirely opposed to his sense of an
enveloping blackness, the coming chaos where order is anni-
hilated. Yet, even as he moves in the wagon toward Mottstown
with his chosen pattern established, the black shoes keep
their symbolic import: "the black tide creeping up his legs,
moving from his feet upward as death moves" (p. 321).[7]

Joe's capture sustains the dual style which, in his last
days especially, becomes so emphatic. His getting a haircut
and shave prior to capture, the calm and passivity with which
he accepts capture (he doesn't actually give himself up),
imply the meekness of a Negro or the contemptuousness of
a white man, deliberateness or indifference. The categories
of human behavior accepted by the southern community are all
evident in Christmas's conduct, yet in such a mixture that
Christmas is behaving as neither black nor white: "'he never
acted like either a nigger or a white man. That was it. That
was what made the folks so mad'" (p. 331). He is now the
process of both callings, a confluence of forces that violates
the foundations of community life and all the individuals
in that community.

And he sustains that variation of styles right to the
end. Having allowed himself to be captured, without even
trying to get out of the county, he seizes the first opportunity to break away from his captors when they reach Jefferson. Supposedly having agreed to accept a life sentence, he
then arranges what is likely to mean an immediate execution.
Christmas is moving now in a continuous motion of conflicting
orders, a motion that Gavin Stevens, commenting on Christmas's

last hours, must break into blocks acceptable to the dualistic
logic of the community: "'Because the black blood drove him
first to the negro cabin. And then the white blood drove him
out of there, as it was the black blood which snatched up the
pistol and the white blood which would not let him fire it.
And it was the white blood which sent him to the minister....'"
Stevens's analysis of Christmas's dilemma depends on the
assumption that black and white are irreconcilable: "'his
blood would not be quiet, let him save it. It would not be
either one or the other and let his body save itself'" (p.
424). But the safety and peace Stevens presumes here is the
peace Christmas could never accept. This is not his failure
but his triumph, not weakness that deprives him of the security
of structure, but an inhuman strength that is his rise to a
condition above it: design and darkness at one in the supreme
fiction of his life.

In the catastrophe of his murder and castration, Joe
Christmas becomes the completed paradox of conception and
change, the image of what he is and has been:

> soaring into their memories forever and ever. They are
> not to lose it, in whatever peaceful valleys, beside
> whatever placid and reassuring streams of old age, in
> the mirroring faces of whatever children they will con-
> template old disasters and newer hopes. It will be
> there, musing, quiet, steadfast, not fading and not
> particularly threatful, but of itself alone serene, of
> itself alone triumphant. (p. 440)

Like an image of supreme art, a revolving fiction of disparate
forces no longer disparate, he is now that which is beyond
struggle or the endless arguments with self of which the
struggle has been made, beyond dogma and dialectic, crucified
into the black-white man--and therefore beyond the separation
on which that poor phrase of dualism rests. He will be interpreted in the discourse of those who are in life rather than
in art; Gavin Stevens's systematic version of Christmas's
oppositions is the first of these interpretations. But Christmas, as he has always been, although not in a language available to him or us, simply is: "of itself alone triumphant."

Joe Christmas is a Christ figure in this novel because
he grows into manhood with a conviction both of an unintelligible, unresolvable split within him and a need to live this
split into definition, one that is available, as far as he
can determine, nowhere on earth. He owes this conviction to
the existence of a narrative created independently of him,

a mythic structure, fatal, foretelling, in which he believes
and on the basis of which he acts, although he is aware that
this tale of his origins may be false. The biblical Christ,
like Joe, is born into a narrative that precedes him. Also
like Joe, his consciousness is not the plaything of a myth,
but rather the source of a courage to fulfill what has been
foretold, to *be* that atonement of man and God that he believes
is the task of his life and death. We may see Christ as merely
the completion of a structure created centuries before his
existence, the victim not so much of the men who crucify him
as he is of the iron narrative that requires his death in
order for the world to complete its pattern. But we must see
him also as the arbiter of his destiny, not only the God who
becomes a man in order to endure the unwinding of a design,
but as the man who becomes the God through his willingness
to fulfill· that design. It is as if in choosing to complete
what has been foretold he invests the ancient prophecies,
spoken by the lips of men, with meanings larger than they
contain.

Christ berates the man who would save him from the disaster
ahead: "But how then should the scriptures be fulfilled,
that it must be so."[8] And yet he also prays, "My Father, if
it be possible, let this cup pass from me; nevertheless, not
as I will, but as thou wilt." His words from the cross, "My
God, my God, why hast thou forsaken me?" are the triumphant
combination of man and God, the outcry of man caught in the
chaos of seeing his death without end, and the whisper of God
who composes the meaning of that death by quoting a psalm
centuries old, transposing chaos into a unifying design. The
quotation confirms the oneness of past and present: from the
cross it establishes both the validity of prophecy and the
identity of the man who speaks: "Jesus was quoting," Thomas
Mann has written, "and the quotation meant: 'Yes, it is I!'"[9]

Christ's identity as the man–God can be established only
by his pursuing the dualism to the end: for him to be rescued
from his fate by "twelve legions of angels" would establish
his divinity but not his humanity. On the cross the anguished
sufferer and the God who has fulfilled the prophecies are one,
suspended in space like a divine image of the experience and
meaning of being human. The death confirms the unique wholeness of his life, in which the human and divine, flesh and
spirit, have become the inseparable languages of each other.

The basic form of Christ and Christmas is the same; and
both come to horrify those communities whose insistent divisions they have chosen to resolve. This element of outrage is,
of course, more emphatic in the case of Christmas, whose
agony and confusion drive him to murder, whose tale is not

told by a believer, as in the Gospels, but by the writer doomed
to membership in the community. The violence of introducing
a new vision to a world convinced it can do without it is
everywhere in the story of Christmas. Faulkner's Christmas,
unlike the dull echo of Christ we find in *A Fable*, is a new
and striking creation of the *act* of vision, of what it might
mean to invent and live a meeting of contradictions: of man
and God, of design married to the darkness that destroys and
signifies.

NOTES

1. Alfred Kazin, "The Stillness of *Light in August*," in
William Faulkner: Three Decades of Criticism, ed. Frederick J.
Hoffman and Olga Vickery (New York: Harbinger Books, 1963),
p. 251.

2. William Faulkner, *Light in August*, photographed copy
of the first printing, 1932 (New York: Random House, Modern
Library, n.d.), pp. 107-8. Subsequent page references within
this chapter will be to this edition.

3. In *Faulkner's "Light in August": A Description and Interpretation of the Revisions* (Charlottesville: University Press
of Virginia, 1975), Regina K. Fadiman demonstrates that in
an earlier draft of the novel Faulkner made Christmas's black
blood a matter of fact rather than conjecture. She also shows
that Chapters 6 through 12, containing the long flashback
of Christmas's life leading up to the murder of Joanna Burden,
were written only after most of the action in the narrative
present was completed. Once simply a part (usually off-stage)
of the Lena-Byron-Hightower story, Christmas "ultimately came
to dominate the novel," as Faulkner "became more interested
in the inner workings of Joe Christmas's mind" (pp. 64-66).

4. F.R. Leavis, *The Great Tradition* (New York: New York
University Press, 1950), p. 180.

5. Vickery, *The Novels of William Faulkner* (Baton Rouge:
Louisiana State University Press, rev. ed., 1964), p. 69.

6. Friedrich Nietzsche, *The Birth of Tragedy and The
Genealogy of Morals*, trans. Francis Golffing (New York:
Doubleday, 1956), p. 66.

7. The inconsistency in the novel as to whether Christmas
was captured on a Friday or Saturday (on p. 322 it's a Friday;
on pp. 331 and 343 it's Saturday) is owing, like other in-

consistencies in the novel, to the revisions Faulkner made, chiefly his raising the story of Christmas to central importance. See Fadiman, *Faulkner's "Light in August,"* p. 51.

8. Biblical quotations are all from Matthew: Revised Standard Version.

9. Thomas Mann, *Essays*, trans. H.T. Lowe-Porter (New York: Alfred Knopf, 1957), p. 320.

II. Symbols and Myths

FROZEN MOVEMENT IN *LIGHT IN AUGUST*

Darrel Abel

I. Symbol

Faulkner's *Light in August* does not (except within the arbitrary perspective of any given character in the novel) delineate a single complete action with a beginning, a middle, and an end. For Faulkner's reality, like Bergson's, is a "becomingness"--not static, but dynamic; not formed, but fluid. To Faulkner, "The present does not exist, it becomes...."[1] According to Bergson, "Reality is mobility. There do not exist *things* made, but only things in the making, not *states* that remain fixed, but only states in process of change."[2]
A writer's insight into this moving reality, his escape from the static and particular into the vital and general, is intuitive. It is the poetic faculty alluded to in "Tintern Abbey," by which "the heavy and the weary weight/ Of all this unintelligible world is lightened" and "We see into the life of things." Bergson defines intuition as *"knowledge which establishes itself in the moving reality and adopts the life itself of things"* (p. 227). He contrasts "intelligence," as an effort to know reality by hypostatizing and analyzing it, with "intuition":

> To think intuitively is to think in duration. Intelli-
> gence starts ordinarily from the immobile, and recon-
> structs movement as best it can with immobilities in
> juxtaposition. Intuition starts from movement, posits
> it, or rather perceives it as reality itself, and sees
> in immobility only an abstract moment, a snapshot taken
> by our mind, of a mobility. Intelligence ordinarily
> concerns itself with things, meaning by that, with the
> static, and makes of change an accident which is sup-
> posedly superadded. For intuition the essential is

From Boston University Studies in English, *3 (Spring 1957), 32-44. Reprinted with permission.*

change: as for the thing, as intelligence understands
it, it is a cutting which has been made out of the
becoming and set up by our minds as a substitute for
the whole. (p. 39)

Bergson calls artists men who "are born detached," and who
have "a much more direct vision of reality" than other men
(pp. 162-63).

   If Faulkner has, as I think, a similar conception of reality in flux, and a similar theory of the imaginative writer's
gift and function, his technique must master a paradox: in
order to fix reality in a literary construct, it must freeze
movement. "Faulkner appears to arrest the motion at the very
heart of things; moments erupt and freeze, then fade, recede
and diminish, still motionless."[3] In Bergsonian terms, the
artist's "intelligence" must make "cuttings" out of the "becoming" which his "intuition" perceives: "Our mind, which
seeks solid bases of operation, ... has as its principal
function, in the ordinary course of life, to imagine *states*
and *things*.... It substitutes for the discontinuous the continuous, for mobility stability.... This substitution is
necessary to common sense, to language, to practical life"
(p. 222).

   The resource of the intuitive artist in conveying his
intuitions to practical men, who must have reality represented
to them in "states" and "things," is symbolism. Intuition
"will have to use ideas as a conveyance. It will prefer,
however, to have recourse to the most concrete ideas, but
those which still retain an outer fringe of images. Comparisons and metaphors will here suggest what cannot be expressed"
(p. 48). "No image will replace the intuition of duration
[i.e., of "becomingness," of "mobility"], but many different
images ... will be able, through the convergence of their
action, to direct the consciousness to the precise point
where there is a certain intuition to seize on" (p. 195).
Although symbolization is the artist's best expedient for
communicating his intuitive knowledge of the mobile and continuing reality, it is still only a suggestive makeshift;
it conveys no absolute insights, only relative conceptions:
"*Relative is symbolic knowledge through pre-existing concepts,
which goes from the fixed to the moving*" (p. 227). "Relative"
knowledge "depends on the viewpoint chosen and the symbols
employed," but "absolute" knowledge (i.e., "intuition of
duration") "is taken from no viewpoint and rests on no symbol"
(p. 187). Symbolism is merely a means by which "we lean our
communication up against a knowledge that our interlocutors
already possess" (p. 81).

In *Light in August* Faulkner attempts to contrive through
symbols an immobile representation of mobility, and at the
same time to suggest how "relative" and arbitrary any distinct
and arranged version of mobile reality must be. He endeavors
to represent a fluid reality in the static terms "necessary
to common sense, to language, to practical life"; and at the
same time to disclose that the static images through which
he makes the fluid reality visible are merely arrested and
discontinuous blinks—what Bergson calls "snapshots" or "cuttings made out of the becoming."

Such a symbolic shuttering of reality controls the narration from the opening pages, which offer an image, immediately
augmented into a symbol,[4] of the mule-drawn country wagons
in which Lena Grove made her enchanted, ineluctable progress
from Alabama into Mississippi; "backrolling now behind her
a long monotonous succession of peaceful and undeviating
changes from day to dark and dark to day again, through which
she advanced in identical and anonymous and deliberate wagons
as though through a succession of creakwheeled and limpeared
avatars, like something moving forever and without progress
across an urn."[5]

In this figure the countryside across which Lena travels
is, like the "silent form" of Keats's urn,[6] a designated
image or visible metaphor of eternity. The stories of Lena
Grove and Joe Christmas constitute the "legend" (or "brede"
or "frieze") seen against this immutable image of eternity.
A legend is both an inscription and an old story, especially
an "old story" in the colloquial sense of something happening
over and over again from time immemorial. Against the background of countryside which is Faulkner's equivalent of the
"silent form" of Keats's urn, the comic and pathetic leaf-
fring'd[7] legends of Lena Grove and Joe Christmas are seen to
be, although interesting as individual histories, even more
significant as expressions, moments, postures, phases, of a
human reality into which all personal realities fade. The
stillness of urn and countryside represent, not immobility
itself, but "deserts of vast eternity"—so vast that in such
perspective all particulars and moments are lost.

Faulkner's somewhat peculiar use of the word "avatar,"
in characterizing the progressive appearances or apparent
progress of both Lena Grove and Joe Christmas through space
and time, makes their stories legends of arrested human
striving like the "brede/ Of marble men and maidens" on the
urn. Lena "advanced ... as though through a succession of ...
avatars"; Joe, "as in numberless avatars" (Chapter 1, p. 5;
Chapter 10, p. 217). The main signification in Faulkner's
use of the term "avatar" is of course simply "embodiment."[8]

The avatar-figure, which converts personal histories into a
mere succession of envisagements of a continuous and moving
process of human "becoming," determines the conception of the
other characters in the novel too. In Faulkner's sense of
"avatar," Hightower's whole inert existence is a kind of prolonged or aborted avatar, in consequence of his belief "that
I skipped a generation.... I had already died one night twenty
years before I saw light" (Chapter 20, p. 452). Even Byron
Bunch philosophically questions his own determinateness as a
self, his own identity: *"You just say that you are Byron
Bunch.... you are just the one that calls yourself Byron Bunch
today, now, this minute"* (Chapter 17, p. 402). Faulkner apparently uses the avatar-figure to indicate that a person's
sense of distinct and stable identity is simply a hypostatiza-
tion of the streaming subjective life in which he transiently
exists and which his private consciousness defines for him
as *his* life.

   A less conspicuous device of Faulkner's for indicating
that the "fixed" is only an arbitrary arrest of the "moving"
is his frequent mention of the omnipresent muted hum of
natural life,[9] furnishing a vague, monotonous, repetitious,
generalized accompaniment to foreground action. Thus Joe
Christmas, voicing his finally definite intention to murder
Joanna Burden, heard around him "a myriad sounds, ... voices,
murmurs, whispers: of trees, darkness, earth; people: his
own voice; other voices evocative of names and times and
places ..." (Chapter 5, p. 98). As he entered the house later,
to commit the deed, "The dark was filled with the voices,
myriad, out of all time that he had known, as though all
the past was a flat pattern. And going on: tomorrow night,
all the tomorrows, to be a part of the flat pattern, going
on" (Chapter 12, p. 266). After Christmas's capture, as
Hightower hears from Mrs. Hines the story of his early life,
"through the open window there comes now only the peaceful
and myriad sounds of the summer night" (Chapter 16, p. 365).
And later, as Hightower is alone in his house, struggling to
suppress his humane impulse to sympathize with and help "poor
mankind": "Beyond the open window the sound of insects has
not ceased, not faltered" (Chapter 16, p. 370). These generalized, remote, anonymous voices of changing, enduring reality
constitute an audible image of the continuous and moving,
just as urn and countryside are its visible image.

   If, then, *Light in August* eschews classical form--lacks
a single complete action with a beginning, a middle, and an
end--it does so because there is no alpha or omega in Faulkner's alphabet of reality. His novel ends, but his story
does not: it is merely a harsh and prolonged suspiration

swelling out of and subsiding into the "myriad voices, out
of all time." Faulkner's story is about convergent or connected
human destinies, which have as their nexus the burning of the
Burden house, an event which any individual character views
as a fixed and understood reality, but which is in fact a
symbol capable of as many significances as the various individuals who view it are enabled to read into it from their
own experience, their own ideas. To the stranger who brings
Lena to Jefferson, it is merely "a house burning" (Chapter 1,
p. 26). But as a crucial moment in each of the human histories
which converge in it, it is variously interpreted. To each, it
brings "light in August" in a different way, provides a glaring but transient interval of illumination and realization.

II. Story

"There is at least one reality which we all seize from
within, by intuition and not by simple analysis. It is our
own person in its flowing through time, the self which endures"
(p. 191). "If, instead of claiming to analyze duration ...,
one first installs oneself in it by an effort of intuition,
one has the feeling of a certain well-defined *tension*, whose
very definiteness seems like a choice between an infinity of
possible durations" (p. 218). The central perception offered
to readers of *Light in August* is expressed in Bergson's sentence, "The higher the consciousness, the stronger is this
tension of its own duration in relation to that of things"
(p. 105). Such a "tension" requires a consciousness of at
least two "possible durations": the intuition of our own
duration, "which we all seize from within"; and the intuition
of some possible duration more comprehensive than our own.
Duration consists of "the addition to the present feeling,
of the memory of past moments" (p. 211). "The distinction
between our present and past is ..., if not arbitrary, at
least relative to the extent of the field which our attention
to life can embrace" (p. 179). Thus, intuitions grasp "durations" which vary infinitely in comprehensiveness. They may
include awareness of immediate and instant reality, or of
our whole lives since birth, or of generations of our family,
or of the continuing life of the human species, or of the
vast transcendent flux in which the *élan vital* endlessly
reshapes reality in novel and more complex forms.
    Of the major characters in *Light in August*, the one with
least awareness of "this tension of its own duration in relation to that of things" is Lena Grove, for her intuition
of her own duration is a very contracted one, and she has no

intuition of any other duration. Her "attention to life"
embraces only what immediately confronts her; there is little
addition to her present feeling "of memory of past events."
She cares nothing for her own past or for her family, and
never thinks of them; she is fully content with the moment
which she occupies, and with the bliss of being in it. As the
book opens, she reflects, "*Although I have not been quite a
month on the road I am already in Mississippi*"; and as it
ends, she says, "Here we aint been coming from Alabama but
two months, and now it's already Tennessee" (Chapter 1, p. 1;
Chapter 21, p. 480). The brief span of her attention to the
past is clearly marked in such reflections: the only past
she ever speaks of is a very recent one, and she speaks of it
only as the antecedent of the present in which she is almost
wholly engrossed. Her consciousness has "an inwardlighted
quality of tranquil and calm unreason" (Chapter 1, p. 15).
"The duration of things" is not measured for her by the tides
of God or the clocks and calendars of man, but solely by the
elemental urges and responses of her nature to her immediate
surroundings. She knows no reality beyond her subjective
moment. She represents ordinary naive mankind, inviolably
innocent because it cannot enter the realm of ideas. To Hightower she stands for "*the good stock peopling in tranquil
obedience to it the good earth*" (Chapter 17, p. 384). She is
too unsophisticated to comprehend good and evil. Faulkner
assigns her the first and last speeches of the novel because,
just as hers is the least conscious and sophisticated, so
is it the most elemental and enduring, aspect of humanity.
She is one of Sandburg's "people who live on," a primitive
character like Hardy's "man harrowing clods."

   If *Light in August* at all anticipates Faulkner's later
statement, in his Nobel Prize acceptance speech, that "man
will not merely endure: he will prevail," it does so by identifying the "crucified" Joe Christmas with Lena's child,
and by exhibiting her calm and confident onward travel at
the end of the story. The hate, mistrust, and evil will which
impel mankind to crucify some of its members are counter-
balanced by the love, trust, and good will tendered to Lena
and her child. Lena prevails, not by her understanding, but
by her complacent trust in others, a trust amounting almost
to obstinacy and stupidity. Although her story is a comedy
of rustic innocence, a comic pastoral, Faulkner dignifies
instead of disparaging her.

   In contrast, Joe Christmas's story is tragic, or at least
pathetic. Although Lena is hardly more than an expression
of the will to live of the species, Joe is a person struggling
to establish his selfhood, and aware of overwhelming influ-

ences extending into his life from a long reach of time and
a broad range of human relationships. He saw his own history
as a struggle to gain status in white society, or, failing
that, to revert to primitivism. A long passage near the end
of Chapter 5 serves as figure for his life. It relates how,
on the night before he murdered Joanna Burden, he wandered
into the Negro section of Jefferson, Freedman Town, "like a
phantom, a spirit, strayed out of its own world, and lost....
It was as though he and all other manshaped life about him
had been returned to the lightless hot wet primogenitive
Female." He ran in frantic revulsion "out of the black hollow,"
but became calm when he reached a white neighborhood with
"clustered lights: low bright birds in stillwinged and tremulous suspension." He said of the white life around him, "That's
all I wanted.... That dont seem a whole lot to ask." As he
walked on, he saw behind him "the far bright rampart of the
town ... and ... the black pit from which he had fled ...
black, impenetrable, in its garland of Augusttremulous lights.
It might have been the original quarry, abyss itself" (Chapter 5, pp. 106-8).

In retrospect Christmas saw his career as a vain striving
to emerge from the black, primitive, earthy, female, passionate
"allmother of obscurity and darkness" (Chapter 10, p. 216)
into light, civilization, manliness, volition, identity. In
the course of this vain striving, his hatred of the "lightless
hot wet primogenitive Female" grew into a complex obsession.
His first indelible impressions, at the orphanage, were of
females, sex, guilt, and the rejection of Negroes as inflic-
tions divinely and irrevocably decreed. At the McEacherns',
throughout his boyhood, these impressions were all confirmed
and deepened. His first experience of sex made it for him
thereafter simply an overmastering lust: "something liquid,
deathcolored, and foul" (Chapter 8, p. 178). After his young
innocence and affection had been outraged by the malformed
whore Bobbie Allen (an episode grotesquely caricaturing
love's young dream), he tried to coerce by injury and hate
the world into which he could not find a way by generosity
and love. Even at the age of five in the orphanage he had
learned to believe that "*I am different from the others*"
(Chapter 6, p. 129), and he never was able to surmount the
difference.

After his decisive rejection by the white world, he tried
to return to primitive black life. In Detroit

> He lived with negroes, shunning white people.... He
> now lived as man and wife with a woman who resembled
> an ebony carving. At night he would lie in bed beside
> her, ... trying to breathe into himself the dark odor,

the dark and inscrutable thinking and being of negroes,
with each suspiration trying to expel from himself the
white blood and the white thinking and being. And all
the while his nostrils at the odor which he was trying
to make his own would whiten and tauten, his whole being
writhe and strain with physical outrage and spiritual
denial. (Chapter 10, p. 212)

Christmas failed to recover "the dark and inscrutable thinking
and being of negroes," not because they refused to accept him,
but because his upbringing had conditioned him against it.
He had not gained a place in the white world, but he had been
unfitted for a place in the black world. His was the tragedy
of "black blood" in a "pale body," an antagonism of two possibilities so equal in strength that each negated the other.
Thus Gavin Stevens summed up his tragedy:

It was not alone all those thirty years [of his personal
existence] ..., but all those successions of thirty
years before that which had put that stain either on
his white blood or his black blood, whichever you will,
and which killed him.... his blood would not be quiet....
It would not be either one or the other. (Chapter 19,
p. 424)

Thus Faulkner shows that the conviction of his outcast
fate which dogged "Christmas, the son of Joe" (Chapter 16,
p. 364) grew in his mind like a fatality. When he anticipated
murdering Joanna Burden, he did not acknowledge that he willed
to do it, but that he was fated to do it: *Something is going
to happen to me*" (Chapter 5, p. 97). When he murdered her,
he "believed with calm paradox that he was the volitionless
servant of the fatality[10] in which he believed that he did
not believe" (Chapter 12, p. 264). He transvaluated murder
into something like a creative act, however, since it was
for him a symbolic annihilation of the world which had denied
his claims to selfhood and status. Joanna Burden was his
appropriate victim, for she combined in one person the three
elements of coercion which Joe had experienced: femaleness,
Calvinism, and obsession with color-difference.[11]

Since Christmas could not find a secure life anywhere,
his only alternative was to die: to accept and hasten the
doom that he thought was determined for him. After the murder,
as he looked at his feet in the black Negro shoes that he
had put on to throw the pursuing bloodhounds off the scent,
it "seemed to him that he could see himself being hunted by
white men at last into the black abyss which had been waiting,
trying, for thirty years to drown him and into which now and
at last he had actually entered, bearing now upon his ankles

the definite and ineradicable gauge of its upward moving"
(Chapter 14, p. 313).

   Just as Lena represents the comedy of ordinary life, so
does Joe represent the tragedy of extraordinary life. Hated,
corrupted, and persecuted from the hour of his birth, he was
not only accused of being evil by those who "crucified" him
for righteousness' sake (Hines in the name of God, Grimm in
the name of patriotism and society); he *was* evil, for he had
been imbued with all the sin and corruption of humanity; he
was a scapegoat burdened with the accumulated evils of his
generation. But even his persecutors were not responsible for
the tragedy. Although Hines and Grimm were persecutors rather
than victims, although Lucas Burch was Judas rather than
Christ, all alike were servants of the general and traditional
obsessions which assigned their roles in the tragedy. Byron
Bunch's opinion about the town of Jefferson's long harassment
of Hightower applies equally well to Christmas's "crucifixion":
"the entire affair had been a lot of people performing a play
and ... now and at last they had all played out the parts
which had been allotted them" (Chapter 3, p. 67).

                         III. Coda

   "Installed in universal mobility, ... consciousness contracts in a quasi-instantaneous vision an immensely long
history which unfolds outside it. The higher the consciousness, the stronger is this tension of its own duration in
relation to that of things" (p. 105). Gail Hightower is the
most significant character in *Light in August* because only
he attained the higher consciousness which "contracts in a
quasi-instantaneous vision an immensely long history which
unfolds outside it." Hightower suffered even more than Joe
Christmas, for he who experiences most suffers most. Hightower
tried to maintain that he had "bought immunity" (Chapter 18,
p. 292) from involvement in the affairs of living men, but
his long-suppressed humanity impelled him "to come back into
life" (Chapter 13, p. 284) to assist at a birth and try to
prevent a death. His identification with the human beings
whose fates, when he was forced to sympathize with them,
illustrated both the hopeful and tragic possibilities of the
life he had evaded made him comprehend the general fate of
mankind, which is to serve the compulsive ideas which are its
inheritance. Hightower's own story is an exaggerated rendering
of the truth that all men are directed by ancestral ghosts
and do not fully possess their own realities. He had chosen
to withdraw into his ancestral ghost, rather than to let the
human past summed up in him enter the present; but his story,

like Joanna Burden's and Joe Christmas's, shows the persistence
through generations of a pattern of transmitted ideas and
tendencies which effectually make each inheritor their instrument, because they are not externally dictated to him but are
constitutive of his own character.

Because Hightower had so long lived a "dead life in the
actual world," "dissociated from mechanical time" (Chapter 16,
p. 346), had not enacted a vital role in the present, he was
able, like God in a high tower in a medieval mystery play,
to see that present with detachment. He had breadth of understanding and depth of compassion, and rose to contemplation
of those principles of human action, those conditions of human
life, which are so recurrent in time that they seem ulterior
to time, and "tease us out of thought/ As doth eternity." If,
in a naturalistic cosmos, Joe Christmas is Jesus Christ, Gail
Hightower is God Himself. Lena Grove, a pagan generatrix, is
mankind aware of its existence only through participation in
the burgeoning life of nature; Joe Christmas lives and dies
in a world of ideas of good and evil; but Gail Hightower,
by his intuition of "universal mobility," philosophically
transcends both the natural and moral worlds.

The concluding revery of Hightower (to whom light in
August comes more effulgently than to any other character,
although all the witnesses of Christmas's death, like the
witnesses of the crucifixion of Jesus, have a half-compre-
hended enlightenment) shows him in an instant when "consciousness contracts in a quasi-instantaneous vision an immensely
long history which unfolds outside itself." In his agony of
comprehension, of realization, Hightower sits "in the lambent
suspension of August into which night is about to fully come,"
and all the faces of the recent past rise before him, but
"not shaped with suffering, not shaped with anything: not
horror, pain, not even reproach. They are peaceful, as though
they have escaped into an apotheosis" (Chapter 20, p. 465).
The figure which structures his revery is a rapidly revolving
wheel of thought,[12] or consciousness, which slows and stops
to focus the static images and characters which perception
distinguishes in the continuous, moving reality. But the
wheel in rapid revolution is a halo full of faces that "all
look a little alike, composite of all the faces which he has
ever seen" (Chapter 20, p. 465).

In this apocalyptic instant in Hightower's vision the
faces of Christmas and Grimm, in mortal life obsessed and
murderous opponents, "fade and blend." "Then it seems to
[Hightower] that some ultimate dammed flood within him breaks
and rushes away. He seems to watch it, feeling himself losing
contact with earth, lighter and lighter, emptying, floating...."

[He thinks,] 'With all air, all heaven, filled with the lost
and unheeded crying of all the living who ever lived, wailing
still like lost children among the cold and terrible stars ...'"
(Chapter 20, p. 466). Thus, for an instant, Hightower escapes
from the static and discontinuous appearances which constitute
reality to ordinary perception: leaves the temporal world of
frieze and legend and enters the eternity of the urn-world
itself. When, by philosophic intuition, man is able to "arise
from a frozen vision of the real ... to perceive all things
sub specie durationis," "all things acquire depth,--more than
depth, something like a fourth dimension.... What was immobile
and frozen in our perception is warmed and set in motion.
Everything comes to life around us.... A great impulse carries
beings and things along. We feel ourselves uplifted, carried
away, borne along by it" (p. 186). In the Dionysian dance of
life there comes a serene moment of Apollonian vision.

The climactic symbol of *Light in August*, the lambent
wheel which Hightower sees in his highest moment of vision
as an image of eternity, is an archetypal symbol whose richness can be best apprehended in comparison with literary
parallels. The most obvious is Dante's recurrent conjunction
of images of light and a rapidly revolving wheel in the
Paradiso (e.g., Cantos i, xii, xxviii), especially the elaborate image of the circle of fire, or rapidly whirling wheel
haloed with light, which Dante views in the ninth heaven
(Canto xxviii). Dante quotes in connection with this image
a passage from Aristotle's *Metaphysics* on the *primum mobile*,
the "unmoved mover" which is the center and source of this
dazzle of cyclic movement. Similarly, Plato's *Timaeus* desig-
nates the stars in their courses as "a moving image of eternity"--a passage which may be the source of the famous opening stanza of Henry Vaughan's poem "The World":

> I saw Eternity the other night
> Like a great ring of pure and endless light,
>   All calm, as it was bright,
> And round beneath it, Time, in hours, days, years,
>   Driven by the spheres
> Like a vast shadow moved, in which the world
>   And all her train were hurl'd.

I think it likely that such reminiscences, whether conscious or not, have contributed to Faulkner's symbol of the
haloed wheel of Hightower's vision. If Hightower, like Dante,
is regarded as one who, while still in mortal life, is
afforded a vision of eternity in all its phases, his experience exhibits something of hell, of purgatory, and of heaven.
His inferno consists of his witnessing and participating in

the complicated tragedy of human evil and mortality which is
consummated in the "crucifixion" of Joe Christmas. His purgatory is the initial stage of his revery after Christmas's
death, when finally, in "a consternation which is about to
be actual horror," he admits his guilt as an "instrument of
[his wife's] despair and shame," while "sweat begins to pour
from him, springing out like blood" (Chapter 20, p. 464). He
sees, beyond his own guilt, the determinism which fixed this
complicity in evil upon him: "if I am the instrument of her
despair and death, then I am in turn instrument of someone
outside myself" (Chapter 20, p. 465). Purged by his abandonment of delusion, his admission of truth, he enters his para-
dise, his moment of perception of an eternal truth which leaves
his stale and corrupt "body empty and lighter than a forgotten
leaf and even more trivial than flotsam lying spent and
still ...; so that it can be now Now"[13] (Chapter 20, p. 466).

But, although *Light in August* contains a *Divina commedia*,
a *Comédie humaine* encompasses it: Lena, the almost primitive
embodiment of the human species' persistent effort to seek
attachments and find durable satisfactions in local, temporal,
and personal terms, is presented to us first and last. Her
primacy in the story does not mean, I think, that Faulkner
rejects Hightower's vision of reality for her view of it,
but rather that he regards Lena's reality as the almost uni-
versally and constantly available one, and Hightower's as a
difficult, fleeting, and rarely attainable one.

NOTES

1. Jean-Paul Sartre, "Time in Faulkner: *The Sound and
the Fury*," trans. Martine Darmon, in Frederick J. Hoffman
and Olga W. Vickery, *William Faulkner: Two Decades of Criticism* (East Lansing: Michigan State College Press, 1954), p.
183. Reprinted from *Situations*, 1, "Le Bruit et la fureur"
(Paris: Gallimard, 1947), pp. 70-81.

2. Quoted by permission of the publishers, The Philosophical
Library, from Henri Bergson, *The Creative Mind*, trans. Mabelle
L. Andison (New York: The Philosophical Library, 1946), p.
222. All subsequent quotations cited by page numbers enclosed
in parentheses in the text refer to this edition.

3. Sartre, "Time in Faulkner," p. 182.

4. I use the terms "image, "symbol," and "figure" in this
paper in the different senses which I think they usually
carry: "image"--a distinct, unified sense-impression of an
object; "symbol"--an image which is the nucleus and sign of

a congeries of not readily explicable meanings and sensations; "figure"--pattern or design, possibly a configuration of images in time or space; also, any kind of trope.

5. Quoted by permission of the publishers, Random House, from William Faulkner, *Light in August* (New York: Modern Library, n.d.), Chapter 1, p. 5. All subsequent quotations cited by chapter and page numbers enclosed in parentheses in the text refer to this book.

6. For more explicit allusions by Faulkner to Keats's "Ode on a Grecian Urn" which show how persistently Keats's urn-symbol has haunted Faulkner's imagination, see Faulkner's article "Verse Old and Nascent: A Pilgrimage," *Double Dealer*, 7 (1925), 130; and "The Bear," *Go Down, Moses* (New York: Modern Library, 1955), p. 297. Norman Holmes Pearson has commented on Keats's urn-symbol as employed in *Light in August* in "Lena Grove," *Shenandoah*, 3 (1951), 3-7.

7. Professor Pearson ("Lena Grove," p. 6) remarks that Lena's family name (Grove) alludes to the "leaf-fring'd"; probably, despite the change of vowel, Burch's name also has this reference. That *Light in August* is "a kind of pastoral" has been noted by Cleanth Brooks in "Notes on Faulkner's *Light in August*," *Harvard Advocate*, 135 (1951), 27.

8. Thus, for example, Faulkner calls the old mulatto Lucas Beauchamp in *Intruder in the Dust* an "avatar" ("Lucas in ten thousand Sambo-avatars") of the Negro in a position of moral superiority to the white man who has injured him (*Intruder in the Dust* [New York: New American Library, "Signet Books"], Chapter 9). In the "Appendix" to *The Sound and the Fury* which he wrote for *The Portable Faulkner*, ed. Malcolm Cowley (New York: Viking Press, 1946), Faulkner speaks of old Brigadier General Jason Lycurgus Compson II as "now completing the third of his three avatars--the one as son of a brilliant and gallant statesman, the second as battle-leader of brave and gallant men, the third as a sort of pri-vileged pseudo-Daniel Boone-Robinson Crusoe." In the same "Appendix" Faulkner tells of Jefferson's mousy librarian spending "her life trying to keep *Forever Amber* in its orderly overlapping avatars ... out of the hands of highschool juniors and seniors": the "avatars" of *Forever Amber*, that is, are the whole succession of forbidden sexy novels which titillate feverish adolescent fancy. "Avatar," in these various in-stances, seems to signify a periodic succession of embodi-ments of an essentially identical reality--or, as in "ten thousand Sambo-avatars," perhaps multiple simultaneous embodiments.

9. Faulkner's "voices, myriad, out of all time" correspond to what Bergson calls "the uninterrupted humming of life's depths" (pp. 176-77). Faulkner externalizes and objectifies the concept by finding an "objective correlative": the summertime chorus of insect-sounds.

10. Most of the principal characters in the novel (Grimm, McEachern, Joanna Burden, and even Gail Hightower) act as if their wills were determined by some overruling necessity. For an excellent brief discussion of the theme of fatality in Faulkner, see Rabi, "Faulkner and the Exiled Generation," in *William Faulkner: Two Decades of Criticism*, especially pp. 132-34.

11. For discussion of the conjoined Negro-sex motifs in *Light in August* see Phyllis Hirshleifer, "As Whirlwinds in the South: An Analysis of *Light in August*," *Perspective*, 7 (1949), 237-38.

12. Faulkner, in representing what Bergson calls "intuition of duration," generally uses cyclic figures. Movement across an urn is of course cyclic movement. Joe Christmas feels that for thirty years he has been running "inside the circle" (Chapter 14, p. 321). Lena thinks of her movement along a country road as being "like already measured thread being rewound onto a spool" (Chapter 1, p. 6). This simile is also used by Bergson to suggest the sense of "our own person in its flowing through time" (p. 191): "It is, if you like, like the unrolling of a spool.... But it is just as much a continual winding, like that of thread into a ball" (pp. 192-93). Richard Chase has discussed the contrasting significances of what he calls "linear discreteness and curve" in "The Stone and the Crucifixion: Faulkner's *Light in August*," *Kenyon Review*, 10 (1948), 539-51 (reprinted in *William Faulkner: Two Decades of Criticism*). I think that his argument, although perceptive and valuable, miscarries somewhat because he thinks in terms of the form of Faulkner's cyclic images, instead of noting that they are essentially images of duration.

13. Faulkner's "now Now" is a verbal device for signaling the moment of Hightower's passage from a temporal now to the Eternal Now. Compare "yesterday today and tomorrow are Is: Indivisible: One" (*Intruder in the Dust*, Chapter 9).

FAULKNER'S GRECIAN URN

Joan S. Korenman

When asked in a 1955 interview to name his favorite poets, William Faulkner began the list with John Keats. Keats was one of his "old friends" whom he had read and admired early in life and to whom he had returned continually over the years.[1] The poem to which Faulkner was undoubtedly most drawn is the "Ode on a Grecian Urn." In addition to singling it out for special mention during another interview,[2] Faulkner quotes lines from the ode in two of his novels, *Sartoris* (1929) and *Go Down, Moses* (1942). At least two other novels, *Light in August* (1932) and *The Mansion* (1959), contain suggestions of Keats's poem. Several critics have noted briefly this repeated use of the "Ode on a Grecian Urn," but no one has discussed in any detail just why Faulkner was so drawn to the poem or the extent to which it figures in his thought and writing.[3] The present paper proposes as a likely basis for this attraction the similarity between the attitude toward time and change expressed in Keats's ode and Faulkner's own feelings about man's involvement in time.

In the "Ode on a Grecian Urn," Keats expresses strong ambivalence toward the transience at the heart of the human condition. Throughout much of the ode, the poet dwells on the superiority of the urn's world, with its freedom from process and personal distress. Gradually, though, Keats reveals his imperfect contentment with the "Cold Pastoral." Human experience, with all its limitations, finally offers a warmth and vitality that permanence and stasis cannot match.[4]

Just as Keats wavers between envy and rejection of the urn figures' immunity from time, so in his writings and public statements Faulkner both deplored man's immersion

Excerpted from Joan S. Korenman, "Faulkner's Grecian Urn," Southern Literary Journal, 7 (Fall 1974), 3-23; *excerpts from pp. 3-6, 13-17, 19-23. The notes have been renumbered. Reprinted with permission.*

in a world of time and change where nothing lasts and yet
affirmed that "life is motion"[5] and must involve change.
Throughout his fiction, Faulkner offers us characters who
seek the sort of stasis enjoyed by the figures on the Grecian
urn. His treatment of these characters is invariably ambivalent.
Some, like Horace Benbow in *Sartoris* and Gavin Stevens in the
later Snopes books, Faulkner regards primarily with amused
detachment; only occasionally does he seem to respect them.
He accords far more serious and ambivalent treatment to those
protagonists whose desire for stasis is bound up with a longing
for the past. Characters in several of Faulkner's greatest
works--Quentin Compson in *The Sound and the Fury*, Gail Hightower in *Light in August*, and Ike McCaslin in *Go Down, Moses*--
struggle to stop time's flow, to prevent time from defiling
their ideal past. Faulkner recognizes his protagonists' inadequacies, especially their tendency to romanticize the past
and their consequent inability to tolerate life in the present;
at the same time, he presents these characters with great
sympathy and compassion. The ambivalence he exhibits toward
them arises from the mixed feelings with which he, like Keats,
regarded the passage of time. As a Southerner trying to recon-
cile his loving allegiance to his heritage with his awareness
of the need for change, the Mississippi writer found in Keats's
ode the expression of a conflict he well understood.

Even as a young man, Faulkner seems to have had Keats's
ode in the back of his mind. In a December 1922 review of
three Joseph Hergesheimer novels, Faulkner wrote of *Linda
Condon*: "It is more like a lovely Byzantine frieze: a few
unforgettable figures in silent arrested motion, forever
beyond the reach of time...."[6] The stasis ("silent arrested
motion") represented here by art is for Faulkner the ultimate
peace, immunity from the destructive march of time. The
achievement of this peace, he suggests, may have been one reason for writing the novel: "One can imagine Hergesheimer submerging himself in Linda Condon as in a still harbor where the
age cannot hurt him and where rumor of the world reaches him
only as a far faint sound of rain. Perhaps he wrote the book
for this reason...." Significantly, Faulkner uses a variation
of the still harbor image a few years later in discussing the
"Ode on a Grecian Urn." Outlining the development of his
literary taste in a 1925 article for *The Double Dealer*, he
wrote: "I read 'Thou still unravished bride of quietness'
and found a still water withal strong and potent, quiet with
its own strength, and satisfying as bread."[7] Here, as in the
Hergesheimer review, still water suggests a resting place,
a refuge from the onrushing stream of time. This association
of still water with Keatsian stasis and peace finds expression

later in Faulkner's novels, in particular *Sartoris* and *The Sound and the Fury.*

. . . .

What Quentin could find only in death--Keatsian stasis, an escape from time and change--the Reverend Gail Hightower in *Light in August* seeks by retreating from life into the past. Born into his parents' old age, Hightower comes to dwell on the glamorous stories told about his grandfather who was killed raiding a chicken coop during the Civil War. Like the story of Bayard Sartoris and the anchovies in *Sartoris*, the chicken-coop raid becomes elevated in the telling, until it exemplifies "that fine shape of eternal youth and virginal desire which makes heroes."[8] In the course of time, the grandfather's past becomes Hightower's sole reality. He denies his own existence, feeling that he was "born about thirty years after the only day he seemed to have ever lived in-- that day when his grandfather was shot from the galloping horse" and that "time had stopped there and then ..." (pp. 57, 59). Rather than risk living his own life in a world less pure and heroic than his vision, Hightower retreats to the moment of his grandfather's "heroism," a moment that offers the fearful idealist both a sense of grandeur and a shelter from the ugly complexities of the present.

Hightower's decision to become a minister is in large measure motivated by his obsession with the past. He envisions announcing to the church elders, "Listen. God must call me to Jefferson because my life died there, was shot from the saddle of a galloping horse in a Jefferson street one night twenty years before it was ever born" (p. 452). He knows that "he went [to the seminary], chose that as his vocation, with that as his purpose" (p. 452). Hightower turns to the Church as his means of going back to the past, of stopping time; not surprisingly, then, he regards the Church as a source of peace:

> He believed with a calm joy that if ever there was shelter, it would be the Church; that if ever truth could walk naked and without shame or fear, it would be in the seminary. When he believed that he had heard the call it seemed to him that he could see his future, his life, intact and on all sides complete and inviolable, like a classic and serene vase, where the spirit could be born anew sheltered from the harsh gale of living and die so, peacefully.... (p. 453)

Like Quentin and other Faulkner characters, Hightower seeks the peaceful stasis represented by the Keatsian "classic and serene vase."

Hightower's intense concentration on the past renders him incapable of participating successfully in the present. He lives only for the coming of twilight each evening. Quentin Compson regarded twilight as "that quality of light as if time really had stopped for a while,"[9] and twilight has effectively the same meaning for Hightower. Each day, as "the final copper light of afternoon fades," he sits by the window listening for his grandfather's galloping cavalry to thunder past. Totally preoccupied with the past, Hightower neglects both his parishioners and his wife. His insensitivity to his wife's needs and desires drives her first to infidelity and eventually to a rather scandalous suicide. The shocked parishioners expect that the minister will give up the congregation and leave Jefferson. They force him to resign his pulpit, but neither threats nor physical violence can persuade him to leave town. At last, the community gives up and simply ignores him. This, of course, is exactly what Hightower wants, for now he can devote himself to his ancestral ghost without the petty distractions of intercourse with society.

Hightower retains only one contact with Jefferson society, Byron Bunch, himself something of a loner. When Byron falls under the spell of Lena Grove, Hightower's life, too, is altered. Through Byron's efforts, the minister comes back in touch with society, at least temporarily; he presides over the birth of Lena's child and he makes a last-minute futile gesture to save Joe Christmas's life. Hightower's sudden involvement in the lives of others and his contact with life's most basic and extreme experiences—birth and death—unsettle him profoundly. He feels compelled to reexamine the course of his own life, and he comes to a painful realization of the futility and destructiveness of that life.

Hightower is not able to live with his new understanding. It is too late for him to be reborn. Instead, he returns to the obsessive image of his grandfather which has haunted him throughout his life. As his head slumps to the window sill, he hears once again the sound of galloping cavalry, "the wild bugles and the clashing sabres and the dying thunder of hooves" (p. 467).

Faulkner's portrayal of Hightower is both critical and sympathetic, exhibiting the same divided feelings that went into his characterization of the past-obsessed Quentin Compson. In Light in August, Faulkner sees the failings of such a character quite clearly and spells them out for us somewhat more explicitly than he did in The Sound and the Fury. And yet, we can still discern a certain approval of Hightower's obsession, "this last left of honor and pride and life" (p. 466). Lest these words be thought to express merely the

warped perspective of the deluded minister, they should be
compared with a statement Faulkner made about Hightower some
years later:

> He had failed himself, but there was one thing that he
> still had--which was the brave grandfather that galloped
> into the town.... [Hightower] had to endure, to live,
> but that was one thing that was pure and fine that he
> had--was the memory of his grandfather, who had been
> brave.[10]

Even as he makes his most pointed criticism of Southern past-
worshipping romanticism, Faulkner proves to be something of
a worshipper himself. As psychiatry has long been forced to
recognize, diagnosis does not always carry with it a cure.

The serene timelessness that Hightower seeks finds embodiment in Lena Grove. At one with nature, the pregnant Lena
moves "with the untroubled unhaste of a change of season"
(p. 47). She lives each moment as it comes and accepts whatever life brings. Her destiny in life, as Hightower recognizes,
is simply to *be*, to fulfill her natural function: "*The good
stock peopling in tranquil obedience to it the good earth:
from these hearty loins without hurry or haste descending
mother and daughter*" (p. 384). Lena is unreflective, possessing
simply a "tranquil and calm unreason" (p. 15). She gives scant
thought to time, and hence does not despair at its passing.
She rarely looks to either the past or the future and thus is
spared the fear of change which plagues the minds of many of
Faulkner's more intellectual characters.

Early in his description of her, Faulkner likens Lena to
a figure on an urn:

> backrolling now behind her a long monotonous succession
> of peaceful and undeviating changes from day to dark
> and dark to day again, through which she advanced in
> identical and anonymous and deliberate wagons as though
> through a succession of creakwheeled and limpeared
> avatars, like something moving forever and without
> progress across an urn. (p. 5)

Once again, Faulkner very likely had Keats's "Ode on a Grecian
Urn" on his mind. Keats contrasts the urn's timelessness with
the frantic, struggling figures whom the urn depicts:

> What men or gods are these? What maidens loth?
> What mad pursuit? What struggle to escape?
> What pipes and timbrels? What wild ecstasy?

Similarly, Lena's "untroubled unhaste" contrasts with Christmas's "mad pursuit" and "struggle to escape" and the "wild

ecstasy" experienced in different but equally warped ways by
Hightower, Joanna Burden, and perhaps even Percy Grimm. In
her identification with the natural world (which remains, though
men pass), and in her serene repose, Lena symbolizes the timelessness suggested by Keats's urn.[11]

Keatsian urn-like timelessness figures significantly in
both *The Sound and the Fury* and *Light in August*, but actual
reference to Keats's poem in these novels is at best oblique.
In *Go Down, Moses*, however, characters speak directly about
the ode and even recite it to each other. Faulkner's use of
the poem here helps us to understand better Ike McCaslin and
his tenacious allegiance to the wilderness.

As a boy, Ike learns of the exploitation and racial injustice that form his heritage. Unlike Gail Hightower, Ike
does not glamorize history. His grandfather's behavior fills
him with shame, not admiration. He sees that his family's
history--which Faulkner explicitly equates with the history
of the South[12]--is too corrupt to support idealization and
nostalgia. But while his rational awareness prevents a High-
tower-like worship of the Southern past, Ike's emotional
commitment resembles that of Faulkner's earlier past-obsessed
Southerners. Unable to sustain an idealized version of the
historical past, Ike turns to the wilderness of his childhood
where "death did not even exist" (p. 327) and shot-down bucks
"still and forever leaped ... forever immortal" (p. 178),
like the immortal figures on Keats's Grecian urn.

. . . .

Ike wishes the wilderness to remain forever just as it
had been in his youth. Faulkner accentuates Ike's desire to
stop time by introducing lines from the "Ode on a Grecian
Urn." The actual quotation occurs during a conversation between fourteen-year-old Ike and his older cousin, Cass. Ike
has rejected a chance to shoot the almost legendary bear,
Old Ben. Cass explains Ike's reluctance to shoot by reading
Keats's ode (pp. 296-97), repeating the lines:

> She cannot fade, though thou has not thy bliss,
> For ever wilt thou love, and she be fair.

By quoting the ode, Cass suggests that the reason Ike did not
shoot Old Ben is that he wished to prolong the wilderness
that he loves and that is symbolized by the bear and the
annual bear hunt. Like Quentin Compson and Gail Hightower,
Ike is seeking in the Keatsian unfulfilled state a way to
defy time and change.

Significantly, Ike thinks back on this Keats conversation seven years later when he renounces what he regards as his tainted McCaslin patrimony. He is again embroiled in a discussion with Cass, who accuses him of relinquishing the land as an escape. Ike does not deny the charge: "All right. Escape," he agrees. He finally admits: "I could say I dont know why I must do it but that I do know I have got to because I have got myself to live with for the rest of my life and *all I want is peace to do it in*."[13] Shortly after Ike says this (p. 295), the look in Cass's eyes reminds him of their Grecian urn discussion seven years before. What all this seems to suggest is that Ike clings to his vision of the timeless, ideal wilderness as an escape from his complex heritage and his present responsibilities. Like Quentin Compson, he wants his world to remain the simple, untainted existence of his childhood. He refuses to accept change as part of the human condition, insisting instead upon the static peace embodied by the timeless woods and Keats's Grecian urn.

For years, critics have debated whether Ike is an ideal character who deserves our moral admiration or a narrow, selfish escapist.[14] Faulkner's own comments have only contributed fuel to the controversy. Discussing Ike with interviewer Cynthia Grenier in 1956, Faulkner observed: "Well, I think a man ought to do more than just repudiate. He should have been more affirmative instead of shunning people."[15] This comment establishes beyond dispute the existence of Faulkner's reservations about Ike, but it cannot be taken as a definitive judgment. Only two years later, at the University of Virginia, the author was asked whether he looked on Ike "as having fulfilled his destiny" and whether the things that Ike learned from Sam Fathers "stood him in good stead all the way through his life." Faulkner replied:

> I do, yes. They didn't give him success but they gave him something a lot more important, even in this country. They gave him serenity, they gave him what would pass for wisdom—I mean wisdom as contradistinct from the schoolman's wisdom of education. They gave him that.[16]

These remarks demonstrate once again the elusive complexity of Faulkner's attitude toward those of his protagonists who try to defy time and change. As a representative and defender of the old times and old values, Ike has the author's admiration. However, when he renounces his patrimony and proclaims, "'Sam Fathers set me free'" (p. 300), Ike is claiming freedom from his responsibilities and from time. This is a claim with which Faulkner may sympathize, but, unlike Ike, he recognizes that it is a claim that cannot be realized.

As we have seen, Ike shares his attraction to Keatsian stasis with a number of other Faulknerian characters spanning almost the entire range of the author's long career. In each case, Faulkner's portrayal is marked by ambivalence, but he seems to approach with most seriousness and passion characters like Quentin Compson, Gail Hightower, and Ike McCaslin who wish to stop time's flow at least partly in order to return to and preserve an ideal past. Theirs is in many ways the desire of the South, and Faulkner's mixed feelings toward them mirror the complexity of his response to his Southern heritage. Born near the turn of the century, Faulkner was brought up in the ways of the Old South, schooled in his family's history and in the beliefs and loyalties of the nineteenth century. And throughout his fiction, his sympathy generally rests with "the old people"--the men and women out of the semi-legendary Southern past who were simpler, more whole, and more honorable than those of the modern age--and with individuals like Will Falls and Miss Jenny Du Pre of *Sartoris* or Miss Habersham of *The Unvanquished* who, being advanced in years and hence almost part of the past themselves, possess some of these same qualities. Faulkner's villains, on the other hand, invariably belong to the modern world. They are men like Jason Compson, Popeye, and Flem Snopes, who honor no ties from the past and completely disregard feelings and scruples as they pursue their personal goals. The author's portrayal of the world they ally themselves with is singularly unflattering. Modern Jefferson consists of

> neat small new one-storey houses designed in Florida
> and California set with matching garages in their neat
> plots of clipped grass and tedious flowerbeds, three
> and four of them now, a subdivision now in what twenty-
> five years ago had been considered a little small for
> one decent front lawn, where the prosperous young
> married couples lived with two children each and (as
> soon as they could afford it) an automobile each and
> the memberships in the country club and the bridge
> clubs and the junior rotary and chamber of commerce
> and ... the wives in sandals and pants and painted
> toenails puffed lipstick-stained cigarettes over shop-
> ping bags in the chain groceries and drugstores.[17]

Almost all of Faulkner's works, from *Sartoris* and *Sanctuary* to *Go Down, Moses*, *Requiem for a Nun*, and the Snopes books, are shaped by the author's belief that the "progress" which accompanies the march of time has replaced the grandeur and individualism of the past with an increasingly commonplace, mass-produced, faceless, irresponsible society in which men care neither for each other nor for the natural world.

However, just as Keats experienced a vague discontent mixed with his envy of the urn figures for whom time has stopped, so Faulkner at times finds himself rationally at war with his emotional commitment to the past and to the notion of stopping time. As a man of the twentieth century, he appreciates the need for progress and change; as a Southerner, he understands the danger of paying too much heed to the ghosts of the past. " ... It's foolish to be against progress," he observed while a writer-in-residence at the University of Virginia.[18] In his role as Faulkner's spokesman, Gavin Stevens comments in *Intruder in the Dust* that "no man can cause more grief than that one clinging blindly to the vices of his ancestors."[19] On various occasions, Faulkner reiterated his belief that time must flow on and men must change: "the only alternative to change is death."[20]

Faulkner never resolves his conflicting attitudes toward time and change. He obviously admires and even envies characters like Dilsey and Lena Grove who can move along easily with the flow of time and accept whatever the passing moment brings. But the characters in his fiction who possess the strength and serenity of a Lena Grove are, like Lena, "primitives"--women, children, Negroes, simple men--people as far removed as possible from their author in both mind and circumstance. Their world is not the world with which Faulkner and his time-ridden characters have to cope, nor into which they can escape. Faulkner's world more closely resembles that described in Keats's "Ode to a Nightingale":

> Where but to think is to be full of sorrow
>   And leaden-eyed despairs,
> Where Beauty cannot keep her lustrous eyes,
>   Or new Love pine at them beyond to-morrow.

Time must pass, life must change; for Faulkner as for Keats, this is the sadness and the essence of the human condition.

NOTES

1. Cynthia Grenier, "The Art of Fiction: An Interview with William Faulkner--September, 1955," *Accent*, 16 (Summer 1956), 168.

2. Jean Stein, "William Faulkner: An Interview," *Paris Review* (Spring 1956), rpt. in *William Faulkner: Three Decades of Criticism*, ed. Frederick J. Hoffman and Olga Vickery (New York: Harbinger Books, 1963), p. 68.

3. Critics who have noted Faulkner's repeated use of Keats's ode include Darrel Abel, "Frozen Movement in *Light in August*," *Boston University Studies in English*, 3 (Spring 1957), 33; Michael Millgate, *The Achievement of William Faulkner* (New York: Random House, 1966), p. 96; Richard P. Adams, *Faulkner: Myth and Motion* (Princeton: Princeton University Press, 1968), p. 12; and J.F. Kobler, "Lena Grove: Faulkner's 'Still Unravish'd Bride of Quietness,'" *Arizona Quarterly*, 28 (Winter 1972), 340-41. The argument of the present paper is presented more fully in the author's doctoral thesis, "Faulkner's Grecian Urn," Harvard University, 1969. An article by Blanche H. Gelfant, "Faulkner and Keats: The Ideality of Art in 'The Bear'" (*The Southern Literary Journal*, 2 [Fall 1969]), which came to the author's attention after the present paper had been completed, advances an argument for Faulkner's attraction to Keats in some respects similar to the one presented here. Gelfant's discussion, however, is limited to *Go Down, Moses*. So, too, is a brief note by William B. Stone, "Ike McCaslin and the Grecian Urn," *Studies in Short Fiction*, 10 (Winter 1973), 93-94.

4. This interpretation is similar to that presented by Douglas Bush, *John Keats: His Life and Writings* (New York: Macmillan, 1966), pp. 138-43. Of course, the question of whether Keats's ode places higher value on life or art has provoked much critical discussion. For a summary of various interpretations, see Robert Gleckner, "Keats's Odes: The Problems of the Limited Canon," *Studies in English Literature*, 5 (Autumn 1965), 577-85.

5. Stein, p. 80.

6. "Books and Things: Joseph Hergesheimer," *William Faulkner: Early Prose and Poetry*, ed. Carvel Collins (Boston: Little, Brown, 1962), p. 101.

7. "Verse Old and Nascent: A Pilgrimage," *William Faulkner: Early Prose and Poetry*, p. 117.

8. William Faulkner, *Light in August* (New York: Modern Library College Editions, 1968), p. 458. All references are to this Modern Library edition and will henceforth be incorporated within the text wherever possible.

9. *The Sound and the Fury* (New York: Random House), pp. 209-10 (editor's note).

10. *Faulkner in the University: Class Conferences at the University of Virginia, 1957-1958*, ed. Frederick L. Gwynn and Joseph L. Blotner (New York: Vintage, 1965), p. 75.

11. Norman Holmes Pearson also discusses Lena in relation to Keats's ode in "Lena Grove," *Shenandoah*, 2 (Spring 1952), 3-7.

12. William Faulkner, *Go Down, Moses* (New York: Modern Library, 1942), p. 293. All references are to this Modern Library edition and will henceforth be incorporated within the text wherever possible.

13. *Go Down, Moses*, p. 288; emphasis added. Ike's words recall the Rev. Hightower's in *Light in August*: "I just wanted peace" (p. 293).

14. Compare, for example, Irving Howe's positive assessment in *William Faulkner: A Critical Study* (2nd ed. rev.; New York: Vintage, 1962), pp. 92-98, with the more critical view expressed by Olga Vickery, *The Novels of William Faulkner: A Critical Interpretation* (rev. ed.; Baton Rouge: Louisiana State University Press, 1964), pp. 132-34. See also the essays and annotated bibliography in Francis Lee Utley, Lynn Z. Bloom, and Arthur F. Kinney, eds., *Bear, Man, and God: Eight Approaches to William Faulkner's "The Bear"* (2nd ed.; New York: Random House, 1971).

15. Grenier, p. 175.

16. *Faulkner in the University*, p. 54.

17. William Faulkner, *Intruder in the Dust* (New York: Random House, 1948), pp. 119-20. Cf. the historical prefaces in *Requiem for a Nun*.

18. *Faulkner in the University*, p. 98.

19. *Intruder in the Dust*, p. 49.

20. "On Fear: Deep South in Labor: Mississippi," *William Faulkner: Essays, Speeches and Public Letters*, ed. James B. Meriwether (New York: Random House, 1965), p. 95.

FAULKNER, THE MYTHIC MIND,
AND THE BLACKS

Lee Clinton Jenkins

Without the permanence of the past, Faulkner has said,
"there would be no grief or sorrow." But one must add that
there would also be no viable conception of freedom in the
future, if one were eternally condemned to keep faith with
the past. Whatever has happened is irrevocable in its determining aspect, Destiny is at the source of life. Nothing is
ever lost. This view may have an application to Faulkner's
fondness for his vision of Keats's urn, where the possibilities
of human behavior, in a suspended state of enactment, are
perpetually arrested in time, in a metaphor of the wholeness
and unity of human action in time. Whatever happens is related
to everything else. All actions are offered up as inheritance
of the group consciousness, in which each individual participates and for which each is responsible. This, one might say,
is the real beauty of consciousness, the transcendent power
of its accumulated heritage in its realization of truth and
perfection, as well as its curse, the collective, irreversible
and unredeemable weight of its capacity for wrongdoing. Guilt,
from this point of view, is forever and unending, because
acts of appeasement--a denial of the consequences of consciousness, its inextricable evil, as exemplified in Isaac McCaslin,
on the one hand, and the sacrificial atonement of sin, as
exemplified in Joe Christmas, on the other--cannot eradicate
the guilt-producing determinants of consciousness, since the
compromising of moral nature in man is an inevitable feature
of his human nature. The act of appeasement in Joe Christmas's
case, for example, confirms the basic imperfection of human
functioning in an act, presided over by Percy Grimm, a knife-
wielding sadist, which is guilt-producing all over again.

*Excerpted from Section I of "Faulkner, the Mythic Mind, and
the Blacks," by Lee Clinton Jenkins,* Literature and Psychology,
*27 (1977), 74-91. Reprinted with permission. The notes have
been renumbered.*

As this applies to the lives of characters in Faulkner,
Blöcker[1] sees the application of the mythic consciousness as
a rebuke to Jean-Paul Sartre's criticisms of the entrapment
of Faulkner's characters living in a "barred future" where
"there is never any progression, nothing which can come from
the future" and "everything is in suspension."[2] For Sartre,
Faulkner denies life of its possibilities and potential for
fulfillment, in terms of the rational assessment, on a literal
level, of life prospects and circumstances which allow for
choices to be made which move one out of the grip of the past
into the future. Without such choice, life is absurd, which
is the way Sartre views Faulkner's "metaphysic," although
he likes his "art." Yet the art itself expresses, as Sartre
notes, the idea of suspension, not in abstract terms, but in
literal ones, in things themselves. The opening passages in
Light in August where Lena sees the approaching wagon reveal
for Sartre the motion arrested "at the very heart of things"
where "moments erupt and freeze, then fade, recede and diminish,
still motionless," while for Blöcker this scene is the very
expression of the mythic: Lena has made her progress through
a "long monotonous succession of peaceful and undeviating
changes from day to dark and dark to day again, through which
she advanced in identical and anonymous and deliberate wagons
as though through a succession of creakwheeled and limpeared
avatars, like something moving forever and without progress
across an urn," and the wagon she is watching approach, as
if hypnotized, seems to "hang suspended in the middle distance
forever and forever ..." (p. 5).

I have explored these matters at some length to establish
a basis for the consideration of the sense of irreversible
personal destiny that many of Faulkner's characters display
as they are seen to be entrapped within the confines of prior
life experiences which must be repetitively reenacted in the
present. I have spoken of how the data of memory is not that
which is recalled out of the past into the present, but is
rather the past subsisting, unaltered by time, in the present,
which constitutes not only memory but the very mode of consciousness. Events in the present, therefore, are absorbed
into and activate the functioning of the omnipresent past,
which is the sole reality in consciousness. For example,
Quentin Compson's fight with Gerald Bland is not rendered
by Faulkner as an event occurring in the present, and Quentin
himself is only aware of it as an expression of his prior
conflict with Dalton Ames in regard to his obsessional concern with vidicating Caddy's honor and his inadequacy as a
male to do so. The actual quarrel with Bland is rendered by
Faulkner only after it has occurred and become history, and

was, when occurring, an obscure and shadowy event in Quentin's mind,[3] as well as in the reader's. Faulkner's opening chapter on Joe Christmas's childhood captures the whole idea of the irremediability and deterministic quality of the past, not subject to conscious deliberation or alteration, with the famous equation, "memory believes before knowing remembers." This would be taken to mean that experience exists in the mind as that which is meaningful and as that which the mind accepts, because it has been "distilled," without the mind knowing or understanding what it accepts, because no process of rational mediation has come into play in consideration of the data of experience that has been accepted--and in Christmas's case, it also seems that no such process of understanding, as a result of the rational appraisal of the givens in his mind, *ever* occurs. As Jean Pouillon points out, this is not a matter of an individual being the sum of his experiences in the conventional sense, or of the idea that "a man is what his past had made him,"[4] because when we ordinarily speak of such a case, we do not think of the present as losing its importance because of the primacy of the past, since it is from the point of view of the present that we determine the existence and significance of the past. But in Faulkner's conception of it, the past is extratemporal; the "past, therefore, not only was but is and will be; it is the unfolding of destiny."[5] The past subsists. What happens in the present is absorbed into it. Benjy, for example, in *The Sound and the Fury*, is the perfect example of the past never being lost; he *is* his past.

Further, the fatality that unfolds in the life of Joe Christmas is not the manifestation of a necessary and inevitable dramatic sequence of events which, if altered, would lose its inevitability. Rather, the things that happen to Joe are an expression of inner compulsion that cause him to act in the same way toward each experience in life; indeed, he seeks out experiences that cause him to act in the compulsive fashion that provides confirmation of the necessity of the manner and mode in which he must act. He does not have knowledge or understanding of his actions or of why he must act, only a sense of the inevitable necessity of doing so. It is this sense of inner necessity which he feels as destiny. And the increase in the sense of destiny, the inevitability of what Joe must do, is achieved by Faulkner through an enlarging of the scope of the past, all of that which is yet to be evoked by and forced upon the present, as Joe's experiences in the present accumulate to bring to bear upon it the fullness of the sense of inevitability of the past repeating itself, since the past exists already as a finished whole. Hence Joanna's murder has already occurred when the novel

opens, and the course of events, subsequently revealed, is
not a registering of a necessary sequence of events--since
anything could happen, and there is no reason why what does
happen *must* happen--but of the inner compulsion which must be
fulfilled, in response to the unalterable dictates of the
accumulated past, which are not recalled but are relived in
the present, which act as if they *were* the present in the
form of the conscious mind being aware of itself.

Pouillon comments on this matter by suggesting that Faulkner distinguishes between consciousness and knowledge and has
his characters function on the level of the former: "consciousness is inevitable, knowledge only a possibility....
Chronology, being a posterior organization of life, belongs
to the domain of knowledge. It is a kind of intellectual
liberation from destiny: it assures us that the past is indeed past even if we feel its pressure on our present."[6]
One would imagine that Pouillon would agree that the liberation he means parallels the emotional and intellectual liberation from the debilitating effects of unresolved conflicts
generated out of past experiences which psychoanalysis, for
instance, seeks to provide for its patients. Hence Christmas
is not so much determined by his past as he is his past, in
the same way that Benjy is, and escape is impossible: "But
there was too much running with him, stride for stride with
him. Not pursuers: but himself: years, acts, deeds omitted
and committed, keeping pace with him, stride for stride...."
(*Light in August*, p. 424).

Driven in this way, Christmas must ever feel responsible
for himself, for the actions which erupt unwittingly out of
his consciousness, in response to the dictates of the past.
Since the past is untouchable and expresses itself as consciousness in the present, Joe must also demonstrate that
clairvoyant knowledge of the future and of what awaits him,
from which he knows he cannot escape. McEachern, similarly,
indicates this facility in the form of the compulsive, trans-
lunary assurance which leads him straight to the dance hall,
the motivating force of which Faulkner does not explain.[7]
The sense of mental oppression and entrapment is rendered
so directly by Faulkner that neither Joe nor the reader can
see how there is always the possibility of taking thought,
of appraising experience, and of achieving liberation from
it, so that it may be seen that what one feels to be destiny
may only be an illusion, if the causes of the feeling can be
made available to analysis. And analysis, as a function of
rational thought, is always a possibility, but Faulkner's
conception of Joe exempts him from such a possibility.

How does this apply to a consideration of Joe's racial conflict, the motivating force of his dilemma? In his most lucid moments, when he speaks of his desire to make of himself what he chooses to be, I think that what he is referring to, if he had sufficient clarity of mind to articulate it, is the possibility of the assertion of the integrity of being, without reference to artificial categories of race and their attendant attributes. It must be remembered that, insofar as he thinks of himself as a black person, there will always be that part of him which seeks self-respect, no matter how degraded the opposed white part views the black portion and wishes to escape from it. Faulkner's conceptional imagination, in presenting the black xenophobia, adequately renders the obsessional quality, from the white point of view, in Joe's mind, but it does not grasp sufficiently the defiant presentation of the yearning for integrity of being that would be appertaining in the black part of Joe's mind. I think Joe, in those lucid moments, is referring to that condition, to paraphrase Sartre's formula, when existence precedes essence, when *being* itself is the highest value in life, and is inviolable, keeping faith with itself, in the way that Lena, for instance, is secure in her being, without reference to artificial classification. But the fierce racial conflict in Joe's mind will not allow him to conceive of himself without reference to imposed racial constructs of identity. At least, that is, he *reacts* as if this were the case. As I have tried to indicate, I do not believe that he *thinks*, since, if he did that, the articulation of an identity that was race-free would not, as the narrative indicates, be an impossibility, nor would he *have* to live outside of humanity to escape its coercion, because he would know within himself the value of his own personhood. He would know that his conflict is the result of artificial categories that can be *dismissed*. It would be a difficult and heroic thing, but not an impossible thing, to one who thinks. But Faulkner does not grant to Joe the capability for rational analysis; thus he does not achieve understanding of his schizoid-like nature. He conforms always, as one critic says, "to that bitter conception of himself which makes him a mental and emotional white in a Negro world, a secret Negro in the white world."[8] This is the circle he travels in until he sustains the violent exacerbation of his conflict in the confrontation with Joanna and commits the deed that casts him in the final role of victim, the sacrificial Black Other who must suffer to expiate the guilt of all. This is not a conscious decision on his part, for he does not think, but a mythic acquiescence

in compliance with psychohistorical dictates that function
beneath reason, that absolve mankind's responsibility for the
black/white dichotomy in a mythic, sacrificial apotheosis.

NOTES

1. Günter Blöcker, "William Faulkner," in *Faulkner*, ed.
R.P. Warren (Englewood Cliffs, N.J.: Prentice-Hall, 1966),
p. 126. This article has been condensed from "William Faulkner,"
from *Die Neuen Wirklichkeiten* by Günter Blöcker, trans.
Jacqueline Merriam (Berlin: Argon Verlag, 1958), pp. 112-23.

2. Jean-Paul Sartre, "Time in Faulkner: *The Sound and the
Fury*," trans. Martine Darmon, *Faulkner: Three Decades of
Criticism*, ed. Frederick J. Hoffman and Olga Vickery (New
York: Harbinger Books, 1963), pp. 227-32. Sartre's essay
reprinted from *Situations I*, "Le Bruit et la fureur" (Paris:
Gallimard, 1947), pp. 70-81.

3. Particular emphasis is given this point in Jean-Paul
Sartre, "Time in Faulkner," p. 228.

4. Jean Pouillon, "Time and Destiny in Faulkner," in
Faulkner, ed. R.P. Warren (Englewood Cliffs, N.J.: Prentice-
Hall, 1966), p. 80. From "Temps et destinée chez Faulkner,"
in *Temps et roman* by Jean Pouillon, trans. Jacqueline Merriam
(Paris: Gallimard, 1946), pp. 238-60.

5. Ibid., p. 81.

6. Ibid., p. 83.

7. Ibid., p. 85.

8. R.G. Collins, "*Light in August*: Faulkner's Stained
Glass Triptych," in *Mosaic*, 7,1 (Winnipeg, Canada: The University of Manitoba Press, 1973), p. 119.

III. Voice and Language

FAULKNER'S JOE CHRISTMAS: CHARACTER THROUGH VOICE

Sister Kristin Morrison, IHM

> *he was hearing a myriad sounds of no greater volume--*
> *voices, murmurs, whispers ... which he had been con-*
> *scious of all his life without knowing it, which*
> *were his life.*--Light in August

Voice as, experientially, the route to person; voice as, structurally, the medium of character: these two concepts are integral to an understanding of Faulkner's narrative technique and of all the strangely intimate knowledge of character it provides. Through all Faulkner's work--but most notably in *The Sound and the Fury*, *As I Lay Dying*, *Sanctuary*, *Light in August*, and *Absalom, Absalom!*--it is voice that constitutes the chief structural principle and that orders character manifestation. In *The Sound and the Fury* and *As I Lay Dying* this is perhaps most clear, for there each voice-unit comprises a chapter and is assigned to an individual character: the structure is mechanical, the revelatory quality of each character-voice relatively obvious. In the last three novels, however, the voice function is more subtle and consequently understanding of it more necessary. Especially is this true of *Light in August*, where the reader's unawareness of the fact of voice and lack of sensitivity to its function easily result in misunderstanding of the novel in general and of the character of Joe Christmas in particular. Only with an understanding of voice--its place in the narrative, its relation to character, its effect on the reader--only then can the reader appreciate *Light in August* and the complexity and dimensionality of Joe Christmas, his manifestation as person.

From Texas Studies in Literature and Language, *11 (Winter 1961), 419-43. Reprinted with permission of The University of Texas Press.*

I. Voice Structure and *Light in August*

Quite simply, voice is the who-said-what of narrative.
Early statements concerning voice and address in literature
are to be found in Plato's *Republic* (III, 392d-394c) and in
Aristotle's *Poetics* (1448a 20-24) and *Rhetoric* (I, 1358a-b).
The most succinct modern statement of this concept is that
of James Craig LaDrière in the *Dictionary of World Literature*;
Professor LaDrière cites four basic types of voice structure:

> (a) one in which a single voice is heard throughout
> and this is the voice of the speaker himself (as in
> the speech of ordinary conversation or a letter in
> which there is not quoted matter), (b) one in which
> a single voice is heard throughout, not that of the
> speaker but that of a personality assumed by the speaker
> in imagination (as in a monologue of Browning, or most
> lyric poetry), (c) one in which a single basic voice
> (that of the speaker in his own person or of an assumed
> personality, *e.g.*, that of one of the characters in a
> story) speaks, but the speech of this voice is inter-
> rupted by direct, verbatim quotation of other voices
> as their speech is reported (as in most narrative),
> and (d) one in which a dialogue of two or more voices,
> which in narration would be quoted, is heard directly
> without the intrusion of a narrator's voice (as in drama,
> where of course action and setting are added to speech).[1]

The progression of these types of structure is, as Professor
LaDrière notes, from "subjectivity" to "objectivity." That
is to say, in the first type, (a) a really existing human
being speaks as himself, from his own subjectivity: this is
outside the province of fiction. In the last three sections
the ultimate speaker--in the case of the novel, the novelist--
presents voices of others, fictive voices. In (b) and (c)
there is the "subjectivity" of a created basic voice (the
voice which ultimately *within the narrative* is speaking) and
objective report of other voices (temporarily assumed by the
basic voice) in quotation; (d) is of course the most objective
of all, for it is the form of drama, entirely exteriorized
speech.
    It is possible that a novel be written in any of the
three latter combinations, although it is the mixed voice
structure of (c) which lends itself most readily to extended
narrative. Bald as this division of voices into basic and
assumed might seem in theory, in practice it works with great
subtlety; in fact, the experimentation with form in the
modern novel is more precisely experimentation with voice

structure: a fact strangely neglected in contemporary criticism, which has concerned itself more with the visual, spatial metaphor introduced by Henry James--point of view--than with the concept of voice.

Since much Faulkner analysis has been in terms of point of view and none specifically in terms of voice, it will be helpful to consider briefly the relation between these two critical concepts. First of all, in bare and obvious signification, free for the time of any historical grounding, it is clear that the one figure is of sight, the other of sound; the one suggests picture, the other, word. Yet obviously the basis of narrative is not painting but saying; and because narrative is made up of words--whether silent or sounded-- there must be a word-sayer, a teller. Narrative is not a matter of picture but of voice. Any picture that results is secondary to voice, is produced by the effectiveness of the voice. Voice constitutes the narrative; picture is the product in the reader's mind of the speaker's words. In their literal signification, then, these terms are clearly distinguished.

Historically, however, the distinction is not so neat. Since such dictums of Henry James as "All [the novel] needs is a subject and a painter"[2] the analogy of narrative with space has dominated critical theory; the same metaphors occur again and again: center of intelligence, point of view, posts of observation in the house of fiction. These are illuminating concepts, but a confusion results from an unrefined use of them; and *point of view* bluntly has been used to cover a multitude of refinements. The greatest confusion arises from the fact that *point of view* is used both in its literal signification and in its signification combined with the concept of voice, as a brief survey of the amorphous use of the term will reveal.

Henry James, to begin with, developing his theory of a character who serves as vessel or center of consciousness, would have as the ideal a person with "the power to be finely aware and richly responsible."[3] Such a finely aware person is Isabel Archer of *Portrait of a Lady* or Strether of *The Ambassadors*, their respective novels for the most part related from their "spatial" points of view. It is their mind's awareness that is the novel's concern, their physical view of events and mental views of those events that is the novel's subject; yet--and this is important-- it is not their voices that narrate. For James, then, the term *point of view* can refer either to the mind in the narrative which "sees" events of the narrative and to some extent their implications (characters such as Strether and Isabel Archer); or to the mind which is the subject of the

narrative and which may be ignorant of events or their implications (a character such as Maisie, James's ironic center).
But it does not refer to the teller of the entire novel, who
is always, for James, the primary author taken for granted
and forgotten.

James's concept of point of view was adapted by Percy
Lubbock in *The Craft of Fiction* as the ultimate in narrative
method. Lubbock, however, has contributed to the present confusion between spatial point of view and narrative voice by
indiscriminate use of the two concepts throughout his work.
Defining point of view (as Henry James never would) as "the
relation in which the narrator stands to the story,"[4] he
distinguishes between the pictorial method (which calls for
a narrator) and the dramatic (which offers to the reader a
"direct sight" of the matter itself while it is passing);
the one is the narrator's point of view, the other--according
to Lubbock--is the reader's point of view.[5] And earlier, as
the ideal example of full dramatization of the mind, Lubbock
had cited James's *The Ambassadors*,

> a story which is seen from one man's point of view, and
> yet a story in which that point of view is itself a
> matter for the reader to confront and to watch con-
> structively. Everything in the novel is now dramatically
> rendered, whether it is a page of dialogue or a page
> of description nobody is addressing us, nobody is re-
> porting his impression to the reader.[6]

There is a real awkwardness here, because, although the novel
may be like drama, it is not drama. However vividly written,
there is not literally a scene to witness, only a scene to
hear about, to read. When Lubbock states that in the dramatic
method there is no narrator, he means there is no obvious
narrator: the narrator does not enter into the story as a
participant or commentator, and the reader does not care who
he is. But there is a voice *telling*, and this is a neutral
basic voice.[7] And what of this dramatic method in which the
point of view is Strether's *and* the reader's? Here Lubbock
uses point of view in two different ways. Speaking of Strether,
he means a spatial point of view (what Strether--as center--
observes and experiences); speaking of the reader, he means
that the reader does not hear the story from a narrator but
"observes" it himself (which, were Lubbock thinking in terms
of word rather than picture, would refer to the basic voice
of the novel).

This inclusion of the concept of voice in the term *point
of view* becomes more obvious in recent theory. Perhaps the
best example is the appendix to Caroline Gordon and Allen

Tate's *The House of Fiction*, where point of view is described
in terms of the authority by which the story is told. Keeping
close to the modes of narrative described by James in his
prefaces and Lubbock in *The Craft of Fiction*, Gordon and Tate
emphasize the narrator rather than the mind which is the subject of the narrative. Thus they distinguish the omniscient
narrator (panoramic report of the story); the effaced narrator
(Lubbock's scenic, dramatic technique); first-person narrator
(which includes both panoramic and scenic techniques); and
the roving narrator (omniscient narrator concealed, in which
the author makes his surmises, summaries, and explanations
in terms of what the central-intelligence character sees and
feels). This emphasis on authority of the narrator and the
distinction of long and short views (panorama and scene, picture, and drama) indicate the definite fusion of the concept
of voice with spatial analogy of narrative in recent use of
the term *point of view*.

It is in psychological fiction that the necessity of an
understanding of voice proper--free of the hazy term *point of
view*--becomes necessary. In 1926 Lubbock stated that with
The Ambassadors the dramatization of experience touches its
limit: there is no further for it to go.[8] And six years later
Joseph Warren Beach, in his survey of the twentieth-century
novel, traced the development of the modern novel as a progressive elimination of the author, citing Joyce's *monologue
intérieur* as carrying James's idea of self-effacement to the
point of unrecognition.[9] Lubbock, with his apparent unawareness of psychological fiction, and Beach, with his complaint
that such fiction exploits the incoherent, both see narrative
in terms of the author's obvious presence or absence rather
than in the relation of voice to character. Is the voice of
the novel inside the mind of the subject-character or outside
it? It is this that distinguishes psychological fiction from
traditional. It is this that makes *The Ambassadors* not the
last word in dramatization: for however closely revelatory
of Strether's consciousness this narrative is, the voice that
narrates is an unidentified omniscience that exists outside
Strether's mind. But in psychological fiction, such as Faulkner's *The Sound and the Fury*, the revelatory voice *is* the
character's mind itself. Characters in such fiction are
centers of intelligence, limited by a single "point of view."

It is interesting that psychological fiction--fiction that
proposes to approximate in words the workings of a mind--has
also been described chiefly by spatial, visual metaphor:
stream of consciousness. This analogy, suggested by another
James, has been preferred by English-speaking critics to what
the French have styled *monologue intérieur*.[10] Yet for all the

spatial quality of the term *stream*, that to which it is
applied is obviously word: it is, in fact, the narration itself which is greatest indication that a passage is mind-voice
and not traditional description: free-flowing, elliptic,
symbolic in quality, rich in association of images, disordered
and *collage*-like so as to approximate the phantasms of the
mind (usually in a state other than reasoning). And although
Robert Humphrey maintains that stream of consciousness is
that kind of psychological fiction which concerns itself with
the pre-speech level of consciousness, "those levels on the
margin of attention"[11]--as opposed to that concerned with
rational, communicable awareness, such as in the novels of
James--it is clear that the novelist to create a likeness of
such pre-speech must, since he is writing, use words: it is
the *way* he uses the words that gives the reader the illusion
of eavesdropping on mental phenomena. And it is very much the
way he uses words which determines whether the narrative is
in the voice of an omniscient narrator, or the narrative is
in the voice of the mind itself. James, for example, describes
Maisie's "point of view" as she is omnisciently observed from
the outside:

> He finished emptying his coffee-cup and then, when he
> had put it down, leaned back in his chair where she
> could see that he smiled on her. This only added to her
> idea that he was in trouble, that he was turning some-
> how in his pain and trying different things. He con-
> tinued to smile.[12]

The first and third sentences describe what Maisie was
able to observe; the middle sentence states objectively the
effect of the observation on her sensibility. Faulkner, on
the other hand, presents Isaac McCaslin's "point of view" in
"Delta Autumn," though in the third person, as an interiorization:

> They had a house once. That was sixty years ago, when
> the Big Bottom was only thirty miles from Jefferson
> and old Major de Spain, who had been his father's
> cavalry commander in '61 and '2 and '3 and '4, and his
> cousin (his older brother; his father too) had taken
> him into the woods for the first time. Old Sam Fathers
> was alive then, born in slavery, son of a Negro slave
> and a Chickasaw chief, who had taught him how to shoot,
> not only when to shoot but when not to; such a November
> dawn as tomorrow would be and the old man led him
> straight to the great cypress and he had known the
> buck would pass exactly there.[13]

Here old McCaslin's mind-voice is itself heard. The sentence
preceding this passage is in the basic voice[14] describing the
old man lying awake facing the night "alarmless, empty of
fret." Then without a transitional phrase the voice is that
of Isaac's own mind; not--and this is important--the precise
words he is thinking (this is rendered usually in italics)
but the "awareness" of his mind, his memory, translated to
word on the page. It is not an exterior omniscience that tells
about Isaac's thoughts; it is rather his mind-voice somehow
verbalized before passing into the mind-ear of the reader.
And though Maisie and Isaac are centers of consciousness in
third-person narratives, the one narrative is objectively
about a psychology, the other is a psychological, subjective
consciousness: the difference is a matter of voice.

It is, in fact, the matter of voice which accounts in
large part for the total effectiveness of Faulkner's novels.
And it is in the matter of voice that Faulkner exercises his
own unique composition of psychological fiction. Of all his
predecessors--Joseph Conrad, Dorothy Richardson, Virginia
Woolf in English; Dujardin and Proust in French; Dostoevsky
in Russian--it is James Joyce whom Faulkner most resembles
in his voice technique. The movement of voice from *Portrait
of the Artist* through *Ulysses* to *Finnegans Wake* is one of
progressive interiorization, toward an elimination not of
the "author" but of any kind of basic voice existing outside
a mind that is subject of the narrative. With minimizing of
the ordering basic voice, as it is replaced almost exclusively
by phantasmagorical mind-voice, the narrative appears incoherent; yet it is not, or should not be, totally incoherent.
Robert Humphrey has pointed out the necessary balance between
"psychological" and "literature" that must obtain in any
successful stream-of-consciousness work:

> The purpose of literature is not to express enigmas.
> Consequently, the writer of stream-of-consciousness
> literature has to manage to represent consciousness
> realistically by maintaining its characteristics of
> privacy (the incoherence, discontinuity, and private
> implications), and he has to manage to communicate
> something to the reader through this consciousness.[15]

Some writers such as Richardson and Woolf have weighted the
balance toward communication by slighting the representation
of the texture of consciousness and by presenting instead
omniscient-voice description of psychic life of characters.
This is much like James's method except for the level of
mind described. Faulkner and Joyce have, however, been concerned with portrayal of various levels of mind-voice, with

representation--through devices such as an approximation of
free association through the workings of memory, senses, and
imagination; the time-space montage; organic punctuation and
typography--of mind as mind. What distinguishes the Faulkner
mind-voice from that of Joyce is the pitch of awareness:
Molly Bloom's soliloquy in *Ulysses* is cast in the idiom and
idea-pattern her mind actually in half-dream-state is using,
and her ideas are those that she could in a waking state
recognize and understand: this is her literal mind-voice.
Faulkner, on the other hand, frequently represents throughout his work not the literal mind-voice of a character but
a heightened voice: a voice that is rooted in the mind of
the character, a voice that issues from that mind yet is
not bound by the limits of intelligence and sensibility which
that mind has by nature, a voice heightened to perception
and articulation of which the mind itself is incapable. Such
a heightening is similar to the phenomenon of possession of
a human medium by a transcendent spirit: the medium speaks,
his voice possessed by the spirit, speaks things of which
he is himself perhaps unaware, even incapable of understanding; yet it is his own voice issuing from his person, his
voice made oracular and transcendent.

The most obvious example of this kind of transcendent
or heightened voice is Addie's chapter in *As I Lay Dying*.
Each chapter in this novel is in the voice of the character
whose name heads the chapter: each speaks his observations
and opinions of Addie's death and the pilgrimage. Addie
herself, however, being dead and encoffined, certainly cannot
speak, yet Faulkner has given her a first-person narration
midway in the novel. It is not her dead lips that speak, nor
the literal voice of her mind, which can no longer function;
it is rather the enduring person of Addie, that innermost
center of her which exists free of body, that speaks ex-
pressing the beliefs and motives which constituted her person yet which she could never have clearly articulated or
consciously perceived. For example, of her husband and her
married life she says:

> He did not know that he was dead, then. Sometimes I
> would lie by him in the dark, hearing the land that was
> now of my blood and flesh, and I would think: Anse.
> Why Anse. Why are you Anse. I would think about his
> name until after a while I could see the word as a
> shape, a vessel, and I would watch him liquefy and
> flow into it like cold molasses flowing out of the
> darkness into the vessel, until the jar stood full
> and motionless: a significant shape profoundly without
> life like an empty door frame; and then I would find
> that I had forgotten the name of the jar.[16]

All Addie's concern here--and elsewhere more explicitly--with word and being, all the distance between them, is far beyond her natural capacity to conceptualize or to express in image and symbol. But this is not her natural voice: it is her heightened voice intoning a kind of self-revelation that occurs frequently in Faulkner's novels.

Addie speaks in the first person; yet there is in Faulkner a heightened voice that speaks in the third person: a character who refers to himself as "he" just as Isaac McCaslin had done. It is this kind of heightening that accounts in large measure for the intensity of the novel *Light in August* and for the dimensionality of the character of Joe Christmas. However, before considering voice as revelatory of Joe's character it will be helpful to summarize briefly the kinds of voices present in *Light in August* and their general sequence of occurrence.[17]

Chapter 1 of the novel, introduced by the magnificent wagon image and the phrase "Lena thinks," is composed of three general levels of Lena's mind-voice plus sections of unidentified neutral omniscience. Lena's most traditional voices are the first and second levels: (1) what she is actually verbalizing in her mind or what she does think aloud and (2) what she is consciously aware of without actually verbalizing (the presentation of this second level in the narrative is therefore not in her precise idiom); these two levels are presented either in quotation marks--single for mind-words, double for spoken--or in italics. Lena's third level of awareness, presented only occasionally, represents what her memory does know expressed in language and sentence structure appropriate to her yet what she is not actually aware of at the moment: as if the voice of her subconscious were possessed by an articulate omniscience that speaks out from her mind what is in its depths. Faulkner quite skillfully orders a definite progression through these three levels of mind: first, the announcement "Lena thinks"; then her literal mind-words, "'I have come from Alabama: a fur piece,'" followed by her conscious awareness, which she does not actually verbalize, expressed in a manner more sophisticated than she is able: *"further from home than I have ever been before. I am now further from Doane's Mill than I have been since I was twelve years old"* (p. 1). This second level is followed by several paragraphs of third level, which develop facts given in her previous unverbalized awareness: "Doane's Mill" triggers two paragraphs of amplification on her weekly trips to town as a child, her parents' death; from that comes memory of her living with her brother, her window-exiting and subsequent plight, her search for Lucas

Burch. One quotation will serve to illustrate Faulkner's
general technique in this third-level consciousness:

> The brother worked in the mill. All the men in the
> village worked in the mill or for it. It was cutting
> pine. It had been there seven years and in seven years
> more it would destroy all the timber within its reach.
> Then some of the machinery and most of the men who ran
> it and existed because of and for it would be loaded
> onto freight cars and moved away. But some of the
> machinery would be left, since new pieces could always
> be bought on the installment plan—gaunt, staring,
> motionless wheels rising from mounds of brick rubble
> and ragged weeds with a quality profoundly astonishing,
> and gutted boilers lifting their rusting and unsmoking
> stacks with an air stubborn, baffled and bemused upon
> a stumppocked scene of profound and peaceful desolation,
> unplowed, untilled, gutting slowly into red and choked
> ravines beneath the long quiet rains of autumn and the
> galloping fury of vernal equinoxes. (pp. 2-3)

The first three sentences are appropriate to Lena: the para-
tactical sentence structure, the simple vocabulary, the
childish fuzzy reference of subject in "It was cutting pine."
This is thus far the literal subconscious musing of a phe-
nomenally musing mind. The next two sentences begin a heightening of her mind-voice with evaluation and prediction beyond
her mind's capacity. The last sentence is, of course, the
ultimate Faulknerian heightening of a normally simple voice:
the complex structure, the rolling length of sentence, the
vocabulary vivid and mysterious and "profoundly astonishing."
There are numerous shifts among these three levels of
consciousness in the first six pages of the narrative. The
remainder of the chapter is for the most part made up of
assumed voices—Armstid, Winterbottom, Mrs. Armstid, Lena—
reported by an omniscient basic voice generally objective
but on occasion rising to report of what a character is
thinking or is not thinking, is feeling or is not feeling.
Chapter 2 begins with a new voice: the mind-voice of
Byron Bunch. Beginning with the phrase "Byron Bunch knows
this," the chapter proceeds for sixteen pages of heightened-
voice memory flashback (with occasional "now" interpolations)
concerning Christmas's arrival in Jefferson and his illegal
activities insofar as Byron knows them. Then begins again
the omniscient basic voice, which summarizes Byron's position in the town and his relation to a character not yet
introduced, Hightower; establishes connection with the end
of Chapter 1 by mentioning that the burning house (which Lena

had noted) is still burning; and finally settles to objective
report of the meeting between Byron and Lena: their visible
reactions, their dialogue.

Chapter 3 begins with an unidentified "he" described by
an omniscient basic voice that is closely identified with
that he (Hightower). Why is this an omniscient basic voice
and not Hightower's heightened voice? When the two techniques
are compared there is little difference between them: the
very heightening--making more perceptive and more articulate--
is tantamount to a kind of omniscience. As far as pitch of
expression they can be exactly the same. The only difference--
a real difference and an important one in its implications--
is that a heightened voice originates in the mind--usually
the subconscious level of mind--of a character whereas the
omniscient basic voice does not belong to any character in
the novel. Yet how can the reader tell where the voice "originates"? Always the heightened voice is introduced by a phrase
or an event which indicates that what follows must be somehow
from the mind of a character even though typographically it
may appear to be conventional narration. The gradual interiorization of Lena's voice at the opening of Chapter 1 and the
obvious "Byron Bunch knows this" that begins Chapter 2 pre-
pare the experienced Faulkner-reader for mind-voice to come.
Chapter 3, however, has no particular indication that the
voice is Hightower's, and the structure of the chapter indicates the voice is speaking about Hightower intimately but
does not issue from him: the first section introduces him
watching and waiting, the assumed voice of a person from the
town explaining briefly to a stranger Hightower's past; immediately after Hightower's mind-thought *"Now, soon"* is reported there is a break in the narrative and the omniscient
voice transfers its attention from Hightower to Byron Bunch,
narrating summarily--not in assumed voices--what the "town"
had told Byron about Hightower (this report is more detailed
than the previous quoted one and reveals the motives and
beliefs and prejudices of the "town" and Byron's reaction
to them); then with a phrase the reader will understand much
later in the narrative--"They have thundered past now," the
"now" serving as link to the end of the first section of the
chapter--the omniscience once again concerns itself with
Hightower in the present just as Byron Bunch comes to visit
him (p. 70).

Chapter 4 is again a descriptive omniscience which reports
what is observable in the conversation between Byron and
Hightower. Much of the chapter consists of exposition in assumed voices of action that has already occurred, and it is
in spots quite complex: the basic voice quotes Byron, who

speaking to Hightower indirectly quotes Brown directly quoting
Christmas (pp. 87-88). This nesting of voices, especially
when a single quoted voice predominates for some time though
the punctuation is inconsistent, can easily confuse the reader
who is not alert to Faulkner's complex, but deliberate and
effective, manipulation of voice.

In Chapter 4 the event of the murder had been made known
several reports removed from the actual happening. The closest
eyewitness report had been Brown's testimony about Christmas's
actions the night before the murder. Chapter 5 begins--with-
out any immediate time-warning to the reader--during that
night before the murder with step-by-step omniscient narration that concerns itself with Christmas's actions and thoughts
and semi-verbalized or unverbalized feelings, attitudes,
beliefs. Few of Christmas's actual words are recorded, but
much that is interior: particularly important is his general
belief *"Something is going to happen to me. I am going to do
something"* (p. 97) which haunts him through that night,
through the next day and the night of that day until finally
at the stroke of twelve "he rose and moved toward the house
[of Joanna Burden]. He didn't go fast. He didn't think even
then *Something is going to happen to me"* (p. 110).

Faulkner is not mechanically consistent in his punctuation
but he is meaningful. It is significant that there is no
period at the end of the last sentence of Chapter 5 because
the thought Christmas is not even thinking now (that is, the
awareness of his subconscious mind) does not end with that
chapter but extends through what is literally and figuratively
the center of the book, the center of the subject: the next
six chapters. Three facts indicate that this center section
of the book is Joe Christmas's mind-voice: the first is the
lack of period just mentioned; the second is the opening
sentences of Chapter 6, "Memory believes before knowing remembers. Believes longer than recollects, longer than knowing even wonders" (p. 111); the third is the structure of
event that frames the heightened-voice flashback.

Careful reading of Chapter 5 indicates that Joe (as well
as the participating reader) expects something to happen.
Joe's thoughts at first and second level of mind are expressed
in italics or in single quotation marks; and the italicized
thoughts do not have end punctuation, a device intended to
indicate their formless, inchoate form, as if they could flow
on indefinitely. With such an endless element as the period-
less final sentence of Chapter 5, with such carefully established tension that something *is* going to happen, with Christmas physically in motion toward Miss Burden's house, it is
natural for the reader to expect on the next page amplifica-

tion of this something that is going to happen; yet what he
finds is the enigmatic phrase "Memory believes before knowing
remembers." This is as obvious a signpost as Faulkner will
ever plant for his reader, who should take as clue the word
memory to discover and gradually to affirm that this section
is a memory flashback, the memory, as it turns out, of Joe
Christmas. Yet this memory is not a matter of knowing or
even wondering, not a matter, that is, of what Joe is conscious of; it is, rather, a matter of believing, that is, of
felt affirmation: some deep interior recognition that does
not exist at the level of concept; it is, in fact, Christmas's
heightened voice keenly perceptive and articulate speaking
from the depths of his mind what his memory contains but
could never conceptualize or verbalize.

   The structure of event framing the flashback most clearly
indicates it to be Joe's mind-voice that speaks. At the end
of Chapter 5 Joe had been purposefully walking toward Miss
Burden's house just before the murder; at the end of the
flashback the reader sees Joe immediately after the murder.
The memory flashback had progressed in time from Joe's childhood and adolescence to the very moment before he murdered
Joanna Burden, but strangely the act of murder itself is never
described in the flashback. What happened in the time inter-
val--between the end of Chapter 5 and the end of Chapter 12--
when the murder was actually committed: Why such a long
flashback there? Why, except to show that when Joe's body is
engaged in the act of murder his mind is elsewhere in both
time and space. This dissociation has a great deal to do with
Joe's character and will be specifically considered later;
it is enough here to note the fact of dissociation--mind
from body.[18] The final pages of Chapter 12 illustrate best
this dissociation for they cleverly reveal the joining once
more of mind and body on the same plane of reality. Joe is
described as "Standing in the middle of the road, with his
right hand lifted full in the glare of the approaching car"
(p. 267); he is picked up by a boy and girl who are for some
unexplained reason terrified of him. When he later flees from
the car he is struck by something heavy and hard:

> The object which had struck him had delivered an ap-
> preciable blow; then he discovered that the object was
> attached to his right hand. Raising the hand, he found
> that it held the ancient heavy pistol. He did not know
> that he had it; he did not remember having picked it
> up at all, nor why. But there it was. 'And I flagged
> that car with my right hand,' he thought. 'No wonder
> she ... they ...' (p. 270)

Here at the level of image is Joe's mind shown to become
aware of his body and its acts. At first his mind had not
even known what his right hand was doing; then he slowly
became aware that it held something; then finally he discovers
that it (not *he*) holds the gun. Conscious understanding comes,
present awareness impinges on past memory, and the flashback
is over.

The remaining third of the novel is composed of chapters
expressed for the most part in the basic voice and in assumed
voices. The "town's" reaction to the murder, Doc Hines's
version of Christmas's childhood, the conflict between Byron
and Hightower, the birth of Lena's baby, the flight of Christmas, the Percy Grimm incident: all are expressed in various
voice forms that occur in the first third of the novel. Although the basic voice describes various intensities of consciousness, there is--with one exception--little heightened
voice. The one exception is, of course, Chapter 20, Hightower's
thoughts before he dies. The second paragraph of the chapter
begins, "He can remember how," and then follows the memory
of his childhood, his marriage, his grandfather. He is weighted
with thought and explicit memory; but then, by means of an
image, Faulkner creates once more dissociation of mind and
body as Hightower dies: cessation of body-matter reality
and intensification of memory-experience:

> The wheel turns on. It spins now, fading, without
> progress, as though turned by that final flood which
> had rushed out of him, leaving his body empty and
> lighter than a forgotten leaf and even more trivial
> than flotsam lying spent and still upon the window
> ledge which has no solidity beneath hands that have
> no weight; so that it can be now Now (p. 466)

The slowing wheel is the image of his ordered thinking, his
awareness of real, sensible experience, his judgment about
actual situations; the *Now* is--and has been consistently
throughout the novel--the symbol of his own unreal memory
experience, the past of honor and pride and life as represented by the cavalry charge. After his realization and admission that he himself is responsible for his wife's death
and despair, he becomes totally absorbed in the quintessential
Now of idealized past: the voice of his conscious mind replaced by the voice of his most inner being recounting the
last few moments of his life.

This general summary of the voices used in *Light in
August* is a mere indication of the voice structure; it surely
is not intended as any kind of "proof." Only the novel itself
is an adequate illustration of Faulkner's multifarious voices

and extremely complex use of them; and it is this fact which
is perhaps the surest sign of a tight, well-organized narrative: that "whole" which a work of art is supposed to be.

II. Voice and Joe Christmas

Someone once said that a stream-of-consciousness novel
cannot be read; it can only be reread. And this is certainly
the case with most Faulkner novels: the reader while he reads
can no more discern an obvious pattern, a logical cause-and-
effect relation from event to event, than can a man as he
lives his life find an order: only retrospect shows the pattern and close relations that were there all along.

The presentation of Joe Christmas's character may seem
to the first-time reader of *Light in August* as unnecessarily
disordered and as, perhaps, disconcerting as that phenomenal
Charles Eames film sent recently by the United States to
Russia for the American National Exhibition in Moscow. The
Eames film--really, seven films, shown on seven large screens
simultaneously--simply cannot be viewed all at once: the
viewer is confronted by picture and must decide his own order
of perception, build his own final impression from all that
is presented. Of course, the reader of *Light in August*, since
he begins on page 1 and progresses through page 480 in order
does not really choose what it is he will perceive; but the
effect is the same, for the novel is written by Faulkner as
if he, the novelist, had stood in a room writing furiously
from the life of Christmas shown simultaneously on many
screens, each with a different emphasis or different interpretation, each running at a different speed.

To understand, then, the character of Christmas as it is
presented in *Light in August*, it is necessary to note the
order and emphasis in which various facets of his character
are presented and to realize that the apparent disorder among
sections is a flaw only by conventional "and-then ..."
standards.

The presentation of Christmas's character falls into two
large sections, one emphasizing the exterior, one the interior: Christmas as seen from the outside by various characters (this presented usually in the voices and interpretations of the characters themselves) or by an omniscience
(the basic voice); Christmas as seen by himself in the confines of his own mind (his own heightened mind-voice). First
introduced in the voices of others, Joe is described there
as a cruel, incomprehensible creature; only after the reader
has been made to think this of him does any interior view

emerge, and it is in this interior view (in his own heightened
voice) that he becomes progressively more amenable to sympathy.
This switch in attitude George Marion O'Donnell has seen as a
failure on Faulkner's part to maintain the (O'Donnell-postu-
lated) theme of Snopes-vs.-Sartoris: for O'Donnell, Christmas
"ought to be the antagonist but ... becomes, like Milton's
Satan, the real protagonist."[19] However, this is more failure
on the critic's part to abandon his own thesis and accept what
the novelist actually has done. It is not Faulkner's "attitude"
that changes but--importantly--the reader's: as he participates
in the novel, hearing both exterior and interior emphases, he
learns more about Joe, sees the conflict between opinion and
fact, the distance between act and motive. It is the totality
of this experience, the combination of voices, emphases, interpretations, that creates Christmas in the reader's mind.

The first mention of Joe Christmas is in Chapter 2, which
opens with the phrase "Byron Bunch knows this." Then begins
a flashback in the mind-voice of Byron Bunch that recounts
Christmas's appearance in town three years prior to the now-
time (1920's) in which Byron remembers. In his heightened
voice, Byron "thinks" of Christmas with all the detachment
of a journalist and with an articulation that transcends the
simplicity of his own character (as it is established elsewhere in the novel):

> [Christmas] carried his knowledge with him always as
> though it were a banner, with a quality ruthless, lone-
> ly, and almost proud. "As if," as the men said later,
> "he was just down on his luck for a time, and that he
> didn't intend to stay down on it and didn't give a
> damn much how he rose up." He was young. And Byron
> watched him standing there and looking at the men in
> sweatstained overalls, with a cigarette in one side of
> his mouth and his face darkly and contemptuously still,
> drawn down a little on one side because of the smoke.
> (pp. 27-28)

This is what Byron "knows," but these are not the words of
his thoughts. The simile, knowledge carried like a banner,
the direct quotation of what others were saying, the detached
comment about himself standing there observing, are all too
sophisticated for Byron naturally, for anything but his
heightened voice.

This first view of Christmas is an unfavorable one, not
that unfavorable judgments are passed by the narrator or that
prejudices are expressed, but that the exteriorly observable
details which Byron honestly (in his heightened voice) reports
are themselves slanted against Christmas's character: he is

definitely rootless, contemptuous, silent, dressed in soiled
city clothes, with an outrageous look, smoke sneering across
his face; he works with a brooding and savage steadiness. The
words *silent*, *contemptuous*, *sullen*, *savage*, recur again and
again. Byron remembers Christmas as being this way; he remembers his sudden acquisition of a new car and his quitting at
the mill, and his own naïve innocence in not knowing how
Christmas made money; he remembers, too, that Christmas lived
in a cabin on the Burden place; he remembers the Burden family,
and finally works to such a high pitch of general reminiscence
about the past that the flashback ends, refined out of existence.

The next mention of Christmas is also unfavorable, for
it establishes the fact of his murdering Joanna Burden, the
precipitating act of the novel; the reader is not at all
surprised, because of his cold and ruthless character as
established by Chapter 2. Here in Chapter 4 the account is
again given by Byron Bunch. This, it has been mentioned, is
not mind narrative but spoken dialogue between Byron and
Hightower placed in the frame of the basic voice, which sets
the scene and describes the reactions of the two men to their
dialogue. Since it is actual conversation which is recounted
and not stream of memory, the circumstances of the murder are
narrated in a direct and colloquial manner by Byron. It is
interesting, however, to note that the two incidents which
he recounts are not ones he himself has actually observed
but ones told him. He explains first to Hightower the relation between Christmas, Brown, and Joanna Burden; then he
describes an example of Christmas's ruthless behavior and
illegal activities:

> "[Brown] was down town drunk one Saturday night and
> bragging to a crowd in the barbershop something about
> him and Christmas in Memphis one night, or on a road
> close to Memphis. Something about them and that new
> car hid in the bushes and Christmas with a pistol, and
> a lot more about a truck and a hundred gallons of some-
> thing, until Christmas come in quick and walked up to
> him and jerked him out of the chair. And Christmas
> saying in that quiet voice of his, that aint pleasant
> and aint mad either: 'You ought to be careful about
> drinking so much of this Jefferson hair tonic. It's
> gone to your head. First thing you know you'll have a
> hairlip.' Holding Brown up he was with one hand and
> slapping his face with the other...." (pp. 73-74)

Vivid and eyewitness-seeming as this description appears,
Byron must be relating it at least secondhand, for it is

remarked several places in the novel that he is never in town
on Saturday night.[20] The second view of Christmas that Byron
recounts is even more unfavorable because for the first time
close personal observations are mentioned. Byron reports conversation between Brown and Christmas as retold by Brown in
claiming the reward money:

> "Then he [Brown] told how he found out that night that
> sooner or later Christmas was going to kill her or
> somebody.... and Christmas said, in that still way of
> his: 'You dont get enough sleep. You stay awake too much.
> Maybe you ought to sleep more,' and Brown said, 'How
> much more?' and Christmas said, 'Maybe from now on.'"
> (pp. 87-88)

This and Brown's statements of Christmas's cool admission after the murder--"'I've done it'" (p. 88)--all corroborate on
the level of incident the general impression left of Christmas in Chapter 2: a thug, cold, silent, cruel.

It is at this point that an awareness of narrative structure, voice structure, becomes important. What is the reader
to think of Christmas so far? He has been shown as hateful:
an unsympathetic character to be held at arm's length. What,
then, of the sudden plunge into his mind that will occur in
the central section of the book? Is this an error on Faulkner's
part, a shift in his attitude toward the "villain"? In these
first four chapters, roughly a fifth of the book, all significant description of Christmas is set in Byron's reporting
voice. Byron, the reader learns, is a man of simplicity,
hesitant goodness; a guileless man who can be trusted to
report things honestly as he sees them. Although Byron's
voice is heightened on occasion to keener perception, refined
articulation, still his own "point of view" is maintained,
his own simple, guileless way of looking at things. In reporting the remarks of other persons about Christmas--and to a
great extent the narrative is secondhand: townsfolk, men at
the mill, Brown--Byron tells truthfully their opinions about
Christmas: the reader can trust that this is truly reported
opinion; what he cannot trust is that the opinion is true.
The townsfolk are shown in several places to be suspect in
their judgment; the clearest indication of this is in a
statement about the town's misunderstanding Byron. This
statement is made by the basic voice alone, the closest one
gets to objectivity in such a narrative, and thus contains
one of the few objective judgments in the novel:

> Man knows so little about his fellows. In his eyes
> all men or women act upon what he believes would moti-
> vate him if he were mad enough to do what that other
> man or woman is doing. (p. 43)

The town has opinions, but they are not to be accepted as a
normative position. And Brown, who is the most explicit con-
demner of Christmas, calling him murderer and Negro, is shown
to be most untrustworthy. Even Byron finds his speech empty:
"a man put no more belief in what he said that he had done
than in what he said his name was" (p. 33). Nor does the marshal
entirely believe Brown's evidence: "'You better be careful
what you are saying, if it is a white man you are talking
about ... I dont care if he is a murderer or not'" (p. 91).
But the reader--like the marshal and, in broader frame of
narrative, like the listening Hightower--is learning as he
goes along. What Brown is saying is partially true, but neither
narrator nor listener yet knows the entire situation. And so
Byron reports what he has heard; the reader accepts.

Only in Chapter 5 does the reader get his first objective
look at Christmas. This, too, for the most part is an external
view: not Christmas as screened through the mind and voice
of some character in the novel but Christmas as objectively
described by the basic voice in an action situation: thus
the reader is one step closer to Christmas though still outside him. The previous descriptions of Joe as cruel, ruthless,
are corroborated when the reader is told immediately:

> [Christmas] stooped, astride Brown, and found his collar
> and hauled him out from beneath the cot and raised
> Brown's head and began to strike him with his flat
> hand, short, vicious, and hard, until Brown ceased
> laughing. (p. 96)

Christmas's thoughts, too, are reported by the basic voice
in a few places; such comments as

> He stood in the darkness above the prone body, with
> Brown's breath alternately hot and cold on his fingers,
> thinking quietly *Something is going to happen to me.*
> *I am going to do something* (p. 97)

and

> he was hearing a myriad sounds of no greater volume--
> voices, murmurs, whispers ... which he had been con-
> scious of all his life without knowing it, which were
> his life, thinking *God perhaps and me not knowing that*
> *too* He could see it like a printed sentence, fullborn
> and already dead *God loves me too* (pp. 97-98)

This is still the basic voice; it in a sense exteriorizes,
speaks *about* certain thoughts of Christmas's mind rather
than opens to view the workings of that mind. But it is a
hint of the interiorization that is to come. For the most

part this chapter describes Christmas the night before the
murder, his restlessness, his foreboding of something about
to happen; it introduces the street image that recurring will
provide thematic rhythm for the novel in general and Joe's
life in particular:

> Nothing can look quite as lonely as a big man going
> along an empty street. Yet though he was not large, not
> tall, he contrived somehow to look more lonely than a
> lone telephone pole in the middle of a desert. In the
> wide, empty, shadow-brooded street he looked like a
> phantom, a spirit, strayed out of its own world, and
> lost. (p. 106)

Here he is, still silent, cold, baleful, but for the first
time attributed with a human quality, a sympathetic quality:
loneliness. And he is haunted by the thought of peace. The
reader is beginning to see Christmas is not an entirely flat
character, not entirely hateful.

Then with Chapter 6 the narrative plunges down into the
very interiority of the hero's mind: "Memory believes before
knowing remembers." As A.A. Mendilow has observed in *Time
and the Novel*, memory is not

> a mechanical reconstruction or recapitulation of the
> past as it was but is rather an emotionally charged
> interpretation of events which changes and shifts as
> the interpreting self grows in time and is altered by
> it.[21]

More than serving as a device of exposition to inform the
reader about past events, the memory flashback of its very
nature is revelatory of the mind that remembers: full of
implications of why certain events are remembered and not
others, why in a particular order and with particular emphasis.
Ultimately, of course, this is all due to the author's selectivity, but within the narrative the items selected are
attributed to the remembering mind and--simply because they
are remembered, consciously or unconsciously--reveal something about that mind.

The flashback section of *Light in August*--Chapters 6 through
12--establishes Joe as a "round," three-dimensional character,
the kind that cannot be expressed in one-sentence summary
or be reduced to mere symbol. For here we see him in the
human context of little-boy-growing-up, with fears and emotions and sufferings. (Yet always the careful reader is aware
that this is Joe's own objectified account of himself and
the entire sweep of his life as he is actually on his way
to murder a woman.) The first memory is of a long corridor,

the street-symbol of his life that Joe sees in retrospect.
Then he remembers the orphanage proper, where he learned fear
and sin and a sense of fatalism and resignation in his encounter with the dietitian, astonishment, shock, outrage, and
revulsion when she does not punish him for what he considered
to be his guilt. At the orphanage, too, he is taunted with
being a Negro.[22] Here he encounters the man who the reader
discovers later is Hines, his fanatical grandfather, a man
who he senses hates him (with his heightened mind the remembering Joe thinks of himself as if he were speaking of someone else):

> If the child [Joe] had been older he would perhaps have
> thought *He* [Hines, who watches him constantly] *hates
> me and fears me. So much so that he cannot let me out
> of his sight* With more vocabulary but no more age he
> might have thought *That is why I am different from
> the others: because he is watching me all the time* He
> accepted it. (p. 129)

At the age of five Joe is adopted by a man whom he cannot
look at because of the man's eyes; a man who the child feels
looks at him with "the same stare with which he might have
examined a horse or a second hand plow, convinced beforehand
that he would see flaws, convinced beforehand that he would
buy" (p. 133). There is a great restrained pathos in the
situation: restraint on Faulkner's part that in writing he
did not sentimentalize; restraint on Christmas's part—an
important facet of his character—that in remembering his
childhood he does not pity himself.

Chapter 7, flashback continued, begins "And memory knows
this; twenty years later memory is still to believe *On this
day I became a man*" (p. 137). What Christmas at thirty singles
out as the day of his manhood is the incident with McEachern,
his foster father, who beat him mercilessly, yet passionlessly,
for not having learned the catechism; he identifies himself
with that hard, cold man:

> They went on, in steady single file, the two backs in
> their rigid abnegation of all compromise more alike
> than actual blood could have made them.... [Joe] was
> looking straight ahead, with a rapt, calm expression
> like a monk in a picture. McEachern began to strike
> methodically, with slow and deliberate force, still
> without heat or anger. It would have been hard to say
> which face was the more rapt, more calm, more convinced.
> (pp. 139-40)

But in contrast with McEachern, Mrs. McEachern symbols for
Joe that possessive affection which he hates:

> It was not the hard work which he hated, nor the punish-
> ment and injustice. He was used to that before he ever
> saw either of them. He expected no less, and so he was
> neither outraged nor surprised. It was the woman: that
> soft kindness which he believed himself doomed to be
> forever victim of and which he hated worse than he did
> the hard and ruthless justice of men. (p. 158)

This is how Joe, walking toward murder, thinks of his pity-
stunted childhood: his dislike for anything as literally dis-
arming as affection; his constant suspicion of "the part ...
which he would not like, whatever it was" (p. 156); his sense
of carrying an unknown guilt and awaiting an inevitable punishment. For another character to say all this would provoke
the reader's dislike for Joe, but for the reader to hear Joe
say this about himself (however deeply in his subconscious)
evokes a genuine sympathy.

The rest of the flashback reveals the progressive hardening of Joe's character and its cause: his meeting with the
prostitute, Bobbie; his beginning to steal, to smoke, to
squint his face against the smoke, to drink; his attack on
McEachern; his rejection by Bobbie. Objectively "bad" as Joe
may seem in this section, the reader feels not dislike or
horror but an incredulous amazement at the innocent sensitivity
and extreme naïvete that compose the interior Joe and around
which he builds his layered hardness. His unawareness that
Bobbie is older than he, that she is a prostitute, that she
is woman in all that to him is loathsome in woman; his remarkable unawareness of anything but what he considers his
own unique relations with her: this naïvete expressed in
reference to sex the reader realizes is indicative not merely
of Joe's adolescent confusion but of his general unawareness
and incomprehension of the world around him. Joe, in remembering, ironically voicing, this incident with Bobbie, does
not pity himself; the reader alone realizes the extent of his
naïvete, one cause of his suffering, and feels pity for what
could have been avoided.

At this point a third important element is introduced in
the development of Joe's character: his sullen coldness, his
innocent naïvete and incomprehension of the world around him;
and now his sense of fate. For all the accusations against
Faulkner as a fatalist, it is of importance to notice that
it is Joe who thinks of himself as determined; that a particular character believes he cannot escape a certain course
of events does not make a novel fatalistic.[23] Again the voice

structure must be stressed: the narrator is still Joe on his
way to murder, perhaps Joe in the act of murder, his mind
dissociated from body, thinking of himself at eighteen, thinking in retrospect that then "he entered the street which was
to run for fifteen years" (p. 210), the street symbolizing
his fated course. Also, when in his encounter with Joanna
Burden he wants to break away but cannot, he thinks, "But
something held him [to remain with her], as the fatalist can
always be held: by curiosity, pessimism, by sheer inertia"
(p. 246). Of the murder itself he thinks before he had done
it as if he had already, inevitably, done it:

> he believed with calm paradox that he was the volition-
> less servant of the fatality in which he believed that
> he did not believe. He was saying to himself *I had to
> do it* already in the past tense; *I had to do it. She
> said so herself* (p. 264)

And later outside the memory narrative, the basic voice repeats the circle image that had haunted Joe and quotes his
own explicit statement: "'But I have never got outside that
circle. I have never broken out of the ring of what I have
already done and cannot ever undo,' he thinks quietly" (p.
321). Whether this is fatalism or determinism in the strict
sense of the words is not important here; what is important
is that Joe feels he could not have escaped his life as it
was, that he was somehow--whether by the effect of his own
acts or by the workings of a malignant fate--swept through an
unavoidable series of events.

The final section of Joe's memory flashback recounts the
time of the murder, the time immediately before and immediately
after; the act itself is not described. This fact is important
because it points to the climax of Joe's dissociation of mind
from body, thought from act. (The entire flashback, it will
be remembered, has been set in such a dissociation, which is
not resolved until Joe "comes to" when mind and body join as
he realizes he holds a gun in his hand.) It is important to
note, too, that the motive for murder is never explained in
the novel, and the reader does not wonder about motive, although this is one of the first things asked by someone who
has heard only summary of plot. The reader, because he realizes
the dissociation of Joe's person, realizes as well that Joe
simply does not have a clearly defined motive: since Joe cannot in mind admit the fact of murder neither can he untangle
what in him drives him to murder.

Thus in the flashback there has been a character-progres-
sion from fearful and lonely childhood through naïve adolescence to final hardening of personality into coldness and

cruelness, natural outcome of what began as a loveless resignation to suffering by a child who had no way to escape suffering. As memory, the flashback shows a greater and greater
detachment from Joe's consciousness so that as he approaches
in mind his actual situation in time and space he comes more
and more to objectify himself, to view himself as someone else,
until finally he is so much "other" that he cannot even re-
count the crucial act of murder. To the reader the information in the flashback coupled with the attitude of Joe toward
himself reveals an aspect of the murderer exterior reports
cannot communicate (and which reporters could not even know):
Joe's own deepest knowledge of himself, the very center of
character.

Here is the emotional climax of the book. The final third
serves the necessary function of answering the many questions
in the reader's mind, neatly finishing off the line of plot,
and--most important of all--painlessly extricating the reader
from the novel, which is done chiefly through the foil-stories
of Lena-and-Byron and Hightower with their graduated intensities, ending with the folk-comic alliance of Lena and Byron.

The final views of Christmas are mostly exterior ones,
ones the reader himself is able to evaluate because he now
"knows" Christmas by a certain direct experience and surely
knows him better than does any character in the book. Doc
Hines recites his version of the story--Christmas, God's
abomination--but this cannot be taken as a correct interpretation, for Hines proves himself a fanatic and mad. Gavin
Stevens, who is not otherwise present in the story, voices
his rational explanation of Christmas's tragedy--white blood,
black blood in conflict within the protagonist--but this, a
little too obviously and neatly "explanation," falls short
of the whole complex reality. Along with these two extremes--
the religious-fanatical and the theorizing-reasonable--is
the abstracting-impersonal: the "town's" reaction, concretized
by Percy Grimm, who sees Christmas not as a person, not even
as an individual Negro, but simply as a race to be punished.
These three groups of opinions round out other characters'
views of Christmas and prove to the reader--who has heard
Christmas's own heightened-voice thoughts about himself as he
commits the murder--that real interior personality is more
complex, more dimensional and multifaceted than any summary
statement or explanation allows.

Indeed, what A.A. Mendilow has observed of character
presentation in the stream-of-consciousness novel is particularly true of Joe Christmas:

> The fixing of personality by external description, by
> labels and definitions and lists of characteristics

has been discarded as false. Instead, personality is seen in the light of its moment-by-moment renewal, as the ever-present past, which changes as it increases with his moving time-field, pours into and through the formation we call a human being.[24]

Joe's moment-by-moment renewal is of course his long memory flashback, with all the impingement of past on present that constitutes him the person he is. The time-space continuum in which he lives interiorly is his own mind and is communicated to the reader by his own heightened voice. The time-space world in which he lives exteriorly is society, which voices its account of him through the omniscient basic voice and through the slanted voices of various characters. If there is, then, a full and adequate statement of the character of Joe Christmas it is the combined recitals of all the voices that speak him in *Light in August*, and if the reader is to know and understand Christmas it is only by his responding to this statement as a listener responds to voice.

NOTES

1. "Voice and Address," *Dictionary of World Literature*, ed. Joseph T. Shipley (New York, 1943), p. 616.

2. *Henry James: The Future of the Novel*, ed. Leon Edel (New York, 1956), p. 33.

3. Ibid., p. 54.

4. Percy Lubbock, *The Craft of Fiction* (New York, 1957), p. 251.

5. Ibid., pp. 253-55.

6. Ibid., p. 170.

7. This Lubbock does admit--the disagreement is largely one of terminology--when he states that in the dramatic method "the mind of the narrator becomes the stage, his voice [as a person] is no longer heard" (Ibid., p. 256). This "stage" would seem to correspond to a neutral basic voice.

8. Lubbock, p. 171.

9. Joseph Warren Beach, *The Twentieth Century Novel* (New York, 1932), p. 411.

10. There is here, too, a looseness of terms. Robert Humphrey in *Stream of Consciousness in the Modern Novel* (Los Angeles, 1958), p. 23, and Melvin Friedman in *Stream of Con-*

sciousness: A Study in Literary Method (New Haven, 1955), p.
3, insist that the term *stream of consciousness* refers to a
genre, *interior monologue* to one technique which the genre
may employ. Yet as Leon Edel observes in *The Modern Psychological Novel* (New York, 1955), p. 56, the two terms have been used
interchangeably in the past.

11. Humphrey, p. 3.

12. Henry James, *What Maisie Knew* (New York, 1922), p. 329.

13. *Go Down, Moses and Other Stories* (New York: Random
House, 1942), p. 351.

14. The term *basic voice* will be used in a more restricted
sense than that given by LaDrière; because of the voice nice-
ties of psychological fiction it will be necessary to distinguish between the narration of an unidentified omniscience
(here called basic voice) and that of the mind of a character
within the novel (mind-voice).

15. Humphrey, p. 62.

16. William Faulkner, *The Sound and the Fury and As I Lay
Dying* (New York, 1946), pp. 464-65.

17. For a useful summary of plot and chronology see B.N.
McElderry, Jr., "The Narrative Structure of *Light in August*,"
College English, 19 (February 1958), 200-207.

18. Jean-Paul Sartre very interestingly analyzes such a
state in his discussion of self-deception, where an individual
does not wish to coordinate or synthesize the two aspects of
his human reality: facticity and transcendence. The example
he gives is of a pleasure both wanted and not wanted, pleasure
given to the body but deliberately not noticed by the consciousness. This applies as well to Christmas's body-act of
murder and mind-absence as it happens, so that his only acknowledgment of murder is *as mind* remembering what body did
(and that, not in detail); see Jean-Paul Sartre, "Self-Deception," *Existentialism from Dostoevsky to Sartre*, ed. Walter
Kaufmann (New York, 1958), pp. 251-52. There are innumerable
such examples of body-mind dissociation throughout *Light in
August*, but Christmas is the only character with such a sustained dissociation.

19. "Faulkner's Mythology," in *William Faulkner: Two
Decades of Criticism*, ed. Frederick J. Hoffman and Olga W.
Vickery (Michigan State College, 1951), p. 57.

20. Immediately after supper Byron rides on his mule
thirty miles into the country to spend Sunday leading the
choir at a country church (p. 43).

21. A.A. Mendilow, *Time and the Novel* (London, 1952), p. 32.

22. The question of Christmas's white-and-black blood is too important to omit and too tied to the sociological implications of the novel to admit of detailed treatment here. A few facts must be kept in mind, however: Christmas's racial origins are never definitely established, and he himself is never certain whether he has Negro blood or not; the real problem of his being black is of concern more to the violent whites he meets than to Christmas himself. He shows a constant dislike for the Negroes (even when he has deliberately lived with them) and only flaunts his possibly black blood when he wants to hurt or shock someone. There is never the personal torment for Joe that is present in the protagonist of a novel such as Sinclair Lewis's *Kingsblood Royal*: Joe is troubled by the engulfing fate that destroys him in the black-white conflict of the South, but he is never interiorly disturbed about *being* Negro or not.

23. At the Nagano Seminar in 1955 in answer to a question about a statement made by one of his characters in *Intruder in the Dust*, Faulkner replied, "Well, now you must remember that that was that character's opinion and it need not necessarily be mine. I'm writing about people, not trying to express my own opinion, so that could have been his and I would have disagreed with him possibly" (*Faulkner at Nagano*, ed. Robert A. Jelliffe [Toyko, 1956], pp. 127-28).

24. Mendilow, pp. 149-50.

VOICE AND VOICES
IN *LIGHT IN AUGUST*

François L. Pitavy

In interviews and class conferences, Faulkner often expressed his unawareness, and disdain, of the intricacies of
technique, which a writer should never allow to "take command
of the dream before [he] himself can get his hands on it."[1]
Yet he never denied the validity of technique, emphasizing
the paramount importance of discipline and work,[2] constantly
referring to himself as a craftsman. There is no contradiction here, only an assertion of the supremacy of the dream
and of the necessity for the writer to retain the freedom by
which he will always "try to be better than [him]self."
    This double-faceted objective is evinced in Faulkner's
early novelistic career. His first two novels are indeed bold,
though not quite realized, experiments, in which the influence
and the exemplarity of Joyce have long been recognized. If
Sartoris (or *Flags in the Dust*, for that matter) is technically
less remarkable, it may be that Faulkner was then engrossed
in discovering the *locus* of his fiction. But it is significant
that the road explored with *The Sound and the Fury* and, even
more radically, with *As I Lay Dying* would be abandoned, and
that Faulkner would invariably refer to the latter as a *tour
de force*; as if this experiment had reached its own limit,
as if the writer--after a necessary time of asceticism when
the anonymous narrator was refined out of the narrative, lin-

*This is a revised and much expanded version of the section
"The Voice" in Chapter 3 of* Faulkner's Light in August, *by
François Pitavy (Bloomington and London: Indiana University
Press, 1973; trans. Gillian E. Cook with the collaboration
of the author), pp. 67-70. A shorter version of this book
appeared in* William Faulkner: As I Lay Dying, Light in August,
*by André Bleikasten, François Pitavy, and Michel Gresset
(Paris: Armand Colin, 1970). Permission to use this material
has been granted by the Indiana University Press.*

guistically abolished so as to clarify the terms of the reflection on poetics evinced in the immediate discourse of those
two poets, Quentin and Darl--had felt the need to break out
of the limitations inherent in the stream-of-consciousness
technique, and to reassert himself as the original narrative
agency in his fiction, that is, linguistically to reassume
the God-like position such as is affirmed, in broader novelistic terms, in the well-known conclusion of the 1956 interview given to Jean Stein.[3]

This reassumption of linguistic fatherhood (the paternal
obsession is nowhere more evident than in the broodings of
Quentin Compson, as well as in those of Stephen Dedalus, the
would-be poet) may be demonstrated in the manipulation of
voice and voices in *Light in August*: the characters in this
novel do speak in their own (fictional) voices, while paradoxically the anonymous narrator never seems to lose control
of them, amplifying them to the point where boundaries become
uncertain, thereby making the narrative voice an admirably
plastic medium.

In fact, in *Light in August*, the distinction is often
blurred between the dramatization of a character's inner consciousness and the discourse of the anonymous narrator.
Faulkner often merges these two methods, immediate discourse
(that is, stream of consciousness) and traditional, mediatized narrative, in such a supple way that he manages to
create an intermediate voice endowed at once with the widest
possible range and with a tone completely its own. Thus he
will describe a character from the outside, while reproducing
the different levels of the character's own voice, so that
the narrative always seems to remain within the range of that
voice. Some modern musicians record a variety of sounds and
then modulate and amplify these raw materials to produce a
unique and personal medium, in which the original sounds are
more or less recognizable according to the modulation and
amplification they have undergone. In the same way, the reader
sometimes does hear the voices of Lena, Byron, or, more
rarely, Joe, but at other times the pitch of their voices
is so modified and amplified as to sound pretty much like
the narrator's; and yet Faulkner's fingertip control never
allows the impression that one is at the center of the character's consciousness to be destroyed. This is indeed a more
elaborate and delicate technique than the one used in Benjy's
section in *The Sound and the Fury*, where the voice always
retains the same intensity and pitch.

In conversations or when a character thinks aloud--when
Faulkner uses double quotation marks--the voice is clearly
that of the character. His own expressions and pronunciation

are respected, and the intensity of the speaker's voice is
consistent.

Sometimes a character formulates his thoughts clearly,
using his own vocabulary, and his voice is still recognizable
even though he is not speaking aloud. The thought is then in
single quotation marks and is usually introduced or followed
by "thinks" or "thinking." One example suffices to show an
intermediary level of amplification and how conscious Faulkner
was of the suppleness of the technique: "[Armstid] says to
himself, between thinking and saying aloud: 'I reckon she will.
I reckon that fellow is fixing to find that he made a bad
mistake when he stopped this side of Arkansas, or even Texas'"
(p. 11).

Often, though, a character's thoughts are semi-conscious,
simultaneous with action or actual speech. Then they are
usually printed in italics and introduced by "thinking," without quotation marks or final punctuation. But they are not
necessarily in the character's idiom: it is his voice, but not
his style, as Faulkner transcends and formulates the character's most fleeting thoughts at their instant of conception,
when they are probably more striking than when they have been
pondered and put into the character's own words. The narrator
thus succeeds in giving expression to evanescent thoughts,
which are too swiftly come and gone for the character himself
to grasp them:

> Then [Joe] looked at [the heifer], and it was again too
> fast and too complete to be thinking: *That is not a
> gift. It is not even a promise: it is a threat* think-
> ing, 'I didn't ask for it. He gave it to me. I didn't
> ask for it,' believing *God knows, I have earned it* (pp.
> 170-71)

> Perhaps he had already expected some fateful mischance,
> thinking, 'It was too good to be true, anyway'; think-
> ing too fast for even thought: *In a moment she will
> vanish. She will not be. And then I will be back home,
> in bed, not having left it at all* Her voice went on:
> "I forgot about the day of the month when I told you
> Monday night." (p. 176)

These two examples demonstrate Faulkner's skillful variation
of intensity or tone. Now, the following extract clearly shows
how the character's voice merges with the narrator's as the
original thought is gradually amplified. Joe, aged seventeen,
remembers the waitress he saw a few months before:

> 'I dont even know what they are saying to her,' he
> thought, thinking *I dont even know that what they are*

> *saying to her is something that men do not say to a*
> *passing child* believing *I do not know yet that in the*
> *instant of sleep the eyelid closing prisons within the*
> *eye's self her face demure, pensive; tragic, sad, and*
> *young; waiting, colored with all the vague and formless*
> *magic of young desire.* (p. 165)

Sometimes the narrator even says that he expresses in his
own voice and words what a character thinks but is unable to
say. This does help somehow to preserve the illusion that it
is the character's voice:

> If the child had been older he would perhaps have thought
> *He hates me and fears me. So much so that he cannot let*
> *me out of his sight* With more vocabulary but no more
> age he might have thought *That is why I am different*
> *from the others: because he is watching me all the time*
> (p. 129)

Finally, the ultimate stage of amplification is used to
give form to what is latent and unexpressed in a character's
mind. In Chapters 6-12, though a framework is set up and recalled again from time to time (variations on "memory" and
"knowing"), the narrative is that of an objective narrator
(far from omniscient) and the chapters concerning Joe's life
seem little different from, say, Chapter 20, Hightower's confession. In fact, the difference is stylistic, not technical.
Faulkner adapts his style to the gradually revealed character
in each case; and Hightower and Joe require very different
styles. One of Faulkner's achievements in *Light in August* is
indeed his way of seeming to present a character from the inside, creating the illusion that the story springs from the
character and is a continuation of his voice, even though the
description may in fact be objective and external. He does it
through vocabulary and tone, not through technique as such.

The advantages of this technique are obvious. The style
can be varied without losing its unity. Faulkner has the best
of both worlds: by amplifying all the vague, fleeting, latent,
or forgotten thoughts of a character without being restrained
by the latter's limited intelligence or consciousness, he
gives the reader the impression that he participates in that
character's life. He retains the emotional force of a subjective, immediate account while giving it the full scope
and suppleness of which a mediatized narrative is capable.
Since a voice thus modulated seems at once external and internal to the character, both emanating from him and enveloping him, a three-dimensional effect not unlike that of stereo-
phonic sound is produced: such reassertion of the narrator's
presence, both powerful and unobtrusive, gives *Light in August*
its specific tone and intensity.

NOTES

1. *Lion in the Garden: Interviews with William Faulkner, 1926-1962*, ed. James B. Meriwether and Michael Millgate (New York: Random House, 1968), p. 244.

2. *Lion in the Garden*, p. 238.

3. *Lion in the Garden*, p. 255.

A STYLISTIC APPROACH TO
LIGHT IN AUGUST

François L. Pitavy

Faulkner probably had little more confidence than his
contemporaries in a language made up of words deprived of
meaning ("words are no good; ... words dont ever fit even
what they are trying to say at," thinks Addie Bundren),[1]
which rarely help communication and often prevent it alto-
gether. However, he did try to make this inadequate tool work
for him by evoking in the reader's mind images and emotions
which would correspond as nearly as possible to his own mental
vision: "One of the great ironies in Faulkner is the creation
of experiential truth ... out of words which are in themselves
held to be insufficient to convey or embody truth."[2] Though
little significant criticism has yet been written on this
aspect of Faulkner's art, the critics are generally agreed
in attributing to him two sorts of style. One is sober and
accurate, describing with rare felicity light and sounds,
outlines and movements, remarkably vivid sensory impressions.
The other is rich, expansive, sonorous, imaginative, and in-
terpretative, exploring all the possibilities of language,
setting aside rules and conventions, spanned and harmonized
by immense movements of prose--to talk of sentences would be
out of place--of which the most remarkable and consistent
example is *Absalom, Absalom!* This rhetoric is the most con-
troversial aspect of Faulkner's art. Even though *Light in
August* and *Absalom, Absalom!* are not written in the same
style, that of the former has a power and a beauty which far
exceed the descriptive style.

*This is a revised and expanded version of Chapter 6, "Stylis-
tic Approaches," of* Faulkner's Light in August, *by François
Pitavy (Bloomington and London: Indiana University Press,
1973; trans. Gillian E. Cook with the collaboration of the
author), pp. 119-50. Permission to use this material has been
granted by the Indiana University Press.*

The style of *Light in August* is indeed difficult to define. By comparison it is easier to analyze Faulkner's rhetoric, which, in its occasionally unbearable excess, reveals its methods. In *Light in August*, the rhetoric never really intrudes except perhaps briefly in the reflections on Joanna's death (p. 273). Likewise, grammatical gymnastics are rare (in the sentence "It was the woman who ...," p. 157, the relative pronoun is not followed by a verb), as are those long parentheses which suspend the sentence so that the reader may simultaneously perceive everything the author wishes him to absorb. Polysyllabic latinate words, which, at their best, are rich in connotations both precise and abstract, and which give a unique sonority and rhythm to, say, *Go Down, Moses* and *Absalom, Absalom!*, are sparingly used, and the same is true of rare or precious words like "banshee," "Juggernaut," "suttee," and such adjectives as "promptive," "abnegant," "maculate," "punctuate."

Before defining and illustrating the actual qualities of Faulkner's style in this novel, we must first remark how conscious and conscientious a craftsman he is. The useful romantic image of a Faulkner driven by his demons and writing in a trance (or indeed in a haze of bourbon) hardly corresponds to the truth. As Faulkner himself has explained in the well-known 1933 introduction for a luxury edition of *The Sound and the Fury* which never came out, *Light in August* was not written with the urgency which characterized the 1929 masterpiece. Even though the author felt some indecision in planning the architecture of the novel, he nevertheless insists in this text on the *deliberation* with which he wrote it, and on the overawareness, due to his thorough knowledge of his trade, which prevented him from being carried away by inspiration.[3] Anyone who has studied Faulkner's manuscripts and typescripts must be aware of the meticulous care which he gave to the details of composition and writing.

Discounting the pasted-up fragments from earlier versions, the manuscript of *Light in August* has relatively few corrections. The writing, in the passages between these collages, is so hurried that often the ends of words are missing and the text is occasionally illegible. Such haste could lead one to suppose that the author was in fact copying from a previous script, correcting it as he went along: that would explain why there are so few visible alterations, not counting the paste-ups. On the other hand, a great many minor changes, mostly stylistic, were made when the novel was being typed out, although there are no visible signs of them on the manuscript. Short insertions, revised or new sentences, and indeed a few long passages seem to have emerged ready-made

from the author's mind to take their place in the final text.
Often, it is only through a comparison of the two texts that
one may appreciate his sure sense of rhythm and sound (in
several places, words or groups of words which are repeated
were so arranged only during the typing of the text), and the
precision with which the vocabulary is gradually adjusted to
correspond with the author's design. The slightest details, of
spelling, punctuation, quotation marks, even of spacing, command his meticulous attention.

There is one document which forcefully shows these qualities in Faulkner: the galley proofs of the novel, now in the
possession of the Humanities Research Center of the University
of Texas at Austin. The copy editor at Smith and Haas several
times took it upon himself to suggest "improvements." Faulkner's
comments, haughty or annoyed, sometimes furious, are those of
a writer admirably sure of himself and confidently refusing
to change any part of a text whose every detail he had already
carefully pondered. (He would only agree to alter obvious
errors.) For instance, the astonishing opening paragraph of
Chapter 6 seemed rather unorthodox to the copy editor, who
wrote in the margin: "construction?"--to which Faulkner replied:
"O.K. damn it" (galley 33). On reading this sentence: "He saw
now that the cabin sat some two feet above the earth" (p. 437),
the editor feared there was some mistake and suggested "set,
instead of sat"--which drew the following from Faulkner: "I
dont think that 'set' is a very good verb. Thanks, though"
(galley 128). Some grammar "mistakes" in the furniture dealer's
account were apparently unacceptable: "Then he came back, with
enough wood to barbecue a steer, and she began to tell him
and he went to the truck and taken out that suitcase and opened
it and taken out a blanket" (p. 473). The editor proposed
changing "taken," which is perfectly normal in this character's
speech, to "took" in each case, at which Faulkner became angry:
"No, damn it!!! O.K. as set" (galley 138). Likewise, Calvin
Burden's vocabulary in this threat to his son surprised the
copy editor: "'I'll learn you to hate two things, ... or I'll
frail the tar out of you'" (p. 229). But Faulkner refused to
change "frail" to "flail," an alteration which would have
diluted the verbal vigor and dimmed the color of his character: "O.K. as set and written. Jesus Christ" (galley 67).
Finally, as a last example of the care he took to preserve
the full flavor of dialects in the spoken word, there is this
thought of Byron: "'I be dog if it dont look like a man that
has done as much lying lately as I have ...'" (p. 374), which
the copy editor questioned tentatively: "Expression O.K.?"--
at which Faulkner's annoyance erupted: "O.K. Why in hell not?"
(galley 129). These few examples, selected from among many

others, conclusively show that the author of *Light in August* was a confident writer, in sure command of his trade.

Precision

The first remarkable qualities of the style in *Light in August* are its precision and sobriety--especially remarkable if the novel is compared with the later ones. For the most part, Faulkner uses relatively short sentences which are easy to understand and which concentrate on reporting accurately the movements, words, and thoughts of the characters. Such precise descriptions give an impression of objectivity, sometimes reminiscent of Hemingway's style, where the narrator almost completely disappears from the narrative, leaving next to no mark of authorial intrusion, so that the reader feels as though he has apprehended *immediately* the objects or actions described or reported. This effect is seen, for instance, in the description of Lena awaiting Armstid's wagon, then climbing into it and sitting by his side, of the brusque Mrs. Armstid in her kitchen and bedroom, of Byron at work, of Christmas methodically striking Brown, and of his every deed and gesture during the twenty-four hours before the murder. The description of Joe at dawn on the Friday when he decides to give himself up is a particularly good example of this minute precision:

> It is just dawn, daylight. He rises and descends to the spring and takes from his pocket the razor, the brush, the soap. But it is still too dim to see his face clearly in the water, so he sits beside the spring and waits until he can see better. Then he lathers his face with the hard, cold water, patiently. His hand trembles, despite the urgency he feels a lassitude so that he must drive himself. The razor is dull; he tries to whet it upon the side of one brogan, but the leather is ironhard and wet with dew. He shaves, after a fashion. His hand trembles; it is not a very good job, and he cuts himself three or four times, stanching the blood with the cold water until it stops. He puts the shaving tools away and begins to walk. (pp. 317-18)

The quality of the style here lies in the fact that the exact verb is the motor or muscle of each sentence. Adjectives and adverbs are sparse, as in some of Hemingway's early stories; apart from the adjective "hard," used twice, and which at this place in the novel is charged with suggestions of Joe's aversion to femininity insofar as it denies his masculinity,

apart from the repetition of the clause "his hand trembles,"
the presence of the phrase "after a fashion" and of the approximation of "three or four times" (clearly authorial intrusions),
the choice of such words as "lassitude," "dim," and the compound "ironhard," the passage is as objective as anything
Faulkner ever wrote, almost a camera view of the character.
Yet the minute precision does not mean that the reader obtains
a detached view: on the contrary, this graphic prose, which
does not seek to involve the reader with violent images or
powerful rhythms, forces him instead to participate directly
in the actions by an almost physical contact: "This prose too
has its own compulsive immediacy.... It becomes almost a literal
transcript of action alone and ... compels empathy, a kind of
motor mimicry."[4]

   The spoken word in *Light in August* is a further illustration of the precision of Faulkner's style. Whether in dialogue
or in the narrators' accounts, each character has a voice which,
in some cases, is easily distinguishable since it renders the
personal inflections and rhythms, the idiosyncrasies of vocabulary, the regional colloquialisms, and the common errors of
speech suggesting a certain social class. Hines, for instance,
is unbelievable; it is unthinkable that he should preach in
Negro churches the supremacy of the white race. Yet as soon
as one hears his demented speech he becomes credible. His
vocabulary is unique, crystallizing his biblico-sexual obsessions ("bitchery and abomination," "womanfilth," etc.). And
Faulkner admirably succeeds in containing the violence and the
colloquialisms within biblical cadences:

> he saw that young doctor coming in lechery and fornica-
> tion stop and stoop down and raise the Lord's abomina-
> tion and tote it into the house. And old Doc Hines he
> followed and he seen and heard. He watched them young
> sluts that was desecrating the Lord's sacred anniversary
> with eggnog and whiskey in the Madam's absence, open
> the blanket. And it was her, the Jezebel of the doctor,
> that was the Lord's instrument, that said, "We'll name
> him Christmas.' ... (p. 363)

The long sonorous latinisms, charged with religious connotations, reinforce the regularity of the binary and sometimes
ternary rhythm of the phrases: "lechery ... fornication,"
"stop ... stoop," "raise ... tote," "fornication ... abomination," "followed ... seen ... heard," "desecrating ... sacred,"
"eggnog ... whiskey." This richly rhythmic language with the
severe authority of the Bible and a long tradition of threatening sermons in the background never loses its colloquial
flavor ("tote," "Doc Hines he followed," "he seen," "them

young sluts that was desecrating"). Lena too is recognizable
by her local dialect (double negatives, wrong verb forms),
by her country style, which still retains archaic forms ("un-
beknownst," "a-going," "a-walking"), and by expressions and
pronunciations peculiar to the South ("right kind," "right
far," "a fur piece," "I et polite"). Even the furniture dealer
has the rich imaginative speech of the countryman, which leads
him to describe Byron as "the kind of fellow you wouldn't
see the first glance if he was alone by himself in the bottom
of a empty concrete swimming pool," and Lena's baby as "a
critter not yearling size" (p. 469).

There is no really striking difference between the spoken
and the narrative language in *Light in August*. It is largely
a difference of intensity rather than of quality, and the
characteristics of the style outlined here can be seen in the
characters' dialogues as well as in the language that may be
specifically ascribed to the anonymous narrator. Indeed,
Faulkner often integrates dialogue and narrative: a fair
number of corrections from the manuscript to the typescript
work toward this end, as he changed some descriptive sentences
to spoken ones, blurring the distinctions between the narrator's comments and those of the characters, as can be seen in
a comparison of the original and final texts of the first
description of Christmas. Here is the manuscript: "He looked
like a tramp. Not a professional hobo in the professional
rags, but like a man down on his luck and not intending to
stay down on it for long and not particularly caring how he
rose above it." In the published book, the first part of this
description, considerably extended and made more suggestive
of the character's spiritual rootlessness, is still ascribed
to the omniscient author, while the second half becomes actual
speech:

> "As if," as the men said later, "he was just down on
> his luck for a time, and that he didn't intend to stay
> down on it and didn't give a damn much how he rose up."
> (p. 27)

Such unobtrusive inclusion of spoken language makes the
description more vivid and the gradual revelation of the
character more natural, as the reader's knowledge of Christmas
parallels that of his fellow workers; thus the reader is not
left with a merely personal, possibly unwarranted, impression
of the character, as it is shared by witnesses whose unmis-
takably living speech retrospectively gives a ring of truth to
the whole paragraph. In a similar way, when typing the novel,
Faulkner changed some narrative sentences into his characters'
own thoughts. For instance, the first of Lena's reflections

in italics on page 6 read in the manuscript: "Then it would
be as though she were riding for a half mile ..."; and Christmas's thoughts on pages 98 and 99: "*I have been in bed now
since ten o'clock* ...," and "*Perhaps that is where outrage
lies* ...," were likewise in the third person. A comparison
of the manuscript and the published book reveals that in the
final text Faulkner often achieved a closer integration of
the third-person narration with spoken language or unspoken
thoughts, thus making his narrative more dramatic and his
characters more vividly perceived and better endowed with an
inner, brooding sort of life.

Intensity

   The language of *Light in August* has an intensity deriving
from what we may call at once accretion and compression. Even
more than James Fenimore Cooper, Faulkner would have earned
Mark Twain's censure, particularly because of his almost in-
ordinate use of adjectives. Yet he succeeds in accumulating
them to such a degree that they carry the whole emotional
weight of a given passage. Lena is summed up, morally as well
as physically, in only five adjectives: "swollen, slow, deliberate, unhurried and tireless" (p. 7). In the manuscript
the first adjective was "pregnant"; the alteration replaces
the abstract term by a word which is not only more graphic
but which also adds alliteration and assonance. On his arrival
at Mrs. Beard's, Byron's voice is described by three adjectives with Latin roots, which, by the repetition of the same
consonants, suggest the character's feverish insistence. In
each case, the stress falls on the first or central syllable,
and the final syllables, heavy and muffled, somehow evoke
the impotence Byron felt in face of the situation: "recapitu-
lant, urgent, importunate" (p. 78). McEachern, too, is contained in the adjectival accretion qualifying him as he takes
home the child he has just adopted: "The man was bundled too
against the cold, squat, big, shapeless, somehow rocklike,
indomitable, not so much ungentle as ruthless" (p. 135). The
respective attitudes of Joanna and Joe are concentrated in
a few well-chosen adjectives, in the description of their
confrontation during the third phase of their relationship:
"Their faces were not a foot apart: the one cold, dead white,
fanatical, mad; the other parchmentcolored, the lip lifted
into the shape of a soundless and rigid snarl" (p. 262).
Finally, Hightower's house is described in the following
series of adjectives: "the house unpainted, small, obscure,
poorly lighted, mansmelling, manstale" (p. 44). When this is

compared with the manuscript version ("the small, poorly lighted, manstale house where the ex-minister lives with what the
town calls his disgrace") it is obvious that Faulkner has moved
the adjectives to the end of the sentence to lay greater stress
upon them, Conrad-wise, and that two of the added adjectives
("obscure" and "mansmelling"), far from being synonymous with
the others, add shades of meaning, and enlarge the vision by
evoking Hightower himself and his whole existence as well as
his house.

Faulkner is not satisfied with the accretion of adjectives
alone (in fact, the technique is used with restraint here
compared to later works): he also tries to exploit the adjectives themselves to their full potential, in particular
widening their range of application by making them sylleptic--
in a loose way. For instance, in describing Lena's journey,
he uses such expressions as "anonymous and deliberate wagons,"
"steady and unflagging hypnosis" (p. 5), or "the red and unhurried miles" (p. 25): "anonymous" refers rather to the
drivers than to the wagons, and "deliberate" to Lena herself;
"steady and unflagging" actually describes the mules' pace,
"red" the road surface rather than an abstract distance, and
"unhurried" the movement of the wagons. The first example
quoted, "anonymous and deliberate wagons," differs from the
manuscript, which reads: "anonymous and slow." The alteration
clearly illustrates Faulkner's concern to give his adjectives
the greatest possible extension. (The word "deliberate" thus
appears once more in this first chapter, in which it always
characterizes the attitude of the young woman.) Again, as she
sits on the steps of the Varner store, Lena remembers her
breakfast, "the decorous morsel of strange bread" (p. 23):
"decorous" in fact describes Lena's manners not the morsel,
and "strange," the Armstid family. The word "morsel" itself
adds to the impression of strangeness and gives the remembered
scene an added dimension of eternity, removing it from its
specific, rather mundane, context, and making it into an experience no longer unique. In the same way, "deliberate" describes McEachern's whole attitude rather than the strap or
the noise of the blows he deals: "the strap ... rose and
fell, deliberate, numbered, with deliberate, flat reports"
(p. 150); "dying," "spent," and "satiate" evoke the lassitude
of lovers whose passion has waned: "they would be stranded
as behind a dying mistral, upon a spent and satiate beach"
(p. 248); and "hurried" refers to the women themselves, not
their clothes: "in bright and sometimes hurried garments"
(p. 273). Sometimes, too, the process is reversed, and the
meaning of the adjective slides, not from subject to object
as in most of the examples just quoted, but from object to

subject: "*the ladies constant and a little sibilant with fans*"
(p. 346). This stylistic mannerism has many effects. Disre-
garding the rules of grammar, the adjective hangs suspended
between subject and object, referring to either or both, thus
preventing analytical developments. This manner of ellipsis
is one way of compressing and intensifying language. In addition, it forces the reader to look at people and objects in
a new light, breaking through the traditional perceptions and
language forms. This in turn contributes to the immediacy of
the style (as in "the slow buttocks of mules," p. 192). In
the end, adjectives so used become sufficient in themselves
to evoke a character, an attitude, or an emotion, almost
making the naming of the subject or the object thus qualified
a redundancy.

The effort toward the compression of language in *Light*
in August is again apparent in the invention of a great
number of compound words. The compound nouns are most frequently connected with Christmas, Doc Hines, and Hightower,
almost shaping into language their obsessions and their rigid
conception of a world where male and female are in a constant
struggle for mastery. The most remarkable of these words do
in fact begin with "man" and even more often with "woman":
"maneyes," "manodor," "manshape," "manvoice," "womenvoices,"
"womangarments," "womanfilth," "womansinning," "womanevil,"
"womanshenegro," and so on. The compound adjectives, ellipti-
cal and vividly suggestive, are even more numerous than the
nouns. They either concentrate an obsession into a single
word that makes it felt at once, physically, as in "fecundmellow," "pinkfoamed," "pinkwomansmelling," "hardsmelling,"
"deathcolored," or they stand for an entire description, as
in the case of "bugswirled," "heelgnawed," "stumppocked,"
"hookwormridden," "pinewiney," "Augusttremulous," "patina-
smooth," "cinderstrewnpacked," "thwartfacecurled." Their
power of suggestion is often increased by the combination of
precise concrete terms with abstract ones, giving them a timeless significance, beyond that of the particular context in
which they appear, as in "diamondsurfaced respectability,"
"creakwheeled and limpeared avatars," "softungirdled presence,"
"shadowbrooded," "branchshadowed quiet," "stillwinged and
tremulous suspension."

Faulkner also makes frequent use of oxymorons, which, by
juxtaposing contradictory terms, give a strange impression
of a reality that remains forever in a state of suspension
while at the same time striking the reader's imagination
by its contradictory aspects, making him share and feel
rather than judge and understand. One typically Faulknerian
example of this technique is "slow and terrific"; others

in this novel include: "the wagon crawls terrifically,"
"terrific ... idleness," "motionless wheels rising," "fumbling
and interminable haste," "fields and woods ... at once static
and fluid," "[Hightower's] face is at once gaunt and flabby,"
or "[Joe's] feet seemed to stray ... at deliberate random."
As in the case of the frequent negative forms, the oxymorons
prevent the substitution of language and logic for experience
and emotion, as Walter J. Slatoff explains: "so long as our
reactions are in a suspension rather than in crystallized
form, they remain feelings and experiences rather than rational
or verbal constructions."[5] But it is even more important to
realize that a large number of such oxymorons, even though
they may almost appear a mannerism or a trick of the trade,
and become one of the sure criteria to recognize Faulkner's
style, as one does the "music" of Racine or that of Mozart,
are indeed signs of the splendid failure inscribed in writing, aiming as they do at rendering the impossible conjunction of time and space, or more specifically at reintroducing
time into what is rather a spatial art, by suggesting at once
motion and motionlessness, the attitude or gesture and the
underlying force, as is also apparent in the remarkable and
often noted expressions of arrested movement or the "sculp-
tural" descriptions, in which the suspension of movement at
its peak of speed or of a gesture at its climax of violence
gives the arrested (but not stationary) image the added momentum of potential movement--implicit time: trying to re-
capture it is precisely the major obsession of Faulkner's
art.

     The density of the style is further enhanced by an econ-
omy of punctuation. Faulkner often accretes his adjectives
without separating them by commas: "The hot still pinewiney
silence of the August afternoon" (p. 5; the adjectives are
still separated in the manuscript), "the lightless hot wet
primogenitive Female" (p. 107), "a big long garbled cold
echoing building of dark red brick ..., set in a grassless
cinderstrewnpacked compound ..." (p. 111). The whole paragraph of which this is part is a remarkable demonstration
of the effects Faulkner can achieve through the absence of
punctuation. These desolate, sinister images of the orphanage,
the prison in which love-starved children are caged, are
not quite assimilated separately although read in succession.
Together they combine to produce a uniquely intense emotion
so much more violent than would be the sum of the minor emotions aroused by each single image. Thus, these unpunctuated
image series are a more sophisticated development of the
compound word--for which Faulkner never uses hyphens in this
novel. To join all these words together into one would only

result in confusion, but by dispensing with all superfluous
punctuation Faulkner makes clear his intention.

Rhythm

Rhythm also contributes to the power of the prose in
Light in August. The pulsations throbbing though the sentences
and rhythmically extending from one to another virtually
destroy the sentence as a unity of prose, even though the
general impression of the novel remains one of measured syn-
tax. Indeed, the author never entangles the reader in in-
ordinately long periods, which dull his faculties of analysis
and abstraction, drugging him into a state of receptivity so
that he may respond *immediately* to rhythm and to the suggestive power of images. Nevertheless, a similar effect is more
subtly and effectively achieved here by the rhythmic undula-
tions which overflow and drown the formal sentence. This observation is substantiated if one listens to Faulkner reading
aloud (there are some recordings), in prolonged, monotonous
rhythms which more often than not do not correspond to the
syntactical divisions. In this novel, the rhythm is largely
dictated by the repetitions of words (which often do not yet
occur to such an extent in the manuscript stage of the text),
by the interplay of sonorities, and by the studied alternation
of strong and weak beats.
      The first illustrative passage is interesting because it
appears on the surface to be completely straightforward, with
nothing outstanding in its vocabulary: its suggestive power
is solely derived from the rhythm. It recounts the life of
the workers in the planing mill and their attitudes on Monday
morning after the weekend break:

> Some of the other workers were family men and some were
> bachelors and they were of different ages and they led
> a catholic variety of lives, yet on Monday morning they
> all came to work with a kind of gravity, almost decorum.
> Some of them were young, and they drank and gambled on
> Saturday night, and even went to Memphis now and then.
> Yet on Monday morning they came quietly and soberly to
> work, in clean overalls and clean shirts, waiting
> quietly until the whistle blew and then going quietly
> to work, as though there were still something of Sab-
> bath in the overlingering air which established a tenet
> that, no matter what a man had done with his Sabbath,
> to come quiet and clean to work on Monday morning was
> no more than seemly and right to do. (p. 36-37)

The first sentence (one has to use the term for reference
purposes) begins with four statements, in pairs ("some ...
were ... and some were," "and they were ... and they led"),
and each pair has roughly seven strong beats alternating
fairly regularly with weak beats. Then the rhythm changes as
a new idea is introduced, still in the same sentence: "yet
on Monday morning they all came to work," and this idea is
taken up again two sentences later in almost the same form.
The sentence ends with two complementary words, "gravity"
and "decorum," both of Latin root, both with an unstressed
ending, matching the subdued attitude of the workers, and
their wish to pass unnoticed. The next sentence echoes the
beginning of the first ("some of them") in three propositions
which expand progressively from three to five strong beats.
The beginning of the third sentence takes up the second part
of the first and, in an almost regular succession of strong
and weak beats, introduces the words "quietly" and "clean,"
which dictate the rhythm of the end of the paragraph, when
the activities of the Sunday are remembered, to the accompaniment of the discreet vibrations of "in the overlingering air."
This apparently insignificant passage was chosen deliberately
for the unerring sense of rhythm it shows. Faulkner's prose,
like Flaubert's, also lives in the sounds of the words, and
should be read aloud or in the head.

The description of Joe swallowing the dietitian's toothpaste literally ad nauseam is another passage which owes its
strength to the repetitive rhythm:

> He squatted among the soft womansmelling garments
> and the shoes. He saw by feel alone now the ruined,
> once cylindrical tube. By taste and not seeing he con-
> templated the cool invisible worm as it coiled onto his
> finger and smeared sharp, automatonlike and sweet, into
> his mouth. By ordinary he would have taken a single
> mouthful and then replaced the tube and left the room.
> Even at five, he knew that he must not take more than
> that. Perhaps it was the animal warning him that more
> would make him sick; perhaps the human being warning
> him that if he took more than that, she would miss it.
> This was the first time he had taken more. By now,
> hiding and waiting, he had taken a good deal more. By
> feel he could see the diminishing tube. He began to
> sweat. Then he found that he had been sweating for some
> time, that for some time now he had been doing nothing
> else but sweating. He was not hearing anything at all
> now. Very likely he would not have heard a gunshot
> beyond the curtain. He seemed to be turned in upon him-
> self, watching himself sweating, watching himself smear

another worm of paste into his mouth which his stomach
did not want. Sure enough, it refused to go down. Motionless now, utterly contemplative, he seemed to stoop
above himself like a chemist in his laboratory, waiting.
He didn't have to wait long. At once the paste which
he had already swallowed lifted inside him, trying to
get back out, into the air where it was cool. It was no
longer sweet. In the rife, pinkwomansmelling obscurity
behind the curtain he squatted, pinkfoamed, listening
to his insides, waiting with astonished fatalism for
what was about to happen to him. (pp. 113-14)

We actually see Joe putting the toothpaste into his mouth
only twice. The words "automatonlike" and "diminishing" may
well suggest that the action was repeated many times; however,
the repetition is more clearly apparent in the variations
played on the word "more," used five times in about as many
lines, and coming after "single mouthful": the recurrence
graphically translates the rising nausea. The parallel between
the start of the two successive phrases ("perhaps it was the
animal warning him") reinforces the effect. The rest of the
paragraph is spanned by the repetition and alternation of
several words: "sweating" (or "sweat"), "hearing" (or "heard"),
"watching," "waiting" (or "wait"); and again by the words
"smear," "worm," "sweet," which echo the beginning of the
passage and lead finally to these amazing compound adjectives,
"pinkwomansmelling" and "pinkfoamed." They link women and
nausea together in Joe's mind, or rather in his body, forever
afterwards, and stamp his aversion with an unforgettable color.
The passage is composed of short, simple sentences, but the
reader forgets their divisions since they do not represent
unities of sense or rhythm. The whole flows on in rhythmic
waves which rise and fall on the repetitions. The passage
also illustrates Faulkner's use of sonority. Even though it
does not seem that he tried aloud what he wrote, as Flaubert
did in his study at Croisset, which he used to call his
"gueuloir," Faulkner, poet and word-musician that he is, must
have listened carefully to his prose in the chamber of his
mind. The waves of rhythm are music in themselves. Moreover,
alliteration and assonance abound in the passage: "cool" is
echoed in "coiled," and all the *s*, *th*, *sh*, and *tch* sounds,
grouped around the words "sweating" and "watching," seem to
prolong the disagreeable sensation of sweating and emphasize
the imminence of disaster. The beginning of the paragraph
makes greater use of the muffled *oo* sounds, and of the plain-
tive *e* sounds ("shoes," "ruined," "tube," "cool," "mouth,"
"mouthful," "room," "knew"; "feel," "seeing," "finger,"

"smear," "sweet"). The music is more insistent toward the middle of the paragraph, where the *e* sounds become obsessive ("By feel he could see the diminishing tube"), reinforced by the many present participles. Faulkner's mastery of rhythm and sonority could be illustrated in many other passages, where the effects are perhaps more striking or more sustained than in the two quoted above; for instance, one thinks of the passages referring to Christmas in the interminable street, or the second phase of his relationship with Joanna, or his death, or to Hightower's wheel and his final vision. Yet the selected passages are convincing in their very simplicity.

Discussing the language of Faulkner's characters, Warren Beck has said: "He has fully mastered the central difficulty, to retain verisimilitude while subjecting the prolix and monotonous raw material of most natural speech to an artistic pruning and pointing up."[6] This refinement of the dialogue is mostly achieved through the skill guiding the cadences and repetitions. In this sense the dialogues in *Light in August* are not greatly different from the narrative, and have similar characteristics, as has already been remarked. Faulkner's work to this end can be seen in a comparison of the original and final versions of the conversation between Armstid and Winterbottom in Chapter 1 (in each case, the passages of interspersed narration have been omitted). First, the original text (which is that of the salesman's dummy, preceding the University of Virginia manuscript; the latter is much closer to the final text):

> "Who is it?" Winterbottom said.... "She couldn't have come very far in that shape."
> "And before she goes much further, she is goin' to have company," Armstid said.... "Maybe she is visitin' around here somewhere."
> "Maybe so," Winterbottom said, "I ain't heard tell though."

Now the final version (p. 7):

> "I wonder where she got that belly," Winterbottom said.
> "I wonder how far she has brought it afoot," Armstid said.
> "Visiting somebody back down the road, I reckon," Winterbottom said.
> "I reckon not. Or I would have heard. And it aint nobody up my way, neither. I would have heard that, too."
> "I reckon she knows where she is going," Winterbottom said. "She walks like it."

"She'll have company, before she goes much further,"
Armstid said.... "She aint come from nowhere close....
She's hitting that lick like she's been at it for a
right smart while and had a right smart piece to go yet."
"She must be visiting around here somewhere," Winter-
bottom said.
"I reckon I would have heard about it," Armstid
said.

The second version does not add any information to the
first: the substance is the same in each. The differences are
only revealing of Faulkner's art, for which reason they are
full of interest. To begin with, the author has replaced the
abstract word "shape" with the more concrete "belly," which
acquires its full weight with Armstid's remark: "I wonder how
far she has brought it afoot." The dialogue now has the true
flavor of actual speech, which the original version lacked,
because of the sonorous and picturesque expression "hitting
that lick," and because of the Southern farmer turns of phrase
("right smart while," echoed in "right smart piece"; these
three expressions do not yet appear in the manuscript). Originally, Faulkner was satisfied with one detail of pronunciation (dropping the final "g" of the present participle),
which is too common a trait to signify any one regional
dialect. He has also concretized more fully the locality:
"around here somewhere" is vague and does not suggest any
actual place, nor does it suit the conversation of men who
know their area and calculate directions in relation to their
own farms; the phrases "back down the road" and "up my way"
are more typical. (He uses "visiting around here somewhere"
later on, when vagueness becomes necessary after the remark:
"She aint come from nowhere close.") Such little details
individualize the two men: although they are only minor
characters, seen only in this first chapter, they are brought
to life through the precision of this truly spoken conversation better than they could have been in a long description.
They are clearly Southern farmers living in a specific region.
    The dialogue is also striking for its cadences. Apart
from the repetition of "maybe," the original version has
none of the echoes which give the final version its internal
rhythm: "I wonder" comes twice, "I reckon" is used three
times, and again at the end (the first "I reckon" was not yet
introduced in the manuscript following the first known text,
that of the salesman's dummy); "visiting" recurs twice, "I
would have heard" three times. The repetitions give the
dialogue the rhythm of speech, unite its various elements,
and, most of all, slow it down, thus altering its artistic
significance. By the repetitions, the author represents in

the text itself the slow ways of these men squatting beneath
the shady wall of a barn, not to be hurried by anything. Thus,
the passage not only gives some information about Lena, it
also characterizes these farmers, the "timeless unhaste and
indirection of [their] kind." The alterations and additions
demonstrate Faulkner's perfect mastery of dialogue.

Imagery

In *Light in August*, and in Faulkner's fiction in general,
certain words or images associated with the characters recur
so persistently that they eventually become symbolic of these
chararacters: Brown is represented as an animal (mule, horse,
fox, grasshopper, snake, rat, etc.), Mame always seems "brass-
haired" or "diamondsurfaced," McEachern is "rocklike," Christmas is seen both in black and white or as a lonely shadow,
Hightower is bathed in sweat, or sitting motionless at his
window, just as Joe is connected with the street, Joanna
with the "dark house" (the former title of the novel), and
Lena with the light in this Mississippi August. Such obvious
remarks do not need much elaboration here, no more than the
expressionist eye imagery regarding the characters.[7] It would
be more to the point and of greater use to examine some of
the significant images running through the book and tighten-
ing its texture. The images connected with sexuality are
particularly worthy of note. Everything which has to do with
sexuality and femininity in *Light in August* is warm, moist,
dark, and thick, and is strikingly evoked in the image of
the well or the pit. At the age of fourteen Christmas stands
on the brink: "he seemed to look down into a black well and
at the bottom saw two glints like reflection of dead stars"
(p. 147). Later on he sees himself in his affair with Joanna
as "a man being sucked down into a bottomless morass" (p.
246), and shortly before he kills her he feels oppressed,
as though he were right at the bottom: "As from the bottom
of a thick black pit he saw himself enclosed ..." (p. 107).
These unwholesome depths are peopled with monsters (octopus
and Medusa), and constitute a dark domain of impurity and
filth. Hence the many images of thick dark water and of
liquid putrefaction: "a whispering of gutter filth," "a thick
still black pool of more than water" (p. 99: cf. p. 246);
"periodical filth" (p. 173); "it was as though he had fallen
into a sewer" (p. 242); "living not alone in sin but in
filth" (p. 244); "something liquid, deathcolored, and foul"
(p. 178); "that rotten richness ready to flow into putrefaction at a touch, like something growing in a swamp" (pp.
247-48).

There are two opposites to this formless, treacherous abyss. The first is the straight, cool street, which has a clear-cut, masculine form. When Joe feels himself being dragged downward, he clings to the idea of the street:

> What he was now seeing was the street lonely, savage, and cool. That was it: cool; he was thinking, saying aloud to himself sometimes, "I better move. I better get away from here." (p. 246)

The second opposite is the hill: Joe escapes from Freedman Town by climbing up the hill, and is only restored to calmness when he reaches the top and breathes the "cold hard air of white people" (p. 107); he dare not look back until he has reached the very top, the exact opposite of the abyss: "he did not look back until he reached the crest of the hill" (p. 108). So the qualities of the male world are the contrasting ones to those of the female world. This male world is frequently characterized by the word "hard"; it is pure, cool, or even cold; its waters are clean and refreshing and as light as dew. Once he has removed the last button from his underclothes, Joe sees no more images of the thick corrupted water which previously filled his mind: instead, symbolically naked, he feels the purifying cool air on his body: "he could feel the dark air like water; he could feel the dew under his feet as he had never felt dew before" (p. 100). After two hours' sleep in the stables, another symbol of virility, he goes outside and breathes in the "clean chill" of the air at dawn (p. 102), feels the grass blades against his legs like "strokes of limber icicles." Then he shaves himself, using the clean waters of a spring for a mirror. When at the age of fourteen he had refused the Negro girl, he had felt the brush upon his body of a still lighter element, a purifying wind: "There was no She at all now. They just fought; it was as if a wind had blown among them, hard and clean" (p. 147).

Throughout this novel, copulation and brutality are inseparable; it is all at once a struggle, a rape, and a robbery: "Even after a year it was as though he entered by stealth to despoil her virginity each time anew" (p. 221). The theme of sexuality is thus equally associated with all the striking images of strife and defeat which characterize Joe's relationship with Joanna: "to struggle," "physical combat," "enemy," "resistance," "surrender," "capitulation," "a defeated general on the day after the last battle" (Chapters 11 and 12).

Even more striking are the frequent references to death in connection with sexuality. The eyes of the Negro girl are

"two glints like reflection of dead stars"; Bobbie's are
depthless and reflectionless, her motionless hands look "as
big and dead and pale as a piece of cooking meat," and she
has "a dead mouth in a dead face" (pp. 202 and 204). In
Christmas's vision the foul liquid pouring from the cracked
urns is "deathcolored"; and when he takes Joanna brutally
for the second time, she is like a corpse (the necrophilia
of "A Rose for Emily" is brought forcibly to mind): "beneath
his hands the body might have been the body of a dead woman
not yet stiffened" (p. 223). At a later stage, he feels as
though each night were the last under the last moon, and by
day Joanna seems to be "a phantom of someone whom the night
sister had murdered and which now moved purposeless about the
scenes of old peace, robbed even of the power of lamenting"
(p. 248)--another image in Faulkner with strong Shakespearian
overtones.

The relationship of Joe and Joanna follows the rhythm of
the seasons, but it is significant that at no time does it
evoke a beginning, a dawn, or a spring, and there are no images
of happy fertility: "During the first phase it had been as
though he were outside a house where snow was on the ground,
trying to get into the house; during the second phase he was
at the bottom of a pit in the hot wild darkness; now he was
in the middle of a plain where there was no house, not even
snow, not even wind" (pp. 254-55). Their passion (if such it
may be called) is set in a wasteland, the desert of love. We
do not know for certain when Joe raped Joanna but it is certain that their relationship itself has no spring, beginning
in September: "It was summer becoming fall, with already,
like shadows before a westering sun, the chill and implacable
import of autumn cast ahead upon summer; something of dying
summer spurting again like a dying coal, in the fall. This
was over a period of two years" (p. 247); and again: "that
final upflare of stubborn and dying summer upon which autumn,
the dawning of halfdeath, had come unawares" (p. 251). Joanna's
menopause coincides with the first frost, and when, manlike
once more, she sends for Joe, it is February (pp. 252-53).
Thus the changing seasons not only describe their relationship through a series of metaphors and similes, but they also
become its appropriate background, its obsessive obbligato.
Lena too, as will be remembered, is characterized in similar
terms: she has the unhaste of a change of season, but since
she belongs to immemorial earth and is eternal Nature, she
contains their passage without being their slave. Images
drawn from nature then are applied with contrasting significance to the two characters embodying two opposed concepts
of Woman. This type of imagery helps to distinguish between

the two aspects of one theme, and to bring two characters
close enough for their differences to be the more obvious.
A further result is that the unity of the work is cemented
beyond the level of the plots themselves.

The unifying function of opposing and complementary images
can be seen even more clearly in the use of the straight line
and the circle. Richard Chase sees them as the central images
around which *Light in August* is built, and finds them more
important than the contrast of light and shadow embodied in
Lena and Joe.[8] Joe's life has the rectilinear, masculine form
suggested by the images of the street and the corridor. (On
one occasion, he is himself compared to a lonely telephone
pole in the middle of a desert.) He is associated with the
street the first time the reader sees him, and on the last
morning before he kills Joanna, the day itself seems like a
corridor: "he could see the yellow day opening peacefully
on before him, like a corridor ..." (p. 104). The image is
discreetly insistent throughout the rest of the chapter: he
reads his magazine straight through, "like a man walking
along a street might count the cracks in the pavement, to
the last and final page, the last and final word" (p. 104),
and he spends the morning in a peaceful valley. This pastoral
avatar of the street has a dual significance: the tranquility
it suggests could either be a prefiguration of the tranquility
he experiences eight days later, or an ironic inversion of
his actual state of mind, for his street is also a prison,
and he must follow it to the bitter end, "to the last and
final page, the last and final word." This idea is even more
pronounced in the next chaper when the first image entering
his memory is that of a corridor: the orphanage is, in his
mind, a long, cold, deserted corridor from which the child
could no more escape than could an animal from a zoo or a
criminal from a penitentiary. Then the image of the street
becomes the central motif of Chapter 10, leading Joe straight
to Joanna's house--and finally to Mottstown, the end of his
enforced journey. Joanna's house is only one more stop along
the way: it is synonymous with the abyss, or the womb, and
totally opposite to the street, so that, although he cannot
escape from it for three years, Joe knows that it is not
his true element and that he will have to leave. From the
darkness of Miss Burden's kitchen he seems to stare into
the street, which is the place where he must live: "the
savage and lonely street which he had chosen of his own will,
waiting for him, thinking *This is not my life. I dont belong
here*" (pp. 243-44; cf. pp. 250-51).

Lena, the complete and self-sufficient being, is associated
with the circle, a symbol of plenitude and eternity. It appears

in the wheels of the wagons in which she travels, "a succession of creakwheeled ... avatars" (p. 5), in the Keatsian urn
around whose sides she moves without progress, in the circular
form of the novel which she opens and closes, and even in her
body, rounded by pregnancy. Yet Lena is also associated with
the straight line of the road and continuous travel. She sets
off from Alabama, crosses Mississippi, and the story ends as
she enters Tennessee. For her, too, the stay at Jefferson
was only a temporary, enforced halt. Faulkner even uses the
corridor image for her: "Behind her the four weeks, the evoca-
tion of *far*, is a peaceful corridor ..." (p. 4). Similarly,
the life of Percy Grimm, Christmas's complementary double, is
associated with the same image: "He could now see his life
opening before him, uncomplex and inescapable as a barren
corridor ..." (p. 426). Miss Burden's life too is bounded by
the walls of a prisonlike tunnel: "She seemed to see her whole
past life, the starved years, like a gray tunnel, at the far
and irrevocable end of which, as unfading as a reproach, her
naked breast ... ached as though in agony ..." (p. 250).

Conversely, the image of the circle is associated with
Christmas too, ever since the dietitian offered him the round
dollar and so threatened his integrity when he was five. His
street eventually curves around on itself to make an imprisoning circle. While Lena's road is always open, crossing the
countryside, Christmas, in all his long years of wandering,
is always symbolically in a street, a closed-in space, bounded
by high walls. The image evoked by the succession of his days
is significant: "it seems to him now that for thirty years
he has lived inside an orderly parade of named and numbered
days like fence pickets ..." (pp. 313-14). When he enters
Mottstown a few days later, he understands the true significance of his imprisoning street: "It had made a circle and
he is still inside of it ... 'But I have never got outside
that circle. I have never broken out of the ring of what I
have already done and cannot ever undo'" (p. 321). In contrast
to Lena's circle, a sign of plenitude and of the natural
cycles, Joe's is that of fatality. Hightower's life, too, is
in the form of a circle, that of self-centeredness and alienation from the rest of humanity, that of his ivory tower. So
the wheel of his vision is an appropriate image for the revolution, in the physical sense of the word, that completes
his experience in the novel. That wheel is the wheel of tor-
ture, for he is wounded and his sweat no longer suggests
tears, but blood (p. 464); it is also the wheel of thought
which finally runs free, liberated by his painful confession
from the braking weight of a dead life; the wheel then becomes
a glowing halo, the August light by which Hightower sees, in

an ecstatic instant, the whole of the humanity to which he
now firmly belongs. Finally, the circle is found again in the
image of the urn, which is associated with Lena, and also
with Christmas and Hightower--which makes the Keatsian urn a
polyvalent symbol in the novel: its timeless and rounded perfection can be a false sanctuary, offering no refuge against
time passing and the arrows of fortune, and it appears to be
cracked and foul--an object of nausea.

This survey of the complementary images of the straight
line and the circle shows how the same symbols are associated
with different themes and characters, sometimes to point out
their differences, and sometimes to highlight their similarities. Running all through the novel as they do, they suggest
that it may be read at a level which reaches further than
the facts themselves. Thus they are important factors in the
architecture and unity of the book--ironic though it may be.

So far only a few images, and those the most noteworthy,
have been discussed, but there are so many that it would be
impossible to mention them all. In fact, at some points,
Faulkner's whole universe becomes an image, the *expression*
of his mental vision, thanks to a proliferation of metaphors
and similes: "as if," "as though," "like," "it seemed," punctuate every sentence at such moments. One example is sufficient
illustration: the second phase of the relationship between
Joe and Joanna, at the beginning of Chapter 12. The tone is
set in the first short paragraph, containing four lengthen-
ing similes which make up the whole of it. Faulkner has obviously abandoned objective description to draw the reader
into a world of images, subjective approximations to his
vision, and the only world, the only reality he offers. The
beginning of the second paragraph settles the reader inside
the metaphor: "The sewer ran only by night." The following
pages seem to describe real places and actual situations,
but one remains inside the metaphorical world created at the
start of the chapter. Evoking the corruptive influence of
Joanna, a malevolent power in the form of two creatures in
a single body, Faulkner once more uses similes, but *inside*
the metaphorical frame already established: "like two moon-
gleamed shapes," "locked like sisters" (p. 246). It is notice-
able that in these pages Faulkner feels compelled to show
this imaginary world's distance from the real world by referring, as though in contrast, to "real" sensations (real
within the space of fiction): "that surrender terrific and
hard, like the breaking down of a spiritual skeleton the
very sound of whose snapping fibers could be *heard* almost
by the physical ear" (p. 242); "he thought of that other
personality that seemed to exist somewhere in *physical dark-*

ness itself" (p. 248; italics mine). Faulkner's world here is
in no way the objective reproduction of an actual situation,
sending the reader back to his own experience or to acknowledged norms: it is rather the projection, through images, of
the author's emotional reactions to a situation which has no
actuality whatsoever outside the realm of the imagination.
The author has absolute control over the entrance to this
world as he has almost completely isolated it from an "objective," referential reality. In this way he can manipulate the
reader's emotions as he wishes, making him share the full
intensity of his own. The images are neither for decoration
nor enrichment: they are the very texture of this world which
has no existence other than Faulkner's imaginings, or phantasms.

This is an expressionist rather than an impressionist
technique. Impressionism is realism pushed to extremes, a
desire to imitate the inimitable and to capture evanescence,
like the Seine at Les Andelys or Reims cathedral swathed in
a unique and insubstantial veil of mist. Expressionism, on
the other hand, seeks not to fix the quality of a given instant, not to make "a moment's monument," but to reconstruct
from the artist's own reactions and the elements of his vision
a coherent reality which does not show fleeting appearances
but the essential qualities, as he has glimpsed them beyond
and through these appearances. The results may appear disturb-
ingly idiosyncratic insofar as the work is the outcome of an
inner compulsion working with elements which may well have
been distorted in passing through the prism of a personality.
James Burnham made this point as early as January 1931, in a
penetrating article which has been strangely omitted from
bibliographies concerning Faulkner: "Faulkner is using the
data of observation only as a material in the construction
of his own world. It is to be judged not as imitation but
as creation, by the emotional integrity, with which it is
formed."[9] In a review of *Absalom, Absalom!*, Clifton Fadiman
noted: "Very few things in the book remain themselves. Each
one reminds Mr. Faulkner of something else."[10] The critic
of *The New Yorker* meant thus to censure an author he steadily
refused to understand, but he has accurately described an art
which seeks less to describe an external reality than to re-
create an inner vision in language which will provoke a
similar vision in the reader's mind. The constant use of
similes, the series of approximations, the translation of
emotions into images (techniques which Fadiman calls the
memory of something else) are the methods Faulkner uses to
bring the reader into a state of empathy so that he may share
the author's vision. Like all expressionist art, Faulkner's
bears the marks of the violence inferred in the projection--

the *ex-pression*--of an inner vision. Just as Soutine's *Rooster*
seems torn, lynched as it were, or as the colors in a Rouault
or a Kokoschka seem to scream out, or as Van Gogh's yellows
are thrust onto the canvas with a sort of frenzy, so Faulkner
translates his vision into a language that can be scorchingly
intense, and loads an emotion-releasing prose with his own
(occasionally discordant) reactions toward a character or a
landscape.

So, the precision of the language in *Light in August* (as
discussed above) does not necessarily imply that Faulkner
creates here a realistic universe. The violent intensity
rather argues for a pervasive sense of unreality, or super-
reality. Like expressionistic art, Faulkner makes use of color
symbolism (black and white), of exaggeration and distortion
in the description of characters, and also of what could be
called a derealization process, as appears in the repeated
references to shades and shadows, phantoms, ghosts, masks,
and dehumanized puppets.[11]

Faulkner's style in *Light in August* has a remarkable unity
of tone. The characteristics we have defined are present all
the time at all levels of the writing. Both dialogues and
the characters' narratives, although written in a truly spoken
language, are as rich in images and carefully worked out
rhythms as the passages presented in the anonymous narrator's
voice. Moreover, Faulkner has great skill in amplifying and
augmenting voices so that the differences between his characters' and the narrator's are smoothed away, leaving the unity
unimpaired. This does not mean, though, that Faulkner's style
has no variety. He subtly modulates his prose to fit each
character. Lena's calm endurance, for instance, is suggested
in the regular rhythms and by the recurrence of words which
become musical motifs, giving the prose a richness and con-
sistence characteristic of the woman herself. In the description of a wagon hypnotically suspended in the Southern light,
the style becomes that of poetry. For Hightower, the style is
more ornate, more complex, even precious and self-conscious,
self-centered as befits the character. Chapter 3 in particular
offers examples of this, in the studied inversions ("by bush-
ing crape myrtle and syringa and Althea almost hidden," p.
52), the use of chiasmus ("the sign, carpentered neatly by
himself and by himself lettered," p. 53), and preciosity in
the handling of words and sonorities ("that instant when all
light has failed out of the sky and it would be night save
for that faint light which daygranaried leaf and grass blade
reluctant suspire, making still a little light on earth though
night itself has come," p. 55). The minister's incoherence in
his sermons is mirrored in Faulkner's deliberate anacoluthon:

up there in the pulpit with his hands flying around him
and the dogma he was supposed to preach all full of
galloping cavalry and defeat and glory ..., it in turn
would get all mixed up with absolution and choirs of
martial seraphim, until it was natural that the old men
and women should believe that what he preached ... verged
on actual sacrilege. (p. 57)

Finally, images and rhythms are exploited to their full effect
in the account of Christmas's life, in some of the finest
pages that Faulkner ever wrote. In fact, these six chapters
have the ring of perfection and they have provided most of
the illustrations for this study of his style. They never
sink into the moralizing rhetoric which can occasionally
become unbearable in a few of the later novels, whose significance at times seems obscured rather than enriched by such
mannerisms. The grandeur of *Light in August* has its source
not only in its subtle structure, the forceful presence of
its characters, and the wealth and variety of its themes, but
also in the mastery of its style, a style in which a poetic
sense of rhythm and sound, a powerful imagination, and a
steady control of technique remain firmly harnessed to the
author's purposes. The remarkable mastery of language places
Light in August alongside Faulkner's greatest masterpieces.

NOTES

1. *As I Lay Dying* (New York: Cape and Smith, 1930), p.
163.

2. Eric Larsen, "The Barrier of Language: The Irony of
Language in Faulkner," *Modern Fiction Studies*, 13 (Spring
1967), 19-31; quotation from p. 30.

3. See the introduction to this collection.

4. Karl E. Zink, "William Faulkner: Form as Experience,"
South Atlantic Quarterly, 53 (July 1954), 384-403; quotation
from p. 402.

5. *Quest for Failure: A Study of William Faulkner* (Ithaca,
N.Y.: Cornell University Press, 1960), p. 242.

6. "William Faulkner's Style," *American Prefaces*, 6
(Spring 1941), 195-211. Reprinted in *William Faulkner: Three
Decades of Criticism*, ed. Frederick J. Hoffman and Olga W.
Vickery (East Lansing: Michigan State University Press,
1960), pp. 142-56; quotation from p. 148.

7. See François Pitavy, *Faulkner's Light in August*, "The Eyes" (in Chapter 3, pp. 63-64).

8. "The Stone and the Crucifixion: Faulkner's *Light in August*," *Kenyon Review*, 10 (Autumn 1948), 539-51.

9. James Burnham, "Trying to Say," *The Symposium*, 2 (January 1931), 51-59.

10. Clifton Fadiman, "Faulkner, Extra-Special, Double-Distilled," *The New Yorker* (October 31, 1936), pp. 62-64.

11. See on this point the stimulating comparison between *Light in August* and O'Neill's *All God's Chillun Got Wings* in Ilse Dusoir Lind's discussion of the influence of expressionism on Faulkner, "Faulkner's Uses of Poetic Drama," in *Faulkner, Modernism, and Film: Faulkner and Yoknapatawpha, 1978* (Jackson: University Press of Mississippi, 1979), pp. 66-81. See also the perceptive remarks of Wright Morris in "The Violent Land: Some Observations on the Faulkner Country," *Magazine of Art*, 45 (March 1952), 99-103.

LIGHT IN AUGUST:
THE EPISTEMOLOGY OF TRAGIC PARADOX

Carole Anne Taylor

Readings of *Light in August* have struggled most frequently
with how to relate Faulkner's sustained contradictions--past
and present, motion and stasis, comedy and tragedy--to the
considerable body of myth and symbol the work invokes.[1] Yet
the sheer density of the novel belies any neat system of
allusion, and its immersion in the language of thinking,
knowing, believing, and remembering suggests that interrela-
tions among mental processes may be as important to formal
and structural definition as are Christian, Greek, or Buddhist
religion. The range of narrative voices provides contesting
perspectives on truth, from the self-limited perspective of
local voices to the global perspective of a lyrical narrator
who utters explicitly epistemological incantations ("Memory
believes before knowing remembers"). The novel's most explicit and sustained metaphors focus attention on the kinds
of knowledge that characterize the mental ages of man. And
the book's structure fuses real and metaphoric ages, purposefully thwarting any reliance on mere chronology in favor of
a cumulative, figurative understanding of the highest level
of truth, available only to tragic consciousness. Narrative
voices, figurative density, and structural complexity all
help to create a kind of epistemological space-time in which
Faulkner demonstrates how the paradox of tragic consciousness
differs from the other paradoxes of mind embraced by the
child, the adolescent, and the adult. My concern here will
be with these interrelated paradoxes of mind and their implications for Faulknerian tragedy.
　　Lena's almost precognitive knowing of the senses presides
over her adult childhood and relates her figuratively to the

From Texas Studies in Literature and Language, *22 (Spring
1980), 48-68.* © *1980 by the University of Texas Press. Reprinted with permission.*

actual childhood of Joe. There has been little effort to
characterize her mode of perception, and too often, she has
been regarded as the ideal woman who saves Byron Bunch from
a "pallid half-life."[2] We first hear of Lena from a narrator
who tells her story in short, declarative sentences, without
selectivity, emotion, or commentary. What Lena "thinks" punc-
tuates the story, and there is a wonderful, comic correspondence between this narrator's perspective and Lena's own.
The narrator presents trivial and significant incidents in
Lena's past without altering his tone, so that even the death
of her parents takes its place as one among many indifferently
perceived facts. Lena's own reasoning about time and distance
endows the approaching and receding wagon with the tangible
presence of her own body:

> 'That far within my hearing before my seeing,' Lena
> thinks. She thinks of herself as already moving, riding
> again, thinking *then it will be as if I were riding
> for a half mile before I even got into the wagon, before
> the wagon even got to where I was waiting, and that
> when the wagon is empty of me again it will go on for
> a half mile with me still in it*[3]

Figurative language is absent from Lena's thinking, for she
reduces abstract concepts to sense impressions and her assertions expand the present by imagining herself riding in the
wagon before its arrival and after its departure. This ability
to manipulate time and distance extends to her thinking about
others:

> 'And if he is going all the way to Jefferson, I will
> be riding within the hearing of Lucas Burch before his
> seeing. He will hear the wagon, but he wont know. So
> there will be one within his hearing before his seeing.
> And then he will see me and he will be excited. And so
> there will be two within his seeing before his remember-
> ing.' (p. 6)

Here, Lena projects her own way of perceiving onto Lucas, so
that the fact of his seeing her becomes more important than
the obvious question of how he will react to her presence.
(The close parallel between her quoted and italicized thought
processes graphically illustrates her self-delusion.)

A different, more neutral narrator, whose voice is only
vaguely heard behind the story, underscores the distance between Lena's language and how others perceive it. This narrator watches as her speech communicates beyond her control,
telling "more than she knows that she is telling" (p. 47).
Appropriately, she "doesn't seem to be listening" when others'

voices are alien to her world view, hearing only those things
which she can record, without mental interference, into her
own consciousness:

> ... while thinking goes idle and swift and smooth,
> filled with nameless kind faces and voices: *Lucas*
> *Burch? You say you tried in Pocahontas? This road? It*
> *goes to Springvale. You wait here. There will be a*
> *wagon passing soon that will take you as far as it goes*
> (p. 6)

Lena's "calm unreason and detachment" rely on her capacity
to act as though linguistic meanings were superfluous, to
resist language. Thus, there lurk no abyss beyond the senses,
no fears for herself or for others, and likewise no empathy,
no ability to imagine beyond herself. The matter of language,
like the region beyond present space-time, passes over Lena
as "trivial and unimportant--slow and terrific without meaning." As she frames her sentences from words she has heard
in others' mouths, language assumes importance only as ritual,
the slow accompaniment to her intuitive sense of things. Like
an autistic child, she cannot generate her own sentences, but
repeats the ritual language of social discourse. No experience
or change in audience affects her story's language, spoken
"with that patient and transparent recapitulation of a lying
child" (p. 22). We last see Lena through the eyes of an earthy
member of the community who is annoyed by her empty chatting
and her habit of offering to do things which she knows she
will not be called upon to perform. He, too, recognizes her
willful separation of language and meaning.

Importantly, Lena's fictional role is circumscribed by
the shifting tonal qualities of those who describe or relate
to her and by the contrasting relation between her metaphoric
childhood and the actual childhoods of others. Lena's fertility and her earthmothering womanhood are not in question,
but her way of knowing, emphatically in the foreground, keeps
her consciousness within the limitations of childhood. Faulkner, unlike many of his critics, refrains from passing any
ultimate judgment on this child-woman, showing us instead
the implications of her immunity from suffering. If Lena
reconciles nature and society, it is because she sees in both
only what reflects herself. Her partial view of the world
may be either comic or not depending upon the narrative situation, but she is removed from the possibility of existential
shock at the cost of perennial stasis (like the figures on
an urn). Protected by her child's way of knowing, her perceptual reduction of experience, she will never confront
epistemological crisis.

In contrast, the story of Joe's childhood begins with the lyrical exposition of "memory believes before knowing remembers," and each successive stage of his development transforms the paradoxical relations that inhere in processes of mind. It is important to reflect on these relations--as the text encourages us to do--rather than to see some vaguely mimetic relation between Joe's confusion and the dense intermingling of what memory believes (and then knows) with what knowing remembers (and therefore has believed). The two are not the same, though necessarily related, and the primacy of belief in the opening lines of Chapter 6 emphasizes that we are seeing more than Joe, who in his present knowledge remembers what he once believed as a child: "Believes longer than recollects, longer than knowing even wonders. Knows remembers believes a corridor in a big long garbled cold echoing building of dark red brick" (p. 111). Having seen the adult Joe moving towards Joanna's house with the slow fatality of someone who can feel "something is going to happen to me" without even thinking it, we are prepared for the retrospective view of childhood as "knows remembers believes." Of course, Joe only thinks he knows, because belief colors in what can and cannot be remembered before the self can frame what it knows of the past. We observe how Joe's childhood knowing shapes the adolescence that will induct him into a manhood where self-limited knowing will protect him, for a time, from fear, and pity, and the exercise of free will.

The meanings which are forever lost to Lena's childlike mode of perception are only temporarily lost to Joe. As with Lena, the senses provide Joe with everything he knows as a child. The incident determining his future, the sexual encounter he hears but does not see, is for him only the backdrop for the smell and taste of the toothpaste, the feel of his own sweat, and the rising sensation of his own vomit in the "pinkwomansmelling obscurity" of his curtained hiding place. The narrator tells us how stupidly the dietitian "foisted upon him more of the attributes of an adult," presuming that his physical presence coincided with understanding. Carried off by Hines in the night, Joe "knew" what he touched and smelled, but only "believed that he knew where he was going." His childhood belief presumes that his experience is no different from that of the other children who have left the orphanage: "He believed that they had been carried out, as he was being, in the dead of night" (p. 128). And when he first confronts McEachern, his knowledge of what is to happen relies on his child's memory: "Perhaps memory knowing, knowing beginning to remember; perhaps even desire, since five is still too young to have learned enough despair to hope" (p. 132). As when he does not listen to the words of the dietitian, hearing only "sounds, rustlings, whisperings, not voices," so Joe is "not listening" when McEachern decides to give Joe his own surname; the child Joe does not respond to the abstracted meanings of words. But though at the time, "He didn't even bother to say to himself *My name aint McEach-ern. My name is Christmas*," there will come a time "when memory no longer accepted his [McEachern's] face, accepted the surface of remembering" (p. 135). Here, and many times after this, a process on the mind's surface distinguishes itself from deeper levels of conscious and unconscious mind.

The structural beauty of Chapters 6 through 9 relies on the subtle interplay of two levels of self-delusion. The adult Joe remembers how as a child there were things he thought he knew, things he believed, that later experience forced him to acknowledge he did not really know. The paradox of a child's wisdom is implicit in narration that both describes the world in terms of a child's perceptions and simultaneously under-mines those perceptions with the voice of experience. The fictional method demonstrates the truth of the narrator's assertion that the child may know both "everything" and "nothing." But the adult Joe, remembering past delusions, operates on present knowledge that is in turn based on his own reconstruction of the past, and the narrative voice re-minds us repeatedly that this present way of knowing is also delusive.[4] The adult Joe remembers with the unreliable memory of one who has the strongest vested interest in contrasting his inadequate past knowing with his present adult knowing: identity depends on projecting present knowledge (necessarily limited) onto past error, providing the self with some security that it will not err again, that it can avoid future crisis. The vulnerability of the whole process leaps from the pages of these chapters, and our sense of Joe's being bound by incomplete knowledge is heightened by a narrative technique that frequently juxtaposes Joe's adult memory with phrases like, "If the child had been older, he would perhaps have thought," "He did not then know," and "It was years later that memory knew what he was remembering." Even the narra-tive voice acknowledges its vulnerability before the past, for it is anonymous rather than omniscient, and its most characteristic constructions build upon a hypothetical "might," "perhaps," or "very likely."

As a man who most frequently "was not listening to anyone anymore than he was talking to anyone," McEachern specifically qualifies himself for stunting the natural growth of a knowl-edge that could incorporate sexual knowledge. Unnaturally, Joe's capacity to understand beyond sensory knowing undergoes

no gradual development, but hardens into the kind of absolute
belief that can only be altered through crisis. Chapter 7
begins, "And memory knows this; twenty years later memory is
still to believe *On this day I became a man*." The narrative
shift simulates the suddenness of the crisis as Joe perceives
it. At the same time, it emphasizes his continued vulnerability, the fact that his manhood (the outcome, after all,
of the adolescence he remembers) involves a struggle to contain knowing within the confines of belief and to avoid
the contradiction between experience and memory that might
shake the foundations of identity. "*On this day I became a
man*" heralds Joe's inaccurate belief, forged in adolescence,
that he became a man in stubbornly confronting McEachern; he
has to believe this because his adult identity is founded upon
it. But there is no personal crisis in his battles with McEachern. Joe acts "mechanically" and his "purely automatic"
gestures· correspond to his certainty about what he may expect
both from McEachern and from himself. Joe's cold rigidity
mirrors McEachern's "stolid and rocklike" postures as the two
act out, amid the dense imagery of stone and wood, a scene
that seems to Joe "logical and reasonable and inescapable."
Indeed, Joe takes awful pride in perversely fulfilling McEachern's own statutes of manhood as he triumphs in that implacable, masculine certainty that dominates his memory of how
and when he became a man. For both the adult McEachern and
the adolescent Joe for whom he serves as the exemplar of
manhood, cruelty is firmly allied with the certain contain-
ment of present knowing within the confines of belief; both
find ecstasy in self-flagellation and both beat the same
horse as though it were a part of themselves. The adolescent
Joe tries to adopt McEachern's model of manhood and its assumption of "omnipotence and clairvoyance," but the narrative
mode consistently undermines his belief, showing us before
the fact its transience and vulnerability.

McEachern does not threaten Joe's adolescent illusion of
understanding as do women, with the uncertain mystery of
their sex, their compassion, and their insistence on feeding
him and conspiring for him. Women force him to confront other
ways of knowing that graphically demonstrate how identity
has been based on delusive memory, on wrong knowing. Knowledge about menstruation initiates Joe's anxiety both because
it shows that there is something actual and sensual that his
own senses have not experienced and because it places volition within a fated cycle; he fears the implications of the
fact that women do not always have control of their own bodies
and cannot escape "the temporary and abject helplessness of
that which tantalised and frustrated desire" (p. 173). He

tries to immunize himself from this new knowledge by immersing his hands in the blood of a sacrificial sheep; then he tries to accommodate the physical fact by incorporating it into a revised system of belief, one which admits partly true, partly false categories that desperately and illogically exclude himself: "*All right. It is so, then. But not to me. Not in my life and my love* Then it was three or four years ago and he had forgotten it, in the sense that a fact is forgotten when it once succumbs to the mind's insistence that it be neither true nor false" (p. 174). When Bobbie's menstrual cycle does confront his own life and love, he runs to the woods where "In the notseeing and the hardknowing as though in a cave he seemed to see a diminishing row of suavely shaped urns in moonlight, blanched. And not one was perfect. Each one was cracked and from each crack there issued something liquid, deathcolored, and foul" (pp. 177-78). As with his first intro- duction to sex, he vomits, a gesture which in its fateful lack of control represents the exact nature of the crisis. Still, the physicality of menstruation and sex violates neither the emotional sanctity of his relation to a love he holds "as if no one had done this before" nor the security that whatever his past mistakes, he may *now* at least willfully control experience on the basis of what he knows and believes. Yet even when sexuality no longer shocks him, when he has learned of women's bodies "with the curiosity of a child," his emotional innocence cannot imagine that Bobbie does not feel as he feels. We remember that it is not sex but Bobbie's compassion over his lack of money that first leaves him with a "spirit wrung with abasement and regret and passionate for hiding," when he utters the first of the book's ritual incan- tations of despair: "*It's terrible to be young. It's terrible. Terrible*" (p. 170). Previously, Joe has acknowledged limita- tions to his knowing, but only of a special kind, thinking "I don't even know," but believing, "I do not know yet." But Bobbie's getaway confirms that he has been wrong about love, that she has "done this before," and he is left with only the word "*Bobbie Bobbie*." His paradoxical insistence that things be neither true nor false, characteristic of Joe's adoles- cent knowing, founders when the realities of love and compas- sion force him to see the falsity of present belief.

Chapter 10 begins Joe's adult knowing ("Knowing not grieving remembers"), filling in the chronological time that culminates in the action of Chapter 5. The earlier chapter is framed by Joe's felt premonition that "something is going to happen to me," and the weight of what we know about Joe is strongly carried by figurative description of what "seems" to be, or is "perhaps," "maybe," or "apparently" true. Joe

submits to the passing scene because he feels both that past
acts irrevocably determine present ones and that life is made
up of moments of incomplete knowing, like letters or words
that we perceive individually without knowing their place in
any meaningful progression. The analogy is Faulkner's own and
associates language and meaning with problems of fate and will.
As Joe sits on his cot next to the sleeping Brown, his inner
ear, awakened by the sound of a match whose light vanishes
in midair, *seems* to hear

> myriad sounds ... of trees, darkness, earth; people:
> his own voice; other voices evocative of names and times
> and places--which he had been conscious of all his life
> without knowing it, which were his life, thinking *God
> perhaps and me not knowing that too* He could see it
> like a printed sentence, fullborn and already dead *God
> loves me too* like the faded and weathered letters on
> a last year's billboard *God loves me too* (p. 98)

Because his life seems to be the passive receptacle of successive experiences, "voices," he can imagine God's love only
in retrospect and therefore only as loss. Similarly, the
temporal, serial quality of language determines that by the
time a sentence is printed, it must be "fullborn and already
dead." The progression from word to word or from moment to
moment through time, sometimes seen by Joe as though from the
outside, cannot even be remembered accurately because what
it seemed he knew at the time shaped how he read or lived.
Even before Chapter 10 shows Joe's life following sundry
streets and corridors, Chapter 5 develops the paradox of an
adult consciousness embracing a progression which is both
willed and fated:

> Then he read again. He turned the pages in steady pro-
> gression, though now and then he would seem to linger
> upon one page, one line, perhaps one word. He would not
> look up then. He would not move, apparently arrested
> and held immobile by a single word which had perhaps
> not yet impacted, his whole being suspended by the
> single trivial combination of letters in quiet and
> sunny space, so that hanging motionless and without
> physical weight he seemed to watch the slow flowing of
> time beneath him....
>   When he reached the last story he stopped reading
> and counted the remaining pages. Then he looked at the
> sun and read again. He read now like a man walking along
> a street might count the cracks in the pavement, to
> the last and final page, the last and final word.
> (p. 104)

In the paradoxical relation of parts to the whole, written
language is analogous to the space-time of Joe's adult experience.

The opening lines of Chapter 10 show Joe piecing together
his adult identity as he lies peacefully licking the blood
from his lips "as a child does," not able to act "yet" because
of "the two severed wireends of volition and sentience" (p. 207).
By the time Joe rouses himself to enter "the street which was
to run for fifteen years," he has surrendered active knowing
to the absolutes of a despairing certainty, and over such knowing hover narrative reminders of what he is not *yet* thinking,
what he does not *yet* know. "Doomed with motion," Joe incor-
porates alien truths by forming new absolutes; when he discovers
that he cannot repulse all white women by avowing black blood,
he throws himself entirely into the powers of blackness. Moving
like "numberless avatars," Joe plunges into a passive, fatalistic acceptance of his contrived blackness and adopts the
stealth of a cat, appropriate to the tenuous nature of the
"knowledge" upon which he acts.

In this phase, he comes upon Joanna Burden, and as he
watches her pass through phases reminiscent of his own, he
gradually learns to fear that there is still knowledge which
cannot be accommodated within the way he has chosen to be and
live. When he becomes Joanna's lover, they speak "with speech
that told nothing at all since it didn't try to and didn't
intend to" (p. 219). The dualities become unclear when for
the first time he is drawn into actual communication with
Joanna, who asks how he knows he is "part nigger." For the
first time since "knowing not grieving remembers," Joe must
answer, "I don't know," adding "If I'm not, damned if I haven't
wasted a lot of time" (p. 241). Joanna's explanation of her
own familial past, that one has to act as one has been trained
to act, opens up again the terrible question of volition. And
as he watches Joanna pass into her "inexplicable" nymphomania,
he begins to feel himself out of phase and afraid.

Joe's sense of foreboding and premonition arouses the
thought that this is a street "he had chosen of his own will,"
and yet he finds himself thinking also "*This is not my life.
I dont belong here*" (p. 244). Now it is Joanna who plays the
avatar, passing through stages of wild, sexual abandon in
which she mouths "forbidden wordsymbols." Joanna's condition
bewilders Joe, who sees that "it was as if she had invented
the whole thing deliberately, for the purpose of playing it
out like a play" (pp. 244-45). The capacity to see himself
as though from the outside, spurred by watching in Joanna
"two creatures that struggled in the one body," sparks in Joe
the instinct that his black abyss is "of its own creating."

By the time he has moved from knowing to thinking, and finally
to "thinking fast," Joanna has passed from August to autumn.
Now, Joe's thinking "flashed complete, like a printed sentence,"
and the speed of this thinking matches the contortions of a
threatened psyche. Joanna's voice embodies the threat: "He
dared not try to distinguish the words. He did not dare let
himself know what she was at" (p. 263). And her desperate last
demand coincides with his own calmly despairing crisis: "he
believed with calm paradox that he was the volitionless servant
of the fatality in which he believed that he did not believe"
(p. 264). When he kills Joanna, he is already thinking in the
past tense: "*I had to do it*." Here paradox of mind is a compromise, a defense that sustains adult identity.

As Joe flees, he experiences a resurgence of thinking which
brings him to a revelation of apocalyptic intensity and to a
different level of paradox. Attention to the explicitly religious imagery of apocalypse in *Light in August* has over-
shadowed the fact that revelations about time and history (including one's own history) are firmly grounded in rituals of
mind.[5] Not just Hightower, with his horses and riders, but
also Byron and Joe undergo crises in identity and knowing that
relate revelation to tragic paradox. Joe's seven days' flight
takes him outside those fated, numbered days that have been
his life. He enters what he thought would be the black abyss,
but what is in fact "a gray and lonely suspension." The earth
loses solidity, time loses its ordered sequence of light and
dark, and for the first time, Joe loses his sense of the
divisions between black and white, between all the certain
dualities which have for so long pushed him toward arbitrary
and desperate choices. In direct opposition to the uncontrollable urge to vomit, he finds he is immune to the need for
food and sleep. And instead of not listening, he thinks of
the fear in the Negro hands serving him, finding that he can
"hear without hearing them wails of terror and distress quieter
than sighs all about him"; he thinks of a past when "they were
afraid. Of their brother afraid" (p. 317). He sees even his
own capture as though from without, and in one of the book's
most eloquent images, he acknowledges the terrible effort of
balancing mental processes such that they frame and protect
identity: "*Here I am I am tired I am tired of running of
having to carry my life like it was a basket of eggs*" (p.
319). At the end of Chapter 14, when he reenters time, he
enters the black abyss which signals his return to what he
has been and done. But there exists a profound difference between the former Joe and the Joe who feels pity and fear for
others, who has loosened his hold on arbitrary, certain knowing. Joe's revelation is structurally related to epistemological

crises in Byron and Hightower, and the dimensions of tragic
paradox are marked out by the figurative interaction of metaphors of mind. Though the stories of all three are interwoven
(and not chronological), it is important that Byron's revelation follows Joe's related crisis but precedes Joe's death;
we will see realized in Joe a tragic consciousness which Byron
approaches but relinquishes. And Hightower, entrenched in his
romantic escapism, is drawn slowly but forcefully toward the
book's penultimate chapter, one which illustrates the potency
of bearing witness to tragic action.

The significance of Byron's crisis grows out of our involvement with his characteristic way of knowing, and with the ascendant vulnerability of that knowing. Initially, Byron shows
himself to be different from all the other characters in that
his adulthood follows no history of childhood or adolescence,
but presents itself directly with this sentence: "Byron Bunch
knows this: It was one Friday morning three years ago" (p. 27).
Everything that follows the colon, a fifteen-page account of
Brown and Christmas at the planing mill, is seen as it registers
on the consciousness of Byron. The speaking voice reiterates
what "Byron thought," "seemed to Byron," or "Byron believed,"
and implicitly endorses the sensitivity and reliability of
Byron's observations about others; only Byron's silence about
himself implies some narrative reservation about the extent
of Byron's knowledge. Characteristically, Byron records impressions as appearances only, as things which "seem" or are "as
if" true. He describes, for example, how Brown tells anecdotes
to Christmas even though Christmas "did not even seem to hear
his voice. As if the other were a mile away, or spoke a different language from the one he knew" (p. 36). Byron emphasizes
what will later matter so much to the narrative voice, the
"unawares" quality of Brown's and Christmas's actions, their
habit of "not listening," and their tendency to emptiness and
diffusion.

In fact, the first act of the narrator who steps away from
what Byron "knows" is to acknowledge a limitation of his own
vision which we have not felt to be a limitation of Byron's.
The townspeople think that Byron works overtime for the pay,
and the narrator acknowledges the possibility: "Perhaps this
is the reason. Man knows so little about his fellows. In his
eyes all men or women act upon what he believes would motivate
him if he were mad enough to do what that other man or woman
is doing" (p. 43). This gnomic truth about how men perceive
others does not apply to Byron, who does not project his own
beliefs and motivations onto others. And the established
superiority of Byron's knowing, which he carries with him into
his first encounter with Lena, makes it a particularly power-

ful moment when the narrator announces that there is something
Byron does *not* know: "Her tone is quiet, but Byron is already
in love, though he does not yet know it" (p. 50). The moment
coincides with Byron's telling against his will the identity
of the scurrilous father of her child; and as he suffers the
profound embarrassment of the faux pas, a comic dimension to
his character emerges. This comic limitation of Byron's knowledge makes possible a sustained structural irony as Byron and
Hightower perceive each other's failure in self-awareness.
As Byron fumbles and gropes within his new vulnerability, and
as Hightower shrinks from involvement, their relations become
a kind of counterpoint between pity and fear, emotions which
can upset the equilibrium of identity because pity can become
as strong as empathy (threatening the "I-Am") and fear can
mount to terrible despair (threatening volition). Both of
Byron's roles, as perceiver and as perceived, are sustained
as he moves towards the crisis which will show his capacity
for tragic consciousness at its height; moments later, he will
slip permanently into his comic role and entirely relinquish
his status as a reliable perceiver.

Byron's epistemological crisis has never, to my knowledge,
been identified as such, and critical indifference to Byron's
complexity has missed the significance of the culmination of
his explicitly tragic and comic dimensions (Byron as perceiver
and Byron as perceived). Lena's wailing brings down upon Byron
the fact that he has not really believed in the reality of
Lena's pregnancy, and this self-knowledge is in his mind,
"galloping in yoked and headlong paradox," as he urgently
seeks a doctor. The vulnerability of his past knowing overcomes
him ("'If I had known then,' he thought, 'If I had known then.
If it had got through then'"), and he feels himself pursued
by something clawed with lurking. When he returns too late
with the doctor, the sound of the child's cry coincides with
a blow: "the clawed thing overtook him from behind" (p. 379).
The knowledge that Lena is not a virgin, that he will have to
get Lucas, and that he has been living in the hopefulness of
an illusion strikes him with "terrible" force. As with Joe's
related experience, Byron's crisis involves the recognition
of how total past error has been, how language and meaning
have been manipulated to fit identity: "*like me, and her, and
all the other folks that I had to get mixed up in it, were
just a lot of words that never even stood for anything, were
not even us, while all the time what was us was going on and
going on without even missing the lack of words*" (p. 380). A
richly suggestive symbolism accompanies the crisis, and the
paradoxical knowledge imaginatively revealed to Byron is explicitly named "tragic." After depositing Lucas in front of

Lena's door, Byron thinks to himself, "Now I can go," and he
begins to climb a hill which distances him from both Lena and
his former life. As he climbs, he conceives of the horizon as
"the edge of nothing" and envisions himself having ridden over
the edge into a nothingness where "trees would look like and
be called by something else except trees, and men would look
like and be called by something else except folks. And Byron
Bunch he wouldn't even have to be or not be Byron Bunch" (p.
401). He imagines the indifferent and "inescapable" horizons
saying, "*All right. You say you suffer. All right. But in the
first place, all we got is your naked word for it. And in the
second place, you just say that you are Byron Bunch. And in the
third place, you are just the one that calls yourself Byron
Bunch today, now, this minute*" (p. 402). Perched as he is
above the two ways of being he has known, not looking back,
Byron's symbolic vision places him momentarily both inside
and outside his own identity. Personifying the horizon as a
kind of fate which is neither portentous nor threatful but
merely oblivious, he can both experience his own suffering and
see it as from without. He can even imagine the ultimate paradox: that Byron Bunch is not Byron Bunch, but just a feeble
way of naming a present ("today, now, this minute"). Lena's
timelessness reduces all space and time to a present inseparable
from identity; here, Byron's being within timelessness manifests the insignificance of the present in relation to the
universal dimensions of an inescapable space-time which includes and yet surpasses personal identity.[6] Antithetical to
volition, this paradoxical knowledge sustains itself only
briefly, and Byron says to himself, "I might as well have the
pleasure of not being able to bear looking back too" (p. 402).
Like Orpheus, he loses much in turning around, for as he turns,
the transcendent vision leaves him and he discovers that he
has not realized how high he has climbed or what the vista
beneath him encompasses. He sees Lena's cabin at the center
of his vision, and at this moment, he loses the potential for
tragedy: "Then a cold, hard wind seems to blow through him.
It is at once violent and peaceful, blowing hard away like
chaff or trash or dead leaves all the desire and the despair
and the hopelessness and the tragic and vain imagining too"
(pp. 402-3).

The consequences of Byron's relinquishing his potential
for "tragic and vain imagining" are powerful and immediate.
Instead of thinking about his actions or perceiving himself
as he acts, he acts "before he is aware that his brain has
telegraphed his hand" (p. 403). Now, the narrator tells us
the things which Byron is *not* thinking, a list suggestive in
all its details of the things which Byron as the reliable per-

ceiver would have thought. We see Byron give himself over to
the present moment with abandon; he becomes a man who is going
to get "whipped" though he does not know it *yet*. After being
beaten by Brown, Byron lies bleeding quietly, much like Joe
and Hightower after related crises. But only for Byron does
the imagery of childhood describe a mental retreat from the
kind of paradox that threatens the "I-Am":

> his mind is filled with still shapes like discarded and
> fragmentary toys of childhood piled indiscriminate and
> gathering quiet dust in a forgotten closet--Brown. Lena
> Grove. Hightower. Byron Bunch--all like small objects
> which had never been alive, which he had played with in
> childhood and then broken and forgot. (p. 416)

The metaphor of childhood is sustained as Byron watches an
approaching train with "boylike absorption." He focuses on
Brown jumping on a passing car and the narrator comments:
"Still Byron is not thinking. 'Great God in the mountain,' he
says, with childlike and almost ecstatic astonishment; 'he
sho knows how to jump a train. He's sho done that before.'
He is not thinking at all" (p. 417). This childlike state, a
vivid contrast to his earlier "tragic and vain imagining,"
parallels Lena's non-thought processes in which mechanical detail takes precedence over the obvious significance of an event.
As the last car passes, the narrator sees Byron engulfed by a
world "too huge for distance and time": "It is as though he
has already and long since outstripped himself, already waiting at the cabin until he can catch up and enter" (p. 418).
Italicized thought processes affirm this new confinement of
the future in present time: "*And then I will stand there and
I will* ... He tries it again: *Then I will stand there and I
will* ... But he can get no further than that" (p. 418). Just
as Lena perceives time and distance in such a way as to pre-
clude future anxiety, so Byron now perceives only the physical
facts of his meeting with Lena: "*Even if I cant seem to get
any further than that: when I will open the door and come in
and stand there. And then I will. Look at her. Look at her.
Look at her--*" (p. 418). A stranger in a wagon, strongly
reminiscent of Lena's wagons, stops and tells Byron that there
has been excitement in the town. Byron is now the informed
rather than the informer, and the stranger's words incredibly
and powerfully juxtapose this newly limited, childlike Byron
with a dimension of his former self: "I thought maybe you
hadn't heard. About an hour ago. That nigger, Christmas. They
killed him" (p. 418). Byron's thoughts and feelings about the
most important and terrible event in the book are never known;
he has chosen to live in Lena's world and has lost his capacity

both for pity and fear and for the more extreme self-transcen-
dence of tragic paradox.

Byron, then, retreats from tragic paradox, and the terms
of his withdrawal explain much about Joe's attainment of tragic
consciousness. Joe, too, is seen from without after his crisis
in knowing, but for the reason that his new knowledge cannot
be shared. It can and does, however, produce strong responses
in others. The bulk of Chapter 19 concerns what the town or
Gavin Stevens surmises and how Percy Grimm tracks down Joe.
Importantly, Grimm reincarnates Joe's adult way of knowing
prior to the book's present time, its August. Reaching adulthood from a despairing adolescence, Grimm has the same need
for surrendering volition to what is clear and definite, the
same extreme fatalism, and the same commitment to avoiding
active knowing, "ever again having to think or decide." Un-
surprisingly, he moves amid the same imagery: the barren corridor, the weightlessness, the habit of not listening, "rocklike" or "prophetlike" attitudes, and that speed or motion
that is in fact only stasis (a violent futility reminiscent
of Baudelaire's "La Cloche fêlée," where the wounded man dies
"sans bouger, dans d'immenses efforts"). He hunts down Joe as
though playing in a play, with "lean, swift, blind obedience
to whatever Player moved him on the Board," and his defensive
habit of mind embraces the paradoxical compromise in which
adult experience is both present and past, lived in the present
but perceived like the movement of written language, "fullborn and already dead." The omnipresence of Grimm's mode of
knowing and being, parallel to that of McEachern and an earlier
Joe, makes all the more dramatic the moment of Joe's crucifixion; Grimm's terrible, castrating fury makes a henchman
vomit, while the "pure consciousness" in Joe's eyes registers
with transcendent force on those who watch:

> For a long moment he looked up at them with peaceful and
> unfathomable and unbearable eyes. Then his face, body,
> all, seemed to collapse, to fall in upon itself, and
> from out the slashed garments about his hips and loins
> the pent black blood seemed to rush like a released
> breath. It seemed to rush out of his pale body like the
> rush of sparks from a rising rocket; upon that black
> blast the man seemed to rise soaring into their memories
> forever and ever. They are not to lose it, in whatever
> peaceful valleys, beside whatever placid and reassuring
> streams of old age, in the mirroring faces of whatever
> children they will contemplate old disasters and newer
> hopes. It will be there, musing, quiet, steadfast, not
> fading and not particularly threatful, but of itself
> alone serene, of itself alone triumphant. (pp. 439-40)

The ascendance, the sublimity of Joe's death is captured in
language which inverts the terms of Joe's earlier, defensive
knowing. No wind rushes through him (as it did earlier, and
as it does when Byron and Hightower retreat from tragic paradox); we hear only the rush of his own blood. Instead of motion
which is stasis, we have the motion of a rocket moving upward
and beyond sight; or rather, we have a trope transformed into
the metaphoric truth embodied in that trope. First, Joe "seemed"
to rise, and then "seemed" changes to the "are" and "will be"
of lyrical prophecy. Joe, caught in the stillness of death,
actually soars into their memories "forever and ever," and this
memory is the only mental event in the book of unqualified
permanence; it will not fade, it is alone serene, it is alone
triumphant.

    As if to demonstrate the implications of such a prophecy,
Faulkner turns immediately to Hightower's quasi-apocalypse.
Hightower's potential for tragedy lies in the extent of his
failure to flee, in his vulnerability to the extremes of pity
and fear. His characteristic expression of shrinking and denial
indicates a latent awareness he cannot fully repress; he can
avoid contemplating first causes, but he cannot avoid a
mysterious sense of abyss, most powerfully embodied in the
sexual mystery. Like Joe, he has tried to buy immunity from
"half-delight and half-terror"; he wants to grow old "without
learning the despair of love." Hightower's ritualistic twilight moments--when he welcomes the phantoms that will release
him into the stopped time of his grandfather's galloping horse--
are part of his attempt to transform language beyond meaning,
and he counts on this imaginative transformation of old wounds
to protect him from receiving new ones. His sign, growing up
pathetically out of the "tragic and inescapable earth," no
longer functions as a message, and we find him repeatedly
associated with the dimness of artificial half-light, with
Tennyson (presumably with the austere aestheticism of "The
Palace of Art"), and above all, with those galloping words
which he intones without pretense of meaning, like "a eunuch
chanting in a language which he does not even need to not
understand" (p. 301).

    Joe's death compels Hightower to act and to think, and in
doing so to confront what he knows and has known. Hightower's
memory--now a strongly subversive faculty--revises its relation to prior phases of believing and knowing. Like that of
Joe and Joanna, Hightower's childhood is filled with phantoms
and fading shadows, and memory begins to reconstruct how these
phantoms became a part of what "that same child now thinks"
(p. 452). He sees that his adolescent desire for immunity has
colored "the very face and shape of love," and his memory

reconstructs how the sexual urgency of a desperate woman forced
him to change his notion of knowing (echoing Joe's response to
sexual mystery): "So this is love. I see. I was wrong about it
too" (p. 455). As has the young Joe, the young Hightower has
rejected further error by electing the quiet certainty of despair, telling himself, "That's the rule. I see now." Like the
grandfather who could "see no paradox in the fact that he took
an active part in a partisan war and on the very side whose
principles opposed his own," he has tried to protect the illusory world from the actual one, "lest paradoxical truth outrage itself" (p. 458). Now recognizing that he perceives only
what is of his mind's own making, Hightower sees how eternal
youth and virginal desire must make credible heroes whose deeds
nevertheless border on the unbelievable; he sees how he has
framed his own family legend around "And I believe. I know."
As he approaches nearer and nearer to acknowledging the full
extent to which he has armed himself against truth, he tries to
shove present awareness away from its dangerous connections to
the past: "That's past now. That's bought and paid for now." A
wheel of faces pulls him into acts of recognition until,
finally, he quails before the merged faces of Joe and Percy
Grimm. Yet thinking speeds on as though detached from the
will; he sees he has been hiding "from his own thinking," and
incants: "*I dont want to think this. I must not think this.
I dare not think this*" (p. 464). His mind hovers on the verge
of what Faulkner has already shown, that is, that mental events
are not past, present, or future, that he has shaped his own
knowledge to protect himself from acknowledging that he has
been executioner as well as martyr, torturer as well as victim. But the thundering phantoms arrive in time to turn back
the self-revelation which paradoxically undermines identity,
and like Byron, he ultimately avoids the tragic implications
of epistemological crisis.

Throughout *Light in August*, paradoxical relations among
processes of mind characterize the crises of all ages, so that
mental acts align themselves to protect identity, whether with
the perceptual self-centeredness of the child, the will toward
open-ended, partly true, partly false categories of adolescence, or the determined self-limitation of a despairing
adulthood. The lyrical narrative voice in *Light in August* may
assume omniscience, but other narrative voices follow the
speculations of what "most folks" know, or even concede narrative authority to a furniture dealer (limited by the context
of his bedroom) or a Gavin Stevens (limited by his deterministic view of Joe's victimization). Without these choric voices,
we would sense no demonstrable difference by which to gauge

how tragic knowing undermines any paradoxical knowing which
presumes its own ability to verify and justify the past. Like
other characters, those with the potential for tragedy may
seek immunity from new knowledge by denying meaning and communication, abusing language, adjusting belief and memory to
sustain present knowing, and avoiding pity, fear, and love.
But unlike others, they suffer an essentially epistemological
crisis which entails a threat to the fragile and paradoxical
compromise of adult identity. Joe imagines himself ready to
surrender with, "*I am tired ... of having to carry my life
like it was a basket of eggs*"; Byron looks over a vista where
"he wouldn't even have to be or not be Byron Bunch"; and Hightower sees a personal indictment in the merged faces of Joe
and Percy. Grimm. And all three move towards identification
with universal suffering: Joe cringes at the fears he provokes
in others, "afraid, of their brother afraid"; Byron hears the
inescapable horizons say to him, "*All right. You say you suffer. All right*"; and Hightower fails to resist the compassion
wrung from him for "poor man ... poor mankind." (There is a
kind of rhythmic incantation here of the emotive force behind
tragic action.)

All three characters have been shown progressing through
the paradoxes of mind that protect and sustain identity in
the child, the adolescent, and the adult. The crises which
make up the rites of passage from childhood to adolescence,
or from adolescence to adulthood, share epistemological vulnerability with the crisis that brings adult identity to the
point of tragic paradox; yet tragic paradox does not serve
to realign mental processes or move towards a compromise which
will sustain identity. This last crisis provokes "fast" thought
in which all the dualities fuse and merge, and the self feels
and knows at the same time the disjunction between present
and past knowing, between this space and all space, and between the self and others. Joe, Byron, and Hightower each move
toward the acknowledgment that in thinking of the past as
knowable, they have ignored how we reconstruct a past which
will preserve present identity.[7] They resist, of course, a
knowledge that threatens separateness, intuiting that total
empathy with others necessitates surrendering the will to
survive. Both Byron and Hightower purge themselves--as if by
a cold, hard wind--of the kind of paradoxical knowledge implied
by "tragic and vain imagining." Only Joe explicitly labels
his new feeling as a kind of knowledge and understands that
in reentering space and time, he commits himself to a still
vulnerable knowing, to the necessity for choice in a life that
is already chosen: "'I have been further in these seven days
than in all the thirty years,' he thinks. 'But I have never

got outside that circle. I have never broken out of the ring
of what I have already done and cannot ever undo'" (p. 321).
We see Joe working towards the inexpressible consciousness that
does not reduce time to the present time of individual identity,
but which acknowledges others by putting the self in a shared
present, their present. The experience of our shared separateness, a unifying experience, can happen only to someone who
suffers and yet sees his own suffering as though it were the
suffering of another. In previous transitions, sudden vulnerability was caused by the realization that what was assumed to
be "knowledge" was in fact only "belief" and based on delusive
memory. These earlier transitions show us processes of mind
groping towards some resolution which will sustain identity in
the form of a new epistemological compromise. But the movement
towards tragic consciousness embraces a form of paradox that is
fulfilled and self-sustaining, one that does not demand resolution.

In *Light in August* characters are brought closest to the
paradox of tragic understanding in moments of crisis when they
are forced to realize the fragility of the epistemological
compromise which has sustained their own sense of adult identity, when they acknowledge that they do not know what they
have always known and that they are connected to things they
have assumed separate. It is not right to describe these
moments as antirational, because the abandonment of knowledge
is in the direction of another kind of knowledge, still very
much of the mind. Its difference from previous knowledge has
less to do with the distinction between rationality and irra-
tionality than it does with levels of thinking and with the
active integration of mental processes. Indeed, such vision
involves a kind of hyper-rationality which is driven by its
own force despite willful resistance. Significantly, both
narrative method and the central metaphors of language, meaning, and imagining implicate the reader in the choric sensibility and suggest that the novel's treatment of tragic awareness is self-referential. Tragic imagining draws characters
out of identity and releases them from temporal and spatial
constraints, rather as the novel draws us out of identity
and into a fictional space-time. But like Byron and Hightower,
we have not experienced tragic knowledge, only the effects
of imagining tragedy. Because tragic understanding implies
unity, a sense of being merging the self and the other, it
therefore implies death. Because it is imagined--a second-
order experience of those who watch Joe die or we who read
the book--tragic knowing can only be expressed figuratively,
and the figurative idiom of all epistemological crisis in
Light in August is of course paradox. Only Joe, at the moment
of his death, achieves the fullness of paradoxical under-

standing that is tragic. At that moment, epistemological paradox does not involve balancing processes of mind in order to
piece together an identity based on difference. Rather, in a
state "empty of everything save consciousness," contradictory
intuitions about the nature of knowledge stand revealed in
the unity of a shared separateness, the certainty of uncertain
knowing, the choice that is necessary, and the timelessness
(within the mind) of events which happen in time.

NOTES

1. François Pitavy's *Faulkner's Light in August*, trans.
Gillian E. Cook (Bloomington: Indiana University Press, 1973),
provides a good survey of mythological approaches to *Light in
August* and reaches the convincing conclusion that any attempt
to attach the work to a particular body of myth necessarily
reduces the work as a whole. The central issue, of course, has
been the work's relation to Christian tradition, so much so
that one critic has drawn territorial boundaries between "intimidated secular critics" and those willing to come to terms
with Faulkner's theological interests (John Wesley Hunt,
William Faulkner: Art in Theological Tension [Syracuse: Syracuse University Press, 1965], p. 17). Although much of my
argument suggests broad correspondences with Faulkner's theology, my secular emphasis does imply a coherence that can be
appreciated within or without other frames of reference.

2. Cleanth Brooks, *William Faulkner: The Yoknapatawpha
Country* (New Haven: Yale University Press, 1963), p. 69. In
the tradition of Brooks, subsequent critics tend to emphasize
the lyrical exposition of Lena's fertility and her sense of
timelessness at the expense of considering the implications
of her childlike limitations and her capacity for self-deception. The eulogizing of Lena as the feminine ideal appears
in perhaps its most exaggerated form in Sally R. Page's
Faulkner's Women: Characterization and Meaning (Deland, Fla.:
Everett/Edwards, 1972), in which Lena comes to represent not
only the courage and endurance of women but also the "joyous
triumph of comedy." In fact, Ms. Page consistently alters the
evidence to fit her argument. Lena's interest is "focussed on
her unborn child" only when its movements surprise her; her
mind is as caught up in the taste of sardines and the pleasures
of travel, in present sensation of any kind. Nor does Lena
"allow" Lucas to escape because she intuits that Byron is more
"worthy" (p. 142); she simply adapts, and if she has any
contrastive sense of the two men, it must be that Byron is
the more manipulable. The levels of character portrayal here

suggest that Lena's ideality is a part of more complex relations between comedy and tragedy.

3. William Faulkner, *Light in August* (New York: Harrison Smith and Robert Haas, 1932), p. 6. All subsequent references are to this edition.

4. Importantly, the primacy of belief in earlier chapters yields to delusive knowing here, and the narrative progression demonstrates the implications of "Memory believes before knowing remembers." The distinction is between memory (unwilled belief about the past) and remembering (willed knowledge—or reconstruction—of the past), and bears relation both to the Freudian insight that neurosis necessarily implies some form of amnesia and to the memory theorist's skepticism about how memory may be justified. For an explication of such problems in memory theory, see Charles Landesman, "Philosophical Problems of Memory," *Journal of Philosophy*, 49 (1962), 57-65.

5. Ilse Dusoir Lind ("Apocalyptic Vision as Key to *Light in August*," *Studies in American Fiction*, 3 [1975], 133-41) offers a valuable study of the relation of Faulkner's myth-making to apocalyptic writing. Though she does not explicitly concern herself with either epistemology or tragedy, much of what she describes as syncretism has obvious relevance to my epistemological description of tragic consciousness.

6. For an interesting discussion of Faulkner's "timelessness," see Carolyn Porter's "The Problem of Time in *Light in August*," *Rice University Studies*, 61 (1975), 107-25. Although she does not always differentiate between perspectives on time, Ms. Porter explicates, in Bergsonian terms, the fictional coherence of the novel's time zones. Her apt observation that death is allied with form in the novel and life with formlessness suggests but one reason why tragic consciousness necessarily implies death.

7. Stanley Cavell's essays "Knowing and Acknowledging" and "The Avoidance of Love: A Reading of *King Lear*" (both in *Must We Mean What We Say?* [New York: Charles Scribner's Sons, 1969]) provide a particularly lucid account of the epistemological issues raised by tragic consciousness. He suggests that something in tragedy (acknowledging) goes beyond the kinds of certainty implied by knowing and believing, and examines many of the time-honored conventions of tragedy in the context of questions about how we possess knowledge of others and what it means to acknowledge another's pain. In rereading Cavell's essays after writing this one, I am struck by how many of his observations have direct relevance to my own argument about *Light in August*. As a particular example,

his assertion that the sadness within comedy is its own
limitation--some emptiness, some separateness--does much to
explain the inadequacy of seeing the character of Lena as a
triumphant affirmation. More generally, Cavell's argument shows
how tragedy arises from epistemological confusion, and even
suggests that its opposites are to be found in childlike
fears, adolescent separateness, and adult certainty that implies
a kind of willed amnesia (not, however, connected as "ages
of man" in Cavell as they are in Faulkner). Most generally,
his sense that the work of modern tragedy "is not to purge us
of pity and terror, but to make us capable of feeling them
again" supports my own intuition that Joe has so often been
described as a victim and so rarely as a character of tragic
stature partly because we habitually look for some recognizable
catharsis in works aspiring to tragedy. But here, catharsis
has been transformed: instead of finding himself through love,
Joe finds that there is no context in which to express his
love. Joe's revelation must remain figurative, and pity and
fear are aroused rather than purged--which is why the book
cannot end with his death. In Cavell's words, "Our tragic
fact is that we find ourselves at the cause of tragedy, but
without finding ourselves" (p. 349).

Appendix

THE CHRONOLOGY OF *LIGHT IN AUGUST*

Stephen Meats

William Faulkner gives the reader only two definite dates
of importance in *Light in August*. The first is 1865, the year
Gail Hightower's father returns from the Civil War.[1] The second is 1866, the year Joanna Burden's father, Nathaniel,
returns to his family after a sixteen-year absence (231). Two
dates--very meagre evidence. And yet from these two facts we
can construct with astonishing precision a very detailed
historical chronology involving events stretched over a period
of more than a hundred years.

Some of the most brilliant and compelling passages in the
novel deal with this historical material, for example, the
155-page flashback dealing with Joe Christmas's past (111-
265). Despite its inherent interest, however, the historical
material is of importance mostly as it bears upon the events
of the eleven days which constitute the present time of the
novel. For example, only with the assistance of the historical
material can we calculate the present time of the novel:
August 1932.[2] Also, the historical material supplies the
reader with a comprehensive knowledge of the personal and
family histories of the novel's seven main characters. Thus,
by filling in the past, Faulkner is attempting to equip the
reader to understand what motivates (or compels) these characters and so to understand better the outcome of the narrative
of events in the present time.

The chronology of events in the present time is even more
complex than the historical chronology, and as all readers
of the novel know, Faulkner presents it in a less than
straightforward fashion. Much can be gained in understanding
the sequence and relationships of events by straightening out
the present-time chronology. In doing this, one can also gain
a special appreciation of Faulkner's subtle and complex vision
and of the awesome power of the mind behind the art.

Following is a day-by-day, hour-by-hour chronology of
the present time of the novel. Exact times are provided for
those events which Faulkner himself places at specific times.

Other times are given by approximate hour when it can be determined, or by a more general designation such as morning, afternoon, or evening.

Friday: Early morning (just after midnight): Joe Brown/
                 Lucas Burch comes to the cabin drunk and Joe
                 Christmas beats him. Christmas goes for a walk
                 in his underwear, rips off his last button, and,
                 while naked, curses a white woman in a passing
                 car. He then goes to a stable to sleep--approxi-
                 mate time: 2:30-3:00 A.M. (95-101)
                 Dawn: Christmas wakes in the stable, returns to
                 the cabin, dresses, takes razor, soap, and a
                 magazine, and then leaves. (101-3)
                 Mid-morning: Christmas shaves at a spring, eats
                 breakfast, and begins to read his magazine.
                 (103-4)
                 Afternoon: Christmas destroys his buried contain-
                 ers of bootleg liquor. (105)
                 Late afternoon: Lena Grove catches a ride with
                 Armstid on her way to Jefferson in search of
                 Lucas Burch. Armstid invites her to eat and
                 spend the night at his farm. (9, 11-12)
                 7:00 P.M.: Christmas eats his evening meal in
                 Jefferson. (105)
                     At approximately this time, Lena Grove talks
                 to Mrs. Armstid in the kitchen and confesses
                 that her name is not yet Burch. (14-18)
                 9:00 P.M.: Christmas passes the barbershop to
                 give Brown/Burch a warning glance and then walks
                 out of town, passing through Freedman Town on
                 his way. (105-7)
                 10:00 P.M.: Christmas encounters a group of
                 Negroes on the road to the Burden house. (109-
                 10)
                 11:00-12:00 P.M.: Christmas sits by a gate out-
                 side Joanna Burden's house. (110)
                     At approximately this time, Mrs. Armstid
                 breaks open her rooster bank to get money to
                 give to Lena Grove. (18-19)

Saturday: Just after midnight: Christmas enters the Burden
                 house and confronts Joanna Burden in her bed-
                 room, and her pistol misfires. (265-67, 270)
                 Between midnight and 11:00 A.M.: Joanna Burden
                 dies or is murdered. (Since Faulkner does not

let us observe her death, we are left uncertain
of its time and circumstances.)
Time unspecified, but shortly after midnight:
Christmas flags down a car with Joanna Burden's
pistol in his hand. (267)
Dawn: *Brown/Burch's lie to the sheriff to obtain
the reward money:* Christmas goes to the Burden
house. Actual activity of Christmas and Brown/
Burch unknown. (88)
7:00 A.M.: *Brown/Burch's lie:* Christmas returns
to the cabin and says, "'I've done it.'" Actual
activity of Christmas and Brown/Burch unknown.
(88)
    At approximately this time, Armstid and Lena
Grove eat breakfast. (19-20)
8:00 A.M.: *Brown/Burch's lie:* Brown rises, cooks
breakfast, and sees the Burden house on fire.
Christmas and Brown/Burch's actual activity
unknown. (89)
    At approximately this time, Armstid takes
Lena Grove to Varner's store in Frenchman's
Bend so that she can catch a ride to Jefferson.
(20-21)
Mid-morning: Lena Grove catches a ride to Jefferson. (24)
    Someone (Brown/Burch?) sets fire to the Bur-
den house. (Speculation--see p. 89)
Just before 11:00 A.M.: Hamp Waller discovers the
fire, finds Brown/Burch in the house, and finds
Joanna Burden's body. (83-85, 89)
11:00 A.M.: Hamp Waller's wife reports the fire
by phone to the sheriff. (85, 89)
After 11:00 A.M.: A crowd begins to gather at
the fire. (271)
    The sheriff begins his investigation of the
apparent murder by questioning a Negro. (All
this action takes place over a period of three
hours.) (273-77)
Approximately 2:00 P.M.: The sheriff and the
crowd leave the fire. (277)
    Lena Grove arrives in Jefferson just as the
sheriff and the crowd reach town. (278)
Mid-afternoon: Lena Grove arrives at the planing
mill where she meets Byron Bunch. (45) He tells
her that Brown/Burch is in Jefferson. (45-51)
After 6:00 P.M.: Byron Bunch takes Lena Grove to
his boardinghouse. (76-77) He breaks his routine

Saturday (cont'd):

and does not leave for the country church. (79)
9:00 P.M.: Brown/Burch returns to Jefferson to
tell his story (lie), lured by the reward money.
(278) (On p. 86, Byron Bunch reports that Brown
arrived at 8:00 P.M. Because the 9:00 time is
in an omniscient passage, I will assume it to
be correct.)

Lena Grove, having eaten, waits for Mrs. Beard
to fix her a cot for the night. (80)

Sunday:

Dawn: The bloodhounds sent for by the sheriff
arrive on a train. (279-80)
Sunrise: Sheriff, posse, and dogs arrive at the
cabin on the Burden place and make a cast for
Christmas's trail. They are unsuccessful. (280)
Approximately 10:00 A.M.: All return to town.
(281)
Night: Youth whose car Christmas flagged down
with the pistol arrives in Jefferson with his
father to report the encounter. They too claim
the reward money. (281) Pursuers go immediately
to the place where Christmas got out of the car
and make another cast for his trail. They find
the pistol where he threw it, but are again unsuccessful in finding his trail. (281-82)

Byron Bunch visits Gail Hightower to tell him
about Lena Grove, Brown/Burch, Christmas, and
Joanna Burden. (70-94)

Monday:

Early morning: Sheriff, posse, and dogs return
to town. (282)

Tuesday:

Early morning: Christmas awakes in a haystack
and asks a farm woman what day it is. He then
runs, falls in a field, and sleeps. (314-15)
Mid-afternoon: Christmas awakes in the field
after sleeping more than six hours without
realizing he has been asleep. (315)
Night: Byron Bunch visits Hightower to tell him
that he is moving Lena Grove to the cabin on
the Burden place. (282-91)

Christmas invades a Negro church in the middle
of a service. (305)

Wednesday:

3:00 A.M.: A Negro from the church arrives in
Jefferson to tell the sheriff of Christmas's
intrusion. (304-7)

8:00 A.M.: Pursuers arrive at the church and the
dogs strike Christmas's trail. (308-9)

Just before 10:00 A.M.: Pursuers reach a Negro
cabin on a false trail. (310-11)

10:00 A.M.: Pursuers surround a cotton house and
find it deserted. (312)

Midday or after: Gail Hightower visits a grocery
and hears that the sheriff has struck a fresh
trail. (291-92)

First dark: Byron Bunch visits Hightower to tell
him that Lena Grove is in the cabin and he is
camping in a tent nearby. (294-300)

Thursday: Sometime during the day, possibly (it may have
been Wednesday), Christmas eats a meal at a
Negro cabin; he remembers the meal Friday
morning. On the night of the day he eats this
meal, he finds that he is attempting to calculate the day of the week. (316-17)

Friday: Dawn: Christmas sits by a spring; he remembers
a meal at a Negro cabin. He then shaves at the
spring. (316-18)

Before mid-morning: Christmas sits by a road,
sleeps, wakes, and asks several passersby the
name of the day. (318-19)

About noon: Christmas gets a ride on a wagon
going to Mottstown. (320-21)

Afternoon: Christmas arrives in Mottstown (either
after 1:00 or after 3:00 P.M.). (321)

Saturday: Morning: Christmas gets a shave, a haircut, and
some new clothes in Mottstown. (331)

Early afternoon: Christmas is captured on the
main street of Mottstown by Halliday. Doc Hines
attacks him, is subdued, and is taken home.
(325-26, 331-32)   (On p. 322 we are told that
Christmas was captured on Friday; all other
evidence, however, suggests that he was captured on Saturday; see especially pp. 330-31.)

Mid-afternoon: Doc Hines and Mrs. Hines arrive
downtown. Mrs. Hines tries to find the sheriff
to get permission to see Christmas. (332-35)

Before 4:00 P.M.: The sheriff arrives and takes
Christmas to Jefferson. (335-38)

4:00 P.M.: The Hineses attempt to rent a car to
to go to Jefferson. (338-39)

Saturday (cont'd):

Percy Grimm begins to organize his platoon. (428).

6:00 P.M.: The Hineses eat at a diner and later go to the depot to await the next train to Jefferson. (339-41)

Nightfall: Percy Grimm has his platoon recruited. (428, 430-31)

Night: Grimm's platoon plays poker and begins its patrols. (430-31)

Sunday:

2:00 A.M.: The Hineses leave Mottstown on the train to Jefferson. (341)

3:00 A.M.: The Hineses arrive in Jefferson. (421)

Time unspecified, but during the day: Byron Bunch visits Gail Hightower to tell him of Christmas's capture and of the arrival of Christmas's grandmother, Mrs. Hines. (342-45)

Evening: Byron Bunch visits Hightower with Doc and Mrs. Hines. They leave Hightower's very late. (348-70)

All through the day and night: Grimm's platoon continues its patrols and its poker game. (431-32)

Monday:

Dawn: Byron Bunch is awakened by Mrs. Hines and sent after a doctor for the birth of Lena Grove's baby. Byron wakes Hightower and sends him to help Lena while he goes on after the doctor. (371-73, 377)

Between dawn and sunrise: Lena Grove's child is born. Byron and the doctor arrive after Hightower has delivered the baby. Byron then slips away. (374-75, 381)

After sunrise: Gail Hightower walks home from the cabin, eats breakfast, and goes to sleep in a chair in his backyard--approximate time, 7:00-8:00 A.M. (381-83)

10:00 A.M.: Byron arranges with Lena to have Brown/Burch brought to the cabin. (390)

Between 10:00 A.M. and noon: The Grand Jury meets. (393)

Byron Bunch quits his job at the planing mill and makes arrangements to move out of his boardinghouse. (391, 395-98)

Between noon and 1:00 P.M.: Byron arranges with the sheriff to have a deputy take Brown/Burch to the cabin to see Lena Grove and the baby. (398-400)

Mrs. Hines falls asleep at the cabin; Doc
Hines sneaks out of the cabin and goes back to
town; Mrs. Hines wakes, discovers Doc is gone,
and follows him. (386-87)
Approximately 1:00-2:00 P.M.: Gail Hightower
wakes, walks back to the cabin to see Lena,
and they talk. (383-91)
Approximately 3:00 P.M.: Hightower leaves the
cabin to go to the planing mill. (391)
   Gavin Stevens probably visits Christmas in
his jail cell. (433) (Speculation based on the
sheriff's comment that Stevens had told him
Christmas would plead guilty and take a life
sentence; Stevens would most likely have formed
such an assumption and reported it to the sheriff
after visiting Christmas.)
4:00 P.M.: Gail Hightower arrives at the planing
mill. (391)
   Deputy arrives at the cabin with Brown/Burch.
Byron is hiding nearby. (400, 403-9)
Just after 4:00 P.M.: Byron leaves the cabin on
his mule, rides to the top of a hill, and
glances back just in time to see Brown/Burch
fleeing out the back window of the cabin. (401-
3)
   Gail Hightower leaves the planing mill for
home. (392)
   Mrs. Hines visits Christmas in his jail cell.
(421) (On p. 423 we are told that Mrs. Hines
got permission to see Christmas in his cell
after the sheriff "had just got back from din-
ner." The exact time of her visit during the
afternoon, therefore, is somewhat uncertain.)
Between 4:00 and 5:00 P.M.: Brown/Burch reaches
the railroad, then goes to a Negro cabin and
writes a note to the sheriff about the reward
money. (410-13)
   Gail Hightower arrives home. (392)
   Christmas makes his break as he crosses the
square in the custody of a deputy. Percy Grimm
and others pursue him. (433)
5:00 P.M.: Christmas is murdered by Percy Grimm
in Hightower's kitchen. (418, 439-40)
   Byron Bunch finds and fights Brown/Burch
near the railroad. (415)
Between 5:00 and 6:00 P.M.: Brown/Burch jumps a
ride on a passing train. (417)
   Byron Bunch starts back to town. (418)

Monday (cont'd):
> 6:00 P.M.: Byron Bunch meets a man on the road
> who tells him of Christmas's murder. (418)
> 9:00 P.M.: Gavin Stevens puts the Hineses on the
> train back to Mottstown. (420) Later in the
> evening, Stevens tells his version of the
> Christmas story to a visiting friend. (421-25)
>   Gail Hightower reflects on his past. (441-67)
> (This takes place at an unspecified time; his
> bandaged head (467), however, makes it seem
> likely that it is Monday evening.)

Three weeks after Christmas's death: Lena Grove and Byron
   Bunch travel to Tennessee with a furniture dealer. (468-
   80)

NOTES

   1. *Light in August* (New York: Harrison Smith and Robert
Haas, 1932), p. 443. Subsequent page references will be to the
first printing of the novel and will be in parentheses in the
text.

   2. When Nathaniel Burden returns to his family in 1866, we
are told that his son Calvin is twelve (233, 237). Later we
are told that Calvin "had just turned twenty when he was
killed" by Colonel Sartoris (235); the year is therefore 1874.
Joanna Burden was born fourteen years after Calvin was killed
(236); her birth year is 1888. Joanna Burden informs Joe
Christmas that she is forty-one at the time she tells him of
her family's history; the month is September (226-27); the
date is, then, September 1929. The night Joanna Burden tells
Christmas her family's history marks the beginning of the
second phase of their relationship (242), which lasts about
two years (247). At the end of these two years, again in
September (251), Joanna Burden tells Christmas that she wants
a child; the date is September 1931. "Just after Christmas"
she tells him that she is pregnant (251); the date is December 1931, or perhaps January 1932. In February (252) 1932,
Christmas finds a note from Joanna Burden signaling the beginning of the third phase of their affair (253). We later
find a reference to "the late twilight of May" in the narrative of her efforts to persuade Christmas to go to school
(263); May 1932. We are then told that the Friday night on
which Christmas sits outside the Burden house waiting to
enter (this is the first day of the present time of the novel)
is "that August night three months later" (264). The date of
the present time is, then, August 1932.

   A convenient cross-check of this date can be calculated
using 1865, the year in which Gail Hightower's father returns
from the Civil War. Twenty-five years later, Hightower discovers the Yankee coat his father wore home from the war (443);
the year is 1890. Gail Hightower is eight at the time (443);
his birth year, therefore, is 1882. In the present time of the
novel, Hightower is fifty years old (44, 345). His age, added
to 1882, also establishes the year of the present time as
1932.
   Although Faulkner does not directly tell us the year of
the present time, he leaves such a trail of definite clues
that it is obvious he wanted his readers to be able to figure
it out. The same cannot be said of the actual dates of the
eleven-day present-time period. In August 1932, the fifth,
the twelfth, and the nineteenth all fell on Friday. Any one
of those days could be the first day of the novel's present
time. So far as I have been able to discern, however, Faulkner
gives the reader no clue as to which Friday it might be. The
conclusion I reach on the basis of this is that although Faulkner wanted the reader to know the month and year of the present
time, he apparently had reasons for not wanting the reader
to know the exact dates. Determining the dates of the present
time, as tempting as it might appear, would therefore seem
to be beside the point. The question which emerges is not
what are the exact dates, but instead, what might Faulkner's
reasons have been for withholding this information? And further, what can the answer to this question contribute to our
understanding of the novel?

Bibliography

I

CHECKLISTS AND SURVEYS OF CRITICISM

American Literary Scholarship (Durham, N.C.: Duke University Press). The annual bibliographical essays on Faulkner have been by Richard P. Adams (1963-64), Robert A. Wiggins (1965-67), Olga W. Vickery (1968), Michael Millgate (1969-72), James B. Meriwether (1973), Karl F. Zender (1974-75), Panthea Reid Broughton (1976-78).

Bassett, John. *William Faulkner: An Annotated Checklist of Criticism*. New York: David Lewis, 1972. A fairly comprehensive listing of criticism, with sections on books, short stories and poetry, topical studies, and other materials (including American and British dissertations). The sections on individual novels list the contemporary reviews, the reviews of the British editions, and the critical articles. The annotations are occasionally inaccurate, and too brief to be of real use.

Bryer, Jackson R., ed. *Fifteen Modern American Authors*. Durham, N.C.: Duke University Press, 1969. Revised, enlarged edition: *Sixteen Modern American Authors*, 1974. The fine bibliographical essay on Faulkner (pp. 223-75), by James B. Meriwether, includes one brief but able page on *Light in August*.

Inge, M. Thomas. "William Faulkner's *Light in August*: An Annotated Checklist of Criticism." *Resources for American Literary Study*, 1 (Spring 1971), 30-57. Inge lists about 220 items, briefly annotated and ordered chronologically in three sections: contemporary American reviews (1932-34), books treating the novel in chapters or sections, and periodical articles (1935-71). Apart from reviews abroad, this is an exhaustive bibliography, particularly useful because it lists many contemporary reviews for the first time.

McHaney, Thomas L. *William Faulkner: A Reference Guide*. Boston: G.K. Hall, 1973. The most complete and accurate chronological listing of writings about Faulkner (including early reviews and foreign articles) from 1924 to 1973. The annotations are detailed and helpful, but not evaluative.

Mississippi Quarterly. "Faulkner: A Survey of Research and Criticism." Every year since 1978, the *Mississippi Quarterly* summer special issue on William Faulkner includes a bibliographical essay, modeled after Meriwether's essay in *Sixteen Modern American Authors*. The selection and evaluation committee is chaired by Thomas L. McHaney.

II

STUDY GUIDES AND
COLLECTIONS OF CRITICAL STUDIES

1. Study Guides

*None are of any interest: they are summaries
of the novel, with occasionally simplistic
or even inaccurate comments.*

Goethals, Thomas. *Light in August: A Critical Commentary.*
New York: American R.D.M. Corporation, 1965.

Juhasz, Leslie A. *William Faulkner's Light in August (A
Critical Commentary).* Monarch Notes and Study Guides.
New York: Monarch Press, 1965.

Roberts, James L. *Light in August Notes.* Lincoln, Neb.:
Cliff's Notes, 1964.

2. Collections of Critical Studies

Inge, M. Thomas, ed. *The Merrill Studies in Light in August.*
Columbus, Ohio: Charles E. Merrill Publishing Co., 1971.
In addition to Faulkner's own commentaries on his novel,
the chapter on Joe Christmas from the book by John B.
Cullen and Floyd C. Watkins, and five useful reviews
dating from 1932-33, the collection contains the follow-
ing articles (see below, Section III): R. Chase, "The
Stone and the Crucifixion"; D. Abel, "Frozen Movement
in *Light in August*"; C.H. Holman, "The Unity of Faulkner's
Light in August"; R.M. Slabey, "Myth and Ritual in *Light
in August*"; J.L. Kimmey, "The Good Earth in *Light in
August*"; J.L. Longley, Jr., "Joe Christmas: The Hero in
the Modern World"; B.R. McElderry, Jr., "The Narrative
Structure of *Light in August*."

Minter, David L., ed. *Twentieth Century Interpretations of
Light in August.* Englewood Cliffs, N.J.: Prentice-Hall,
1969. In its first part, the collection comprises the

D. Abel article, R. Chase's chapter on *Light in August*
from his book *The American Novel and Its Tradition*, and
the three chapters on *Light in August* from their respective books by O.W. Vickery, C. Brooks, and M. Millgate.
As is the habit in this series, the essays are generally
abridged. Part Two, "View Points," consists of brief ex-
tracts of articles and studies giving different opinions
about several problems and characters: the unity of the
work, Protestantism, sex and women, Joe Christmas, Lena
Grove and Byron Bunch, Hightower. B. McElderry's article
comes as an appendix. Minter's introduction is very
creditable, especially on the ambivalence of Christmas,
divided between the forces of death and those of life.

Vickery, John B., and Olga W. Vickery, eds. *Light in August
and the Critical Spectrum*. Belmont, Calif.: Wadsworth
Publishing Company, 1971. This volume offers a larger
selection of sections of books than the other collections.
Apart from Faulkner's own comments on *Light in August*
from *Faulkner in the University*, a one-page chronology,
questions for study and discussion, and a two-page selec-
tive bibliography, it contains the chapters on *Light in
August* from their respective books by J.B. Cullen and
F.C. Watkins, I. Howe, W.V. O'Connor, O.W. Vickery, H.H.
Waggoner, J.L. Longley, W.J. Slatoff, M. Millgate, P.
Swiggart, C. Brooks, R.P. Adams, W. Brylowski, and also
four articles by D. Abel, I.D. Lind ("The Calvinistic
Burden of *Light in August*"), A. Kazin, and C.H. Holman.

III

BOOKS, ARTICLES,
AND CHAPTERS IN BOOKS

The following bibliography lists most of the British,
American, and French criticism of *Light in August* to 1980.
It is on the whole both descriptive and evaluative, especially
for the more recent items. A rating system of asterisks (two,
one, or none) will also help the reader make his selection
for further reading. Doctoral dissertations and early reviews
are not listed (see above in Bassett, Inge, and McHaney). A
good selection of early American and British reviews (thirteen
on *Light in August*) is reprinted in John Bassett, ed., *William
Faulkner: The Critical Heritage* (London and Boston: Routledge
& Kegan Paul, 1975).

**Abel, Darrel. "Frozen Movement in *Light in August*." *Boston
University Studies in English*, 3 (Spring 1957), 32-44.
A still valuable reading of *Light in August* in the light
of Bergson's *The Creative Mind*, often and aptly quoted
by Abel. Faulkner, like Bergson, sees life as a duration
and reality as a flux. To give them literary form, he
suspends movement and makes use of symbols (the urn, the
hum of insects, endless travelling, cyclic images, etc.).
The story of Joe Christmas represents the tragedy of extraordinary life as seen against the comedy of ordinary
life and images of the static and eternal earth. Hightower's final vision is a moment of full enlightenment.

Adamowski, T.H. "Joe Christmas: The Tyranny of Childhood."
Novel, 4 (Spring 1971), 240-51. Christmas waged a lifelong struggle with men who had always appeared right and
infallible. In Mottstown, he finally seeks to break the
circle of his past life, giving up his struggle for identity and accepting the role of "nigger."

*Adams, Richard P. *Faulkner: Myth and Motion*. Princeton, N.J.:
Princeton University Press, 1968, pp. 84-95. Lena and Joe
have a meaning only if they are seen in contrast to each
other, and in the light of mythical and religious parallels

which broaden their significance. The tension between
movement and suspension is seen first through Joe and
Lena, then strangely, through Byron and the three main
characters, who each represent one aspect of human life.

Anderson, Dianne Luce. "Faulkner's Grimms: His Use of the
    Name Before *Light in August*." *Mississippi Quarterly*, 29
    (Summer 1976), 443.

Applewhite, Davis. "The South of *Light in August*." *Mississippi
    Quarterly*, 11 (Fall 1958), 167-72. A historian measures
    Faulkner's fictional world against the real North Missis-
    sippi hill country, deplores his negative view of religion,
    and questions the validity of his "racial views."

Asals, Frederick. "Faulkner's *Light in August*." *Explicator*,
    26 (May 1968), item 74. Draws another, somewhat far-
    fetched, parallel between Joe's affair with Joanna and
    the temptation of Christ. But stresses the ambivalence
    of the lovers: each is a potential savior and tempter for
    the other.

Backman, Melvin. *Faulkner: The Major Years: A Critical Study*.
    Bloomington: Indiana University Press, 1966, pp. 67-87.
    The emphasis is the reverse of that of Cleanth Brooks,
    stressing the isolation and alienation of the individual.
    But Lena's significance and the import of the first and
    last chapters in the novel are somewhat overlooked.

Baker, Carlos. "William Faulkner: The Doomed and the Damned."
    In *The Young Rebel in American Literature*, ed. Carl Bode.
    London: Heinemann, 1955, pp. 143-69. Hightower is doomed
    to save man, Christmas damned to die as an outcast.

Baldanza, Frank. "The Structure of *Light in August*." *Modern
    Fiction Studies*, 12 (Spring 1967), 67-78. A catalogue
    both extravagant (the author makes many unjustified
    analogies) and incomplete (it hardly goes beyond the
    factual level) of what he calls "theme clusters." Re-
    stricts himself to their aesthetic and musical value
    with no conclusion as to their ultimate meaning. Thinks
    that Faulkner's structural method is akin to the short-
    story anthology: his short, static scenes are linked
    thematically.

*Barth, J. Robert. "Faulkner and the Calvinist Tradition."
    Thought, 39 (Spring 1964), 100-20. Traces the development
    of the two elements of the Puritan tradition back to
    Calvin and Luther. Like Hawthorne and Melville, Faulkner
    stands within the orthodox Calvinist tradition. The con-
    cern with evil or corruption and with doom or the "curse"

is examined through his major novels (yet Faulkner is not interested in the relationship between man and God implied in the "curse," but in the human situation itself). Useful, though necessarily sketchy.

*Benson, Carl. "Thematic Design in *Light in August*." *South Atlantic Quarterly*, 53 (October 1954), 540-55. The design of the novel can best be understood as a thematic conflict between rigid self-involvement and alienation, and commitment to a solidarity that transcends the self. Thus Hightower "can serve as an ethic slide rule by means of which we can compute the relative failures and successes of other characters." In spite of some simplifications and misinterpretations, this old article is sensible and balanced.

Berland, Alwyn. "*Light in August*: The Calvinism of William Faulkner." *Modern Fiction Studies*, 8 (Summer 1962), 159-70. Faulkner paradoxically creates a Calvinist world in order to reject its doctrine while adhering to it as an attitude. Calvinism is condemned because of its intransigence, as seen in the thinking and obsessions of several characters, especially Christmas who ultimately refuses to believe in anything but his blackness, associated with sex, that is, original sin. Yet Calvinism endures in Faulkner, as shown particularly in his tortured style (?) and his treatment of time, suspended in the eternity of God's mind.

Bernberg, Raymond E. "*Light in August*: A Psychological View." *Mississippi Quarterly*, 11 (Fall 1958), 173-76. A psychologist's view of the novel: the characters are well motivated, but there is no significant social statement.

Bledsoe, Audrey. "Faulkner's Chiaroscuro: Comedy in *Light in August*." *Notes on Mississippi Writers*, 11 (Winter 1979), 55-63. An article at once debatable and hackneyed, ignoring the recent Faulkner criticism.

**Bleikasten, André. "L'espace dans *Lumière d'aôut*." *Bulletin de la Faculté des Lettres de Strasbourg*, 46 (December 1967), 406-20. Faulkner links space to consciousness, places to people: the road to Lena, the street to Christmas, the house to Joanna, the window to Hightower. Very good article.

Borden, Caroline. "Characterization in Faulkner's *Light in August*." *Literature and Ideology* (Montreal), 5 (1972), 41-50.

Bowden, Edwin T. *The Dungeon of the Heart: Human Isolation and·the American Novel.* New York: Macmillan, 1961, pp. 124-38. Man escapes from loneliness only by self-forgetfulness, sympathy, love. Mediocre analysis, much paraphrasing.

Brooks, Cleanth. "Notes on Faulkner's *Light in August.*" *Harvard Advocate*, 135 (November 1951), 10-11, 27. The major theme of the novel is isolation from the community.

————. "The Community and the Pariah." *Virginia Quarterly Review*, 39 (Spring 1963), 236-53. Enlarged and incorporated into *William Faulkner: The Yoknapatawpha Country.*

**————. *William Faulkner: The Yoknapatawpha Country.* New Haven and London: Yale University Press, 1963, pp. 47-74, 375-81. Studies the individual characters in relation to the community, which stands as the norm and gives the novel its unity. A very reliable analysis of the novel. The notes contain useful discussions of some specific points.

*————. Introduction to *Light in August.* New York: Modern Library College Editions, 1968. A fine general introduction to the novel.

————. "When Did Joanna Burden Die? A Note." *Southern Literary Journal*, 6 (Fall 1973), 43-46. Enlarged and incorporated into *William Faulkner: Toward Yoknapatawpha and Beyond.*

*————. *William Faulkner: Toward Yoknapatawpha and Beyond.* New Haven and London: Yale University Press, 1978, pp. 426-29. By a close reading of the text, Brooks comes to the likely conclusion that Joanna Burden is murdered on August 6, 1932, and that Joe's death occurs on August 15.

Brown, Calvin S. "Faulkner's Geography and Topography." *PMLA*, 77 (December 1962), 652-59. Provides knowledgeable evidence that the Jefferson of *Light in August* is based on Oxford, Mississippi.

————. "Faulkner's Manhunts: Fact into Fiction." *Georgia Review*, 20 (Winter 1966), 388-95. Games the young Faulkner directed for teen-agers in the woods around Oxford may have inspired his frequent use of the manhunt in his fiction.

Brown, William R. "Faulkner's Paradox in Pathology and Salvation: *Sanctuary, Light in August, Requiem for a Nun.*" *Texas Studies in Literature and Language*, 9 (Autumn 1967), 429-49. Makes a point for the "morality" of the novels by discussing the use of pathological murderers as a means to salvation for their societies.

Brylowski, Walter. *Faulkner's Olympian Laugh: Myth in the Novels*. Detroit: Wayne State University Press, 1968, pp. 102-17. *Light in August* is the successful juxtaposition of two opposed worlds, viewed in the light of mythological backgrounds. Faulkner's is a dual conception of the world. But Hightower is all but ignored.

*Burroughs, Franklin G., Jr. "God the Father and Motherless Children: *Light in August*." *Twentieth Century Literature*, 19 (July 1973), 189-202. Another attempt at establishing the unity of the novel, to be found in the tension between a stern, masculine religion, sanctifying work and discipline and mistrusting all manifestations of love and compassion (not the attitude of the Burden and Hightower ancestors, figures of heroic vitality), and feminine figures which, though they can be subversive Eves, represent the opposite self within the individual. Though not consistently realized with sufficient clarity, the argument is of interest and does not merely repeat other studies of the novel.

Cabau, Jacques. *La Prairie perdue: Histoire du roman américain*. Paris: Editions du Seuil, 1966, pp. 214-36. This chapter is little more than an introduction to Faulkner and *Light in August* for the general public. It is a series of trenchant comments, often more sonorous than profound, and in spite of some accurate points, it offers a simplified and superficial view of the novel and of its author.

Campbell, Harry Modean, and Ruel E. Foster. *William Faulkner: A Critical Appraisal*. Norman: University of Oklahoma Press, 1951, pp. 35-37, 68-74, 109-11. Some remarks on the imagery, the thematic unity, and the humor in the novel.

Campbell, Jeff H. "Polarity and Paradox: Faulkner's *Light in August*." *CEA Critic*, 34 (January 1972), 26-31. Hightower's position at the intersection of the two stories, and particularly his final "soliloquy" [sic], resolve the well-known polarity of the novel, in a paradoxical understanding and reconciliation of contraries. Little aware of the critical work on *Light in August*, Campbell sheds no new light on the novel.

*Chase, Richard. "The Stone and the Crucifixion: Faulkner's *Light in August*." *Kenyon Review*, 10 (Autumn 1948), 539-51. Movement and motionlessness, flight and pursuit, images of line and curve create a central pattern in the novel--"a poetry of physics." Though at times too abstract and confused, and distorting the characters (especially

Hightower) to make them fit theory, this well-known and
influential article has often been reprinted.

*————. *The American Novel and Its Tradition*. Garden City,
N.Y.: Doubleday/Anchor Books, 1957, pp. 210-19. Interesting chapter, despite several debatable points. Joe is not
a tragic hero, but a victim (naturalistic view of fatality).
Hightower is the most successfully drawn character in the
book.

Clark, William G. "Faulkner's *Light in August*." *Explicator*,
26 (March 1968), item 54. On Joe's attitude to white
prostitutes.

————. "William Faulkner's *Light in August*." *Explicator*, 28
(November 1969), item 19. On Joe's sleeping in an old
stable (a place associated with punishment) before killing
Joanna.

*Coindreau, Maurice Edgar. "Préface," *Lumière d'aôut*. Paris:
Gallimard, 1935, pp. VII-XV. Translated by George McMillan
Reeves in *The Time of William Faulkner: A French View of
American Fiction*. Columbia: University of South Carolina
Press, 1971. A remarkable and still valuable early essay,
which emphasizes Faulkner's puritanism in his view of
sex, and his masterly command of his medium.

Collins, R.G. "The Game of Names: Characterization Device in
'Light in August.'" *English Record*, 21 (October 1970),
82-87. Discussion of the thematic significance of all
the names in *Light in August*.

**————. "*Light in August*: Faulkner's Stained Glass Triptych."
Mosaic, 7 (Fall 1973), 97-157. This special issue of
Mosaic also appeared in book form, as *The Novels of
William Faulkner*, ed. R.G. Collins and Kenneth McRobbie
(Winnipeg, Canada: University of Manitoba, 1973). *Light
in August* offers three visions of life in the South: the
present South, uncertain of its identity, battling the
darkness in its own blood (Joe Christmas, Hines, Joanna,
embodying in fact community values); the failed, romantic
South of tradition, paralyzed by its inability to perceive its human obligation (Hightower); the simple acceptance of natural life and the future (Lena Grove, Byron
Bunch). The detailed study of the relationship of Joanna
and Hightower to the community is a pointed analysis of
the mind of the South.

Cottrell, Beekman W. "Christian Symbols in *Light in August*."
Modern Fiction Studies, 2 (Winter 1956), 207-13. Christian parallels are found in Joe's life, and in the names

of other characters. An instance of the perverse--to the
point of stupidity--Christomania of some critics.

Cullen, John B., in collaboration with Floyd C. Watkins. *Old
Times in the Faulkner Country*. Chapel Hill: University of
North Carolina Press, 1961. The reminiscences of an in-
habitant of Lafayette County, Mississippi, who knew Faulkner and hunted with him. Gives numerous possible local
sources--historical and geographical--for Faulkner's
works. Regards the locally well-known lynching of Nelse
Patton (who had slashed a white woman's throat) in 1908
as the source of the Christmas story ("Joe Christmas and
Nelse Patton," pp. 89-98).

D'Avanzio, Mario L. "Allusion in the Percy Grimm Episode of
Light in August." *Notes on Mississippi Writers*, 8 (Fall
1975),'63-68. Sees in Percy Grimm ("an ironic Percivale")
a possible reminiscence of Hotspur in *Henry IV* and of
E.A. Robinson's Miniver Cheevy. Conjectural, and unsup-
ported by Faulkner's text.

————. "Bobbie Allen and the Ballad Tradition in *Light in
August*." *South Carolina Review*, 8 (November 1975), 22-29.
Though it is likely that Faulkner used the name Bobbie
Allen ironically, D'Avanzo evinces a partial and poor
understanding of the novel by trying to force a character
into a definite pattern and to recognize literal (to the
point of being ridiculous) similarities.

————. "Doc Hines and Euphues in *Light in August*." *Notes on
Mississippi Writers*, 9 (Fall 1976), 101-6. Points to
similarities between Eupheus Hines and his namesake,
Euphues in Lyly's *Euphues: Or the Anatomy of Wit*, in which
Euphues castigates vice, lewdness, concupiscence, impiety--
the "bitchery and abomination" of womankind.

————. "Love's Labors: Byron Bunch and Shakespeare." *Notes
on Mississippi Writers*, 10 (Winter 1977), 80-86. Purports
to explore the relationship between *Love's Labor's Lost*
[sic] and *Light in August*, so as to show that the romantic
comedy of Bunch's love takes its spirit and tone from
Shakespeare; but mostly this is a description of possible
resemblances. Also some remarks on the opposition of
fertility and sterility, and Keats's "Ode to Autumn."
Little acquaintance with the Faulkner criticism.

Davies, Charles E. "William Faulkner's Joe Christmas: A Rage
for Order." *Arizona Quarterly*, 32 (Spring 1976), 61-73.

Donovan, Josephine. "Feminism and Aesthetics." *Critical Inquiry*,
3 (Spring 1977), 605-8. A feminist's view, and rejection,
of Faulkner's conception of women (one page on *Light in
August*).

Douglas, Harold J., and Robert Daniel. "Faulkner and the
    Puritanism of the South." *Tennessee Studies in Literature*,
    2 (1957), 1-13. "Faulkner's relation to Calvinism resembles
    that of Joe Christmas in *Light in August*, who detests his
    stern Presbyterian stepfather, yet prefers his harsh
    morality to Mrs. McEachern's softness and weakness." The
    (not new) idea is interesting, but apart from a discussion
    of the similarities between *The Scarlet Letter* and *As I
    Lay Dying*, the article remains unsystematic and super-
    ficial.

Dunn, Richard J. "Faulkner's *Light in August*, Chapter 5."
    Explicator, 25 (October 1966), item 11. Misdirected reli-
    gion and frustrated love in Joanna Burden bring Christmas
    to murder her.

Edmonds, Irene C. "Faulkner and the Black Shadow." In *Southern
    Renascence: The Literature of the Modern South*, ed. Louis
    D. Rubin, Jr., and Robert D. Jacobs. Baltimore: Johns
    Hopkins University Press, 1953, pp. 192-206. Christmas
    represents the tragic consequences of miscegenation in
    the South. Faulkner is ambivalent on the Negro problem.

*Fadiman, Regina K. *Faulkner's Light in August: A Description
    and Interpretation of the Revisions*. Charlottesville:
    University Press of Virginia, 1975. The first systematic
    study of Faulkner's manuscript of *Light in August* (a
    document difficult to interpret), from which Fadiman draws
    provocative--though tentative and at times utterly hypo-
    thetical--conclusions as to the genesis of the novel. The
    Christmas flashback (Chapters 6-12) appears to have been
    written after the present action, and to have been inserted
    during the composition of the Virginia manuscript.

Ficken, Carl. "The Opening Scene of William Faulkner's *Light
    in August*." *Proof*, 2 (1972), 175-84. Examines the manu-
    script, the typescript, and the salesman's dummy of the
    opening scene, and concludes that the latter is probably
    the first text.

Ford, Daniel G. "Comments on William Faulkner's Temporal
    Vision in *Sanctuary*, *The Sound and the Fury*, *Light in
    August*, *Absalom, Absalom!*" *Southern Quarterly*, 15 (April
    1977), 283-90. On Faulkner's Bergsonian conception of
    time as duration, and creation of a sense of eternity.
    Inconclusive, and too brief to be more than superficial.

Fowler, Doreen F. "Faith as a Unifying Principle in Faulkner's
    Light in August." *Tennessee Studies in Literature*, 21
    (1976), 49-57. After reviewing other attempts at identify-

ing an organizing theme, Fowler proposes to show that "unquestioning faith in some assertion acts as a major determining force." No wonder such a vague notion fails to be more than a simplistic catagolue of poorly understood scenes—in the light of none too recent criticism.

Frazier, David L. "Lucas Burch and the Polarity of *Light in August*." *Modern Language Notes*, 73 (June 1958), 417-19. Between positive and negative values, Lucas Burch represents meaninglessness. So does the article.

Gavin, Jerome. "*Light in August*: The Act of Involvement." *Harvard Advocate*, 135 (November 1951), 14-15, 34-37. On the theme of sexual adjustment: Christmas murders the religious fanatics who threaten it.

Geismar, Maxwell. *Writers in Crisis: The American Novel Between the Two Wars*. Boston: Houghton Mifflin, 1942, pp. 143-83. Faulkner is here concerned with the Negro and the Female, the twin furies of his Southern Waste Land.

Glicksberg, Charles I. "William Faulkner and the Negro Problem." *Phylon*, 10 (June 1949), 153-60.

Gold, Joseph. "The Two Worlds of *Light in August*." *Mississippi Quarterly*, 16 (Summer 1963), 160-67. Discussing characters in terms of their inhumanity (racial guilt, perverted religiosity, immersion in an unreal past), Gold contrasts Christmas, Hightower, and Grimm with Lena and Byron. The argument is not clearly realized, mostly paraphrastic, and mistaken on Hightower.

Goldman, Arnold. "Faulkner's Images of the Past: From *Sartoris* to *The Unvanquished*." *Yearbook of English Studies*, 8 (1978), 109-24. A survey.

Graham, Don, and Barbara Shaw. "Faulkner's Small Debt to Dos Passos: A Source for the Percy Grimm Episode." *Mississippi Quarterly*, 27 (Summer 1974), 327-31. Dos Passos's sketch "Wesley Everest" (later one of the biographies of *1919*), published in December 1931, is a source for Chapter 19 of Faulkner's novel: same general pattern of patriotism, flight, and castration, the Christ symbolism, even the name (in his correspondence with Cowley, Faulkner uses the name given to the character in Dos Passos's story, Warren Grimm). On the use of the name Grimm, see also Dianne Luce Anderson, "Faulkner's Grimms: His Use of the Name Before *Light in August*." *Mississippi Quarterly*, 29 (Summer 1976), 443.

Green, Martin. *Re-Appraisals: Some Commonsense Readings in American Literature.* New York: Norton, 1965, pp. 167-95. A negative criticism of Faulkner's style, with examples taken from *Light in August.*

Greenberg, Alvin. "Shaggy Dog in Mississippi." *Southern Folklore Quarterly,* 29 (September 1965), 284-87. Lena's story is a kind of "shaggy dog story," showing man's ability to transcend any difficulties.

Greer, Scott, "Joe Christmas and the 'Social Self.'" *Mississippi Quarterly,* 11 (Fall 1958), 160-66. This sociological analysis of the novel explores "the meaning of race identification" in a small Southern town. Christmas is no messiah, but a "marginal man," living in two worlds, yet identifying with neither, as society will not allow ambiguity. Hence his significance is universal.

Griffith, Benjamin W., III. "Calvinism in Faulkner's *Light in August.*" *Bulletin of the Center for the Study of Southern Culture and Religion,* 2 (Winter 1978), 8-10. Christmas is a representation of rigid, extreme Calvinism (a debatable critical commonplace).

Hays, Peter L. "More Light on *Light in August.*" *Papers on Language and Literature,* 11 (1975), 417-19.

Heimer, Jackson W. "Faulkner's Misogynous Novel: *Light in August.*" *Ball State University Forum,* 14 (1973), 11-15.

**Hirshleifer, Phyllis. "As Whirlwinds in the South: An Analysis of *Light in August.*" *Perspective,* 2 (Summer 1949), 225-38. To the reader of the later criticism, this article seems to have had a too often unacknowledged influence, recognizing as it does, aptly though sometimes sketchily, the interrelatedness of the various themes of the novel or the various levels at which the central theme of man's inhumanity can be studied. The article also includes creditable remarks on the imagery in the novel. For its relative inclusiveness, this early article seems more useful than some better-known later thematic studies.

Hoffman, Frederick J. *William Faulkner.* New York: Twayne Publishers, 1961, pp. 69-74. On evil in the novel.

**Holman, C. Hugh. "The Unity of Faulkner's *Light in August.*" *PMLA,* 73 (March 1958), 155-66. The best-argued article on the Christian symbolism in *Light in August,* which the author sees as the only element giving the novel its unity. Christmas's life parallels that of Christ, above all the "suffering servant" of Isaiah. Well-known, often reprinted.

*Howe, Irving. *William Faulkner: A Critical Study.* New York: Random House, 1952. Second edition, revised and expanded, New York: Vintage Books, 1962, pp. 61-70, 200-14. Third edition, revised and enlarged, Chicago: University of Chicago Press, 1975. The author criticizes the novel's lack of unity ("a triad of actions") and the disparity between the physical presence of Lena and Hightower and their symbolic function. Transcending all stereotypes in his treatment of race, Faulkner writes about the duality in man between social and private being.

Howell, Elmo. "Reverend Hightower and the Uses of Southern Adversity." *College English*, 24 (December 1962), 183-87. The adversities of Southern history shape Hightower's vision, which enables him to endure. Mostly paraphrase.

———. "A Note on Faulkner's Presbyterian Novel." *Papers on Language and Literature*, 2 (Spring 1966), 182-87.

Hunt, John W. *William Faulkner: Art in Theological Tension.* Syracuse, N.Y.: Syracuse University Press, 1965, pp. 13-16. On the Christ symbolism in the novel.

Inge, M. Thomas. "Faulknerian Light." *Notes on Mississippi Writers*, 5 (Spring 1972), 29. Faulkner interpreted "light" in *Light in August* as a quality of lambence during autumn in Mississippi.

Jacobs, Robert D. "Faulkner and the Tragedy of Isolation." *Hopkins Review*, 6 (Spring-Summer 1953), 162-83. Reprinted as "Faulkner's Tragedy of Isolation" in *Southern Renascence: The Literature of the Modern South*, ed. Louis D. Rubin, Jr., and Robert D. Jacobs. Baltimore: Johns Hopkins University Press, 1953, pp. 170-90. Quentin Compson, Joe Christmas, and Thomas Sutpen attempt, and fail, to master time, because they do not understand that man should "love and honor and pity and sacrifice."

———. "William Faulkner: The Passion and the Penance." In *South: Modern Southern Literature in Its Cultural Setting*, ed. Louis D. Rubin, Jr., and Robert D. Jacobs. Garden City, N.Y.: Doubleday, 1961, pp. 142-76 (on *Light in August*, pp. 157-63). In contrast to Richard Chase, sees Christmas as a tragic hero, not totally a victim of heredity and environment.

James, David L. "Hightower's Name: A Possible Source." *American Notes & Queries*, 13 (September 1974), 4-5. The name (from Psalms 18:2) suggests ironically man's failure to reach God.

James, Stuart. "Faulkner's Shadowed Land." *Denver Quarterly*,
     6 (Autumn 1971), 45-61.

*Jenkins, Lee Clinton. "Faulkner, the Mythic Mind, and the
     Blacks." *Literature and Psychology*, 27 (1977), 74-91.
     All actions are an inheritance of the group consciousness
     in which each individual participates. To Christmas, being
     is the highest value in life, but he cannot conceive of
     himself without reference to imposed racial constructs
     of identity. Lena Grove is secure in her being without
     reference to artificial classification.

Johnson, Robert L. "William Faulkner, Calvinism, and the
     Presbyterians." *Journal of Presbyterian History*, 57
     (Spring 1979), 66-81. On Faulkner's experiences with
     Presbyterians, and Calvinism in *Light in August*. Faulk-
     ner's "art will elude all doctrinal categories."

Johnston, Walter E. "The Shepherdess in the City." *Compara-
     tive Literature*, 26 (1974), 124-41. The use of the
     pastoral in modern literature involves a fascination with
     the Romantic faith in the individual and with the ideals
     of simplicity and natural wisdom, and the need for pre-
     Christian models to bring order to modern experience.
     But, as in Virgil's first *Eclogue*, the isolation and
     limitation of the pastoral world are never forgotten,
     and the pastoral mode is ironical: such innocence is
     lost and it is folly to try to regain it. The examples,
     often quotations and paraphrase, do not measure up to
     the argument: Lena Grove, Tonka in Robert Musil, Words-
     worth in *The Prelude*, and Molly Bloom in *Ulysses*.

Kaplan, Harold D. "The Inert and the Violent: Faulkner's
     Light in August." In *The Passive Voice: An Approach to
     Modern Fiction*. Athens: Ohio University Press, 1966,
     pp. 111-30.

**Kartiganer, Donald M. *The Fragile Thread: The Meaning of
     Form in Faulkner's Novels*. Amherst: University of Massa-
     chusetts Press, 1979, Chapter 3: "*Light in August*," pp.
     37-68. At once challenging in its premises and somewhat
     disappointing in its demonstration, this approach to
     Light in August should not be dismissed as a rehash of
     the old 1950 criticism (the comments on Kartiganer's
     book in "Faulkner 1979: A Survey of Research and Criti-
     cism," *Mississippi Quarterly*, Summer 1980, are a mis-
     understanding of the book's ambition). To Kartiganer,
     Light in August is about dualism and fragmentation, and
     the incapacity of language to tell them in fictional terms:
     hence it is the inscription of the failure of the novel

to be equal to the story of Christmas who, instead of a single identity, chooses doubleness. Indeed, Christmas insists on living the whole of his identity, that is, order *and* disorder, whiteness and blackness, Apollonian impulse toward design and Dionysian fascination with chaos, but he eventually obtains "triumph" beyond death: thus he is meaning in process. But the novel achieves order only through the writer's manipulations, instead of creating its own order reflected in the consciousness of the characters. This is where Kartiganer's demonstration becomes thesis-ridden. A character such as Lena finds no place in this (non)pattern, and it is only through spurious rhetoric that one can say that Christmas's choosing disorder and order at once makes him an unrealized character in fiction (and in his mind, order and disorder are *not* neatly balanced). In this respect, the matter of narrative voice has not been sufficiently probed: the central part of the novel is not Christmas's narrative; and the anonymous narrator is not omniscient and hence leaves room for ambiguities (which are not recognized). In spite of this, the section on Christmas provides a new and stimulating insight into the significance of *Light in August*.

**Kazin, Alfred. "The Stillness of *Light in August*." *Partisan Review*, 24 (Autumn 1957), 519-38. Frequently quoted article. It underlines the opposition between Lena (country, life) and Christmas (town, rejection of life). Joe's alienation, symbolic of the condition of rootless modern man, is expressed by the distance at which the character seems to appear. This contrast between the acceptance of earth and rootlessness is characteristic of the best American writing.

Kerr, Elizabeth M. *Yoknapatawpha: Faulkner's "Little Postage Stamp of Native Soil."* New York: Fordham University Press, 1969. Superimposes fictional Yoknapatawpha County on actual Lafayette County in Mississippi; numerous references to *Light in August*. Too dogmatic.

————. *William Faulkner's Gothic Domain*. Port Washington, N.Y., and London: Kennikat Press, 1979, Chapter 6: "*Light in August*: Diana in Dixie, or, The Way of the Cross," pp. 107-36. Kerr examines the novel through Gothic glasses systematically, listing and examining places, characters, themes, either as Gothic elements or as their ironic inversions or parodies; but the reasons for the straight or inverted uses of Gothicism are not accounted for. To Kerr's narrow view, everything is or should be Gothic. This study, which repeats most of the commonplaces (and some of the errors) of the criticism of the novel, which

still considers the tracking of Christ symbols as the
epitome of criticism, and which shows little understanding of what narrative technique and writing mean, comes
twenty years too late. A thorough knowledge of the
Faulkner canon is wasted for lack of critical acumen.

*Kimmey, John L. "The Good Earth in *Light in August.*" *Mississippi Quarterly*, 17 (Winter 1963-1964), 1-8. Methodical
analysis of each character in relation to nature, the
immemorial earth. No definite conclusions drawn.

Kinney, Arthur F. *Faulkner's Narrative Poetics: Style as
Vision.* Amherst: University of Massachusetts Press, 1978,
pp. 15-30, 113-18. Proposes an "explication" of the beginning of Chapter 2 of *Light in August* ("Byron Bunch
knows this") as an introduction to a study of Faulkner's
poetics of vision, which does not rely on a single narrative consciousness but makes the reader into the presid-
ing, "constitutive" consciousness. Attempts a similar
demonstration with the beginning of Chapter 6 ("Memory
believes before knowing remembers").

Kirk, Robert W. "Faulkner's Lena Grove." *Georgia Review*, 21
(Spring 1967), 57-64. Paraphrase.

Kobler, J.F. "Lena Grove: Faulkner's 'Still Unravish'd Bride
of Quietness.'" *Arizona Quarterly*, 28 (Winter 1972), 339-
54. Keats's poem and Faulkner's novel develop multiple
levels of time and share a basic structure. Kobler tries
to recognize parallelisms between the two as if Faulkner
had patterned his novel after Keats's ode.

*Korenman, Joan S. "Faulkner's Grecian Urn." *Southern Literary
Journal*, 7 (Fall 1974), 3-23. This fairly comprehensive
article somehow tends to become a catalogue of Keatsian
images in Faulkner, from his review of Hergesheimer's
Linda Condon to *Go Down, Moses*. But the author is aware
of Faulkner's ambivalent attitude toward those of his
characters who try to defy time and thus turn to the
past and images of eternity.

Kunkel, Francis L. "Christ Symbolism in Faulkner: Prevalence
of the Human." *Renascence*, 27 (Spring 1965), 148-56.
Christmas is an inverted Christ figure, and the Corporal
in *A Fable* is a secular Christ.

Lamont, William H.F. "The Chronology of *Light in August.*"
Modern Fiction Studies, 3 (Winter 1957-58), 360-61.
Just a note on the age of Christmas, who dies at 36,
not 33.

*Langston, Albert Douglas Beach. "The Meaning of Lena Grove
and Gail Hightower in *Light in August*." *Boston University
Studies in English*, 5 (Spring 1961), 46-63. Lena is Diana
of the Grove at Nemi and also the Virgin, and Hightower
is the Buddha, or a Bodhisattva (see the use of the word
"avatar"). Though his view of Hightower is stimulating,
Langston errs on some points; and Faulkner's mythical
method (his use of Christian myths, *The Golden Bough*, etc.)
is far less systematic and rigid than Langston would have
it.

Levith, Murray J. "Unity in Faulkner's *Light in August*." *Thot*,
7 (Winter 1966), 31-34. The unity of the novel is thematic.
Useless article.

**Lind, Ilse Dusoir. "The Calvinistic Burden of *Light in August*."
New England Quarterly, 30 (September 1957), 307-29. Good
study of Joanna and Joe, victims of a Calvinist tradition
and education. Well-known article, already reprinted.

————. "Apocalyptic Vision as Key to *Light in August*." *Studies
in American Fiction*, 3 (Autumn 1975), 133-41. From the
premise that Faulkner's approach to myth is consciously
syncretist in imitation of the syncretism of apocalyptic
writing, Lind reviews the various religious schemes of
reference in the novel, but brings no new key to its
understanding. And it is hazardous to surmise that Faulkner's expecting his first child and also his experiencing
guilt over the tragedy of racism when writing the novel
provided the prodding and brooding that produced the
revelations which this work embodies.

*————. "Faulkner's Uses of Poetic Drama." In *Faulkner,
Modernism, and Film: Faulkner and Yoknapatawpha, 1978*,
ed. Evans Harrington and Ann J. Abadie. Jackson: University Press of Mississippi, 1979, pp. 66-81. After discussing Faulkner's interest and experiments in poetic
and expressionistic drama, Lind tries to show that he
did not abandon symbolism and nonrealism in his fiction,
with the example of *Light in August*, compared with O'Neill's
All God's Chillun Got Wings (black and white symbolism,
distortion, pervasive sense of unreality). Stimulating,
but the argument could be further developed.

Linn, James Weber, and Houghton Wells Taylor. "Counterpoint:
Light in August." In *A Foreword to Fiction*. New York:
Appleton-Century-Crofts, 1935, pp. 144-57. By constantly
shifting the point of view, Faulkner moves the reader
around the central objects of *Light in August*. Probably
the first discussion of the novel to speak of counterpoint in relation to its structure.

Longley, John Lewis, Jr. "Joe Christmas: The Hero in the
    Modern World." *Virginia Quarterly Review*, 33 (Spring 1957),
    233-49. Incorporated into *The Tragic Mask*.

————. "Faulkner's Byron Bunch." *Georgia Review*, 15 (Summer
    1961), 197-208. Incorporated into *The Tragic Mask*.

————. *The Tragic Mask: A Study of Faulkner's Heroes*. Chapel
    Hill: University of North Carolina Press, 1963, pp. 50-62,
    192-205. Byron Bunch is caught between virtuous inactivity
    and the risk of corruption through involvement with Lena.
    Joe Christmas is a tragic hero in the classical and the
    modern senses. "He is the modern Everyman." Too much
    summary of the story and not enough critical discussion.

Loughrey, Thomas F. "*Light in August*: Religion and the Agape
    of Nature." *Four Quarters*, 12 (May 1963), 14-25.

McCamy, Edward. "Byron Bunch." *Shenandoah*, 3 (Spring 1952),
    8-12. Byron Bunch is at the center of the novel, moving
    from Hightower, tyrannized by the past, to Lena's world
    of hope and optimism.

McDonald, Walter R. "Coincidence in the Novel: A Necessary
    Technique." *College English*, 29 (February 1968), 373-82.

McElderry, B.R., Jr. "The Narrative Structure of *Light in
    August*." *College English*, 19 (February 1958), 200-207.
    In spite of the title, little more than a summary of the
    novel.

Malin, Irving. *William Faulkner: An Interpretation*. Stanford:
    Stanford University Press, 1957, pp. 53-64. On opposition
    as a structural device.

Meats, Stephen E. "Who Killed Joanna Burden?" *Mississippi
    Quarterly*, 24 (Summer 1971), 271-77. As "there is no posi-
    tive evidence in the novel to indicate who actually commits
    the murder," Meats suggests that, as a revenge of a sort
    against Christmas, Brown might have slashed the throat of
    Joanna, knocked out by Christmas after she had threatened
    him with a pistol. This ingenious theory, based on Christ-
    mas's apparent right-handedness, is just a tenuous surmise,
    however, running counter to the gist of the novel.

*————. "The Chronology of *Light in August*." In *The Novels of
    William Faulkner: Light in August*, ed. François Pitavy.
    New York: Garland Publishing, Inc., 1982, pp. 227-35. An
    original article for this collection. Keeping strictly to
    the evidence of the text, Meats handsomely rounds off
    Brooks's note in *Toward Yoknapatawpha and Beyond*, and
    provides the best chronology to date of events in the
    present time of the novel.

**Millgate, Michael. *The Achievement of William Faulkner*. New York: Random House, 1966. The chapter on *Light in August* (pp. 124-37) is a stimulating study of the thematic and ironical relationships between the three centers of interest and of the mythical connotations surrounding the characters.

Milum, Richard A. "Cavaliers, Calvinists, and the Wheel of Fortune: The Gambling Instinct in Faulkner's Fiction." *Notes on Mississippi Writers*, 11 (Spring 1978), 3-14 (on *Light in August*, pp. 11-13). The Cavalier tradition of gambling is a corruption of the chivalric concept of valor. Hence it is a useful device for portrayal of character and the resolution of conflict. In *Light in August*, gambling is "a last desperate cast in a game already lost" (the Joe-Joanna confrontation). Mostly descriptive, no conclusion.

Miner, Ward L. *The World of William Faulkner*. Durham, N.C.: Duke University Press, 1952, pp. 141-44. On institutional religion as a destructive force.

Minter, David. *William Faulkner: His Life and Work*. Baltimore and London: Johns Hopkins University Press, 1980, pp. 129-32. This intelligent literary biography evinces a thorough knowledge of the Faulkner canon, but brings no new insight into *Light in August* specifically. Minter seems to think that Faulkner began with the idea of Hightower--which is questionable and inconsistent with Faulkner's own assertions and, it seems, with his manuscript.

**Morrison, Sister Kristin. "Faulkner's Joe Christmas: Character Through Voice." *Texas Studies in Literature and Language*, 11 (Winter 1961), 419-43. Though some concepts need to be updated, owing to recent research on voice in fiction, the opening pages of this article, on the notion of voice which should replace that of point of view, inoperative here, are still valid. The bulk of the article, on voice structure in *Light in August* and on the different levels of voice creating the character of Joe Christmas, remains one of the most pertinent studies of the novel.

Moseley, Edwin M. *Pseudonyms of Christ in the Modern Novel: Motifs and Methods*. Pittsburgh: University of Pittsburgh Press, 1962, pp. 135-51. Study of the characters in the light of Christian symbolism. Sees Joe as more of an image of Christ than a parody.

Mulqueen, James E. "*Light in August*: Motion, Eros, and Death." *Notes on Mississippi Writers*, 8 (Winter 1975), 91-98.

Uses Freud superficially and mechanically to show that
Light in August is an inconclusive struggle between Eros
and Death: in the pattern of the novel and in the lives
of the characters.

*Nash, H.C. "Faulkner's 'Furniture Repairer and Dealer': Knit-
ting up *Light in August*." *Modern Fiction Studies*, 16
(Winter 1970-71), 529-31. The furniture dealer and his wife
bring warmth and "sentiment" into the novel, and help
restore natural continuity. They give the Lena-Byron couple
its full significance. Brief but useful comments.

Nemerov, Howard. "Calculation Raised to Mystery: The Dialectics
of *Light in August*." In *Poetry and Fiction: Essays*. New
Brunswick, N.J.: Rutgers University Press, 1963, pp. 246-
59. *Light in August* is built on the related black-white,
male-female polarities. Christmas and Hightower are opposites.

*Neufeldt, Leonard. "Time and Man's Possibilities in *Light in
August*." *Georgia Review*, 25 (Spring 1971), 27-40. Except
for Lena, who lives in a duration "constant with the
temporal rhythm of her environment," all the characters
"betray a pathological awareness of time": Byron has become a human watch until he partakes of Lena's rhythm,
Hightower is caught up in his past until he returns to life,
Joanna is haunted by her past, from which she tries to
escape through Joe, and Christmas is "destroyed by time
because he expends his time struggling against it." The
article also sketchily underlines some resemblances between Joe and Lena.

Nilon, Charles H. *Faulkner and the Negro*. Boulder: University
of Colorado Press, 1962. Reprinted, New York: Citadel
Press, 1965 (on *Light in August*, pp. 73-93). Unfortunately
of little interest. Paraphrase. Reiterates that "the South
must assume moral responsibility toward the Negro."

O'Connor, William Van. "Protestantism in Yoknapatawpha County."
Hopkins Review, 5 (Spring 1952), 26-42. Reprinted in
Southern Renascence: The Literature of the Modern South,
ed. Louis D. Rubin, Jr., and Robert D. Jacobs. Baltimore:
Johns Hopkins University Press, 1953, pp. 153-69. Revised
for *The Tangled Fire of William Faulkner*. Minneapolis:
University of Minnesota Press, 1954, pp. 72-87. Sees
Protestantism as the central issue of *Light in August*.
A few, too brief remarks on the ambivalent view of re-
ligion as both destructive (the church is one of the
agents of Christmas's destruction) and humane (Byron Bunch).
But mostly a paraphrase of the novel.

O'Faolain, Sean. *The Vanishing Hero: Studies in the Novelists of the Twenties*. London: Eyre & Spottiswoode, 1956, pp. 99-134. A negative criticism of Faulkner's style and technique (especially the confused symbolism in *Light in August*).

Palmer, William S. "Abelard's Fate: Sexual Politics in Stendhal, Faulkner, and Camus." *Mosaic*, 7 (Spring 1974), 29-41. The image of castration represents the theme of society's repression of the vitality of the nonconforming individual, as studied in *The Red and the Black*, *Light in August*, and *The Stranger*. Like Julien Sorel, Christmas reacts to the impotency of his schizophrenic frustration with violent aggression against society by means of symbolic phallic extensions (pistol, knife). Though not without use, this study does not really bring the comparison beyond a juxta-position of similarities.

Palumbo, Donald. "The Concept of God in *Light in August*, *The Sound and the Fury*, *As I Lay Dying*, and *Absalom, Absalom!*" *Southern Central Bulletin*, 34 (Winter 1979), 142-46. "A God reveals himself for those characters who believe He will ... while remaining fictitious, absent for most of those who do not."

*Pearce, Richard. "Faulkner's One Ring Circus." *Wisconsin Studies in Contemporary Literature*, 7 (Fall 1966), 270-83. Disputable but stimulating article. Sees *Light in August* as an essentially comic novel with characters like those in a comic strip: tragic characters become grotesque as they struggle with forces beyond their comprehension (image of the chessboard).

*Pearson, Norman Holmes. "Lena Grove." *Shenandoah*, 3 (Spring 1952), 3-7. Lena Grove is the focal point in this novel-- Faulkner's homage to Keats. A good, early study of Keatsian imagery in *Light in August*.

Peckham, Morse. "The Place of Sex in the Work of William Faulkner." *Studies in the Twentieth Century*, 14 (Fall 1974), 1-20. Lena is seen as a character with an "implac-able and ruthless sexual will"--which is a misreading of the text. This study of the tension between idealism and biology is too cursory to be of interest.

*Pitavy, François. "The Landscape in *Light in August*." *Missis-sippi Quarterly*, 23 (Summer 1970), 265-72. The landscape in the novel is always seen through the eyes of the characters or informed by their consciousness. Defined in terms of light and shadow, stillness and movement

(furious immobility), it is a state of mind. (This is a
chapter of Pitavy's book-length study of *Light in August*.)

**——. *William Faulkner: Light in August*. In André Bleikasten,
François Pitavy, Michel Gresset, *William Faulkner: As I
Lay Dying, Light in August*. Paris: Armand Colin, 1970.
Revised and enlarged as *Faulkner's Light in August*. Bloomington and London: Indiana University Press, 1973. A comprehensive study of the novel and of its genesis and history,
with chapters devoted to composition, structure and technique, characters, landscape, themes, style, reception
and interpretations.

Pommer, Henry F. "*Light in August*: A Letter by Faulkner."
English Language Notes, 4 (September 1966), 47-48. Concerns
Faulkner's sentence in the novel ending "He once cursed
Him" (p. 240, 1. 8). The "Him" should be "him," as the
manuscript and the typescript show. In a letter to the
author, Faulkner accepts Pommer's suggestion that it could
be "Ham" (the mythical ancestor of Negroes).

Poresky, Louise A. "Joe Christmas: His Tragedy as Victim."
Hartford Studies in Literature, 8 (1976), 209-22. Because
of a violent, death-oriented religion, Christmas is vic-
timized by his past and in turn becomes victimizer.

Porter, Carolyn. "The Problem of Time in *Light in August*."
Rice University Studies, 61 (1975), 107-25. Lena, Christmas,
and Hightower are studied in terms of the tension between
duration and the need for a structure ordering it. The
tension persists unresolved because the world keeps on
moving. The long, somewhat undigested summary of some of
Bergson's ideas in *The Creative Mind* fails to throw the
promised light in this not clearly realized study. Though
much older, Darrel Abel's article, also making use of
Bergson, is much more useful.

Powers, Lyall H. *Faulkner's Yoknapatawpha Comedy*. Ann Arbor:
University of Michigan Press, 1980, Chapter 5: "*Light in
August*," pp. 89-105. This study of thirteen Yoknapatawpha
novels proposes to show that Faulkner is consistently the
optimistic author asserted in Stockholm and that his coherent "saga" is characterized by comic resolution. To
achieve this, Powers applies three criteria ("dominant
themes"): the self-destructiveness of evil, the second
chance (opportunity given to the characters to try again
and succeed), and the saving remnant ("those in whom our
hope may safely reside"). No wonder such vague and somewhat arbitrary criteria fail to produce more than another
rehash of a character study. In *Light in August*, Christmas

is self-destructive, Lena offers a second chance, and
Byron Bunch is the saving remnant. This summary of each
character's story brings no new light on the novel, and
the formula fails to recognize the ambiguities which the
narrator is very careful to leave unresolved. And the case
for the comic, or the ironical, mode is not precisely new.

*Reed, Joseph W., Jr. *Faulkner's Narrative*. New Haven and London:
    Yale University Press, 1973, Chapter 6: "*Light in August*,"
    pp. 112-44. *Light in August* is a character-dominated
    novel, which finds its consistency, beyond the surface
    time disjunctions, in the individual's response to his
    past, to time and timelessness, to the community. But the
    narrative retains its ambiguities and does not offer a
    sure norm for evaluation. So the movement of the novel is
    dual, revealing at once the subjective and internal, and
    the objective and distant. Interesting though his (not
    too new) reading may be, Reed thus appears to conceal his
    irresolution about the novel by making it systematic in
    the novel--a pirouette of a kind.

Rice, Julian C. "Orpheus and the Hellish Unity in *Light in
    August*." *Centennial Review*, 29 (Winter 1975), 380-96.

Roberts, James L. "The Individual and the Community: Faulkner's
    Light in August." In *Studies in American Literature*, ed.
    Waldo McNeir and Leo B. Levy. Baton Rouge: Louisiana State
    University Press, 1960, pp. 132-53. Incorporated into his
    Light in August Notes.

Rovere, Richard H. "Introduction," *Light in August*. New York:
    Modern Library, 1950, pp. V-XIV (not included in the 1959
    edition). *Light in August* is a moving drama on the theme
    of innocence, but it is a flawed book, "looser in form
    and structure than any of the others and among the most
    implausible in plot." There is not much profit in using
    Christian symbolism to interpret the novel.

Rubin, Louis D., Jr. *Writers of the Modern South: The Faraway
    Country*. Seattle: University of Washington Press, 1963,
    pp. 43-45, 60-62. On Christmas's violence and the absence
    of love.

————. "Notes on a Rear-Guard Action." In *The Idea of the
    South*. Ed. Frank E. Vandiver. Chicago: University of Chi-
    cago Press, 1964, pp. 27-41. A few comments on the South
    of Faulkner's works, which are tragedies about the failure
    of love.

Ruppersburg, Hugh M. "Byron Bunch and Percy Grimm: Strange
    Twins of *Light in August*." *Mississippi Quarterly*, 30

(Summer 1977), 441-43. Examines the parallels between
Byron's chase of Brown and Percy Grimm's chase of Christmas (Chapters 18 and 19).

Sandstrom, Glenn. "Identity Diffusion: Joe Christmas and
Quentin Compson." *American Quarterly*, 19 (Summer 1967),
207-23. These two characters are examined in the light
of psychoanalyst Erik H. Erikson's theory of identity.
"Without benefit of Freud, as he claimed, Faulkner captured
and ordered ... some problems of identity that psychol-
ogists began to itemize and analyze only a generation
later."

Seltzer, Alvin J. "'Hold on! For God's Sake Hold on!': Struggle
and Survival in Faulkner's Whirlpool." In *Chaos in the
Novel: The Novel in Chaos*. New York: Schocken Books, 1974,
pp. 92-119. The intense and frenetic dynamism of Faulkner's
world--a gigantic whirlpool--can be seen in his characters
and his prose. Complete chaos threatens as the character
spins closer to the eye of the vortex: his consciousness
is at once heightened and engulfed. This is another instance of those too numerous indifferent cursory studies.

Sichi, Edward, Jr. "Faulkner's Joe Christmas: 'Memory Believes
Before Knowing Remembers.'" *Cithara*, 18 (May 1979), 70-78.
The novel can only be understood through the personality
and character of Joe Christmas: so Lena, Hightower, and
Byron are not even mentioned in this study which purports
to define the unity of the novel. A superficial, naive,
at times erroneous review of Christmas's life.

Slabey, Robert M. "Joe Christmas, Faulkner's Marginal Man."
Phylon, 21 (Fall 1960), 266-77. With the help of Heidegger,
Kafka, Camus, and Sartre, Slabey tries to see in the
characters of the novel, particularly in Christmas,
"strangers," outcasts from the community--existential
heroes.

*————. "Myth and Ritual in *Light in August*." *Texas Studies
in Literature and Language*, 2 (Autumn 1960), 328-49.
"Joe Christmas is not a 'Christ' figure but a *Golden
Bough* figure." This reading of *Light in August* as a death
and rebirth myth is not devoid of interest, but too rigid
and too narrow to agree with both the theory and the
practice of Faulkner.

————. "Faulkner's Geography and Hightower's House." *American
Notes and Queries*, 3 (February 1964), 85-86. A minor
point concerning the identification of Jefferson and
Oxford: Hightower's back-street house is near "The Ditch."

*Slatoff, Walter J. *Quest for Failure: A Study of William
     Faulkner*. Ithaca, N.Y.: Cornell University Press, 1960,
     pp. 173-98 et passim. Characters and themes remain un-
     resolved, ambiguous. The characteristic form of Faulkner's
     thought is the oxymoron. Some interesting, even provoca-
     tive remarks, but too preoccupied with proving a thesis.

Sowder, William J. "Christmas as Existentialist Hero." *Univer-
     sity Review*, 30 (Summer 1964), 279-84. Joe hates sex
     because it serves life, which appears to him futile and
     filthy. He and Roquentin (*Nausea*) are both "victims of
     existential rape." A comparison with Sartre may be inter-
     esting, but it should not produce a limited and biased
     interpretation of Faulkner, who is no existentialist.

Sternberg, Meir. "Temporal Ordering, Modes of Expositional
     Distribution, and Three Models of Rhetorical Control in
     the Narrative Text: Faulkner, Balzac, and Austen." *P T L:
     A Journal for Descriptive Poetics and Theory*, 1 (1976),
     295-316. *Light in August* illustrates Faulkner's achieving
     of a "primacy effect," "produced only to be shattered and
     ousted by subsequently revealed expositional material."

Stonum, Gary Lee. *Faulkner's Career: An Internal Literary
     History*. Ithaca and London: Cornell University Press,
     1979, passim. In his implementation of the relatively
     new concept of career (the past output being an active
     force in shaping the career as continued production),
     Stonum does not really use *Light in August*. In passing
     remarks, he shows the novel to belong to the referential
     phase of Faulkner's career (in which "the act of repre-
     sentation does not itself come explicitly into question")--
     a point which Kartiganer's study disproves.

Stringer, Gary. *An Introduction to William Faulkner's Light
     in August*. Jackson: Mississippi Library Commission, 1976.
     10 pp. The chief moral of the book lies in the ambivalence
     of morality: the characters are both victims and vic-
     timizers--which is what Hightower comes to understand.
     Although this is a sound conclusion, this presentation
     of *Light in August* repeats the now worn-out remarks on
     Christmas as a Christ figure, and does not come to terms
     with the structure which it had claimed to make clear.
     Useless.

Swiggart, Peter. *The Art of Faulkner's Novels*. Austin: Univer-
     sity of Texas Press, 1962, pp. 41-48, 131-48. On the
     South's puritan mentality in the novel.

**Taylor, Carole Anne. "*Light in August*: The Epistemology of
Tragic Paradox." *Texas Studies in Literature and Language*,
22 (Spring 1980), 48-68. This fresh approach to the novel
studies the characters in relation to their language and
self-knowledge, and to the stance of the anonymous narrator: the range of narrative voices creates "the kinds of
knowledge that characterize the mental ages of man."
Whereas Lena is seen as a child deprived of her own language, repeating the ritualized social language, thinking in terms of her own body, the tragic characters suffer
an epistemological crisis threatening the paradoxical compromise of adult identity: Christmas becomes aware of
the distance between believing (memory) and remembering
(knowledge), Byron recognizes the gap between language
and meaning, and Hightower realizes that he has tried to
protect his illusory world from the actual one.

Terrier, Michel. "*Light in August*: Racisme et sexualité." In
Le Roman américain, 1914-1945. Paris: Presses Universitaires de France, 1979, pp. 235-46. This presentation of
the novel for the general public appears to be a simplified and reductive summary of Pitavy's book, *Faulkner's
Light in August*.

*Thompson, Deborah, ed. "*Light in August*: A Manuscript Fragment." *Mississippi Quarterly*, 32 (Summer 1979), 477-80.
Prints a manuscript page (from Chapter 15) which Faulkner seems to have lost during the revision of his manuscript. The factual differences are unimportant, but the
stylistic and technical ones (not discussed by Thompson)
are of interest.

Thompson, Lawrance. *William Faulkner: An Introduction and
Interpretation*. New York: Barnes and Noble, 1963, pp.
66-80. On Faulkner's use of the "mythical method" and
on his moral vision (fate vs. free will).

*Tuck, Dorothy. "The Inwardness of the Understanding." In John
Unterecker, ed., *Approaches to the Twentieth-Century
Novel*. New York: Thomas Y. Crowell, 1965, pp. 79-107. A
thorough study of the significance of the characters in
relation to each other: the structure is therefore
thematic. Points out the detective-story elements in the
novel.

**Vickery, Olga W. *The Novels of William Faulkner: A Critical
Interpretation*. Baton Rouge: Louisiana State University
Press, 1959. Revised edition, 1964, pp. 66-83. The novel
is seen in the light of the conflict between the private
and public images of each character. Excellent interpretation, almost too coherent.

*Volpe, Edmond L. *A Reader's Guide to William Faulkner.* New York: Farrar, Straus & Co., 1964, pp. 151-74. Sound study of the themes in relation to each character. Hightower remains locked in his past.

*Waggoner, Hyatt H. *William Faulkner: From Jefferson to the World.* Lexington: University of Kentucky Press, 1959, pp. 100-20. Christmas and Lena represent two opposed concepts of mankind. Lena has the last word, but less weight. Sound remarks on the moral ambiguities and aesthetic failings of the novel.

*Watkins, Floyd C. "Language of Irony: Quiet Words and Violent Acts in *Light in August.*" In *The Flesh and the Word: Eliot, Hemingway, Faulkner.* Nashville: Vanderbilt University Press, 1971, pp. 203-15. Faulkner moved from objectiveness to abstraction and moralizing, and the artistic quality of his novels suffered. Mostly a study of language.

*Weisgerber, Jean. *Faulkner et Dostoievski: Confluences et influences.* Brussels: Presses Universitaires de Bruxelles, 1968, pp. 175-88. Views Christmas as a scapegoat for the sins of society. A stimulating comparison with Raskolnikov, who, unlike Christmas, initially enjoys some freedom of choice. Yet tends to make Faulkner more Dostoevskian than he is (there seem to be confluences more than precise influences).

————. "Faulkner's Monomaniacs: Their Indebtedness to Raskolnikov." *Comparative Literature Studies*, 5 (June 1968), 181-93. A comparison of Christmas and several of Faulkner's major characters with Raskolnikov. They share his madness, his estrangement, his pride.

West, Ray B., Jr. "Faulkner's *Light in August*: A View of Tragedy." *Wisconsin Studies in Contemporary Literature*, 1 (Winter 1960), 5-12. The Christian scheme of sacrifice and resurrection is combined with classical tragedy.

Wheeler, Sally Padgett. "Chronology in *Light in August.*" *Southern Literary Journal*, 6 (Fall 1973), 20-42. Such detailed chronology should be accurate and useful: this is not the case, as there are glaring errors in the chronology of the Joe-Joanna affair, and one inconsistency concerning the day of Joe's capture is overlooked. It remains to be shown how the time schemes are "good starting points for extensive study of the basic themes of the novel."

**Williams, David. *Faulkner's Women: The Myth and the Muse.* Montreal and London: McGill-Queen's University Press,

1977, Chapter 6: "Lambence in a Grove: 'An Older Light
Than Ours' in *Light in August*," pp. 157-87. The novel
derives its unity from the controlling presence of the
archetypal feminine found in the Joanna-Lena nexus (Lena
being substituted for Joanna--in the grove). A refreshing
and comprehensive reading of the novel, which enlightens
the ambivalence of the feminine archetype and the various
male characters' responses to it--by which Faulkner exor-
cises the terrible from the good in it. Thus Lena's story
is the stuff of the novel, not just an ironic frame to
the tragedy of Christmas.

Williams, John C. "'The Final Copper Light of Afternoon':
Hightower's Redemption." *Twentieth Century Literature*,
13 (January 1968), 205-15. Shows the progressive changes
in Hightower and his redemption, which consists of his
acceptance of guilt and reintegration into the human
community. Attentive reading of the text, sometimes para-
phrased, but does not allow for the ambiguity of the
character.

Wilson, Robert Rawdon. "The Pattern of Thought in *Light in
August*." *Bulletin of the Rocky Mountain Modern Language
Association*, 24 (December 1970), 155-61.

Wittenberg, Judith Bryant. *Faulkner: The Transfiguration of
Biography*. Lincoln and London: University of Nebraska
Press, 1979, pp. 117-29 et passim. The darkness and
affirmation, despair and hope, which characterize *Light
in August* have their origin in Faulkner's life before
and during the writing of the novel: his affirmation of
his masculine role at home and the beginning of public
recognition, and the grief over the death of his first
child. Thus, the characters are studied in their relationship to William Faulkner, their "creator"--a hazardous
thing to do, which precisely ignores the ambiguities
and distancing involved in the process of creation. On
the whole, *Light in August* is seen as a work of "qualified" commitment, showing Faulkner emerging from darkness.

*Yorks, Samuel A. "Faulkner's Woman: The Peril of Mankind."
Arizona Quarterly, 17 (Summer 1961), 119-29. Good article
on the paradoxical conception of Woman in Faulkner's
novels.

Young, Glenn. "Struggle and Triumph in *Light in August*."
Studies in the Twentieth Century, 15 (Spring 1975),
33-50. A myopic look at some details of the novel blinds
the author to its overall significance, in this article

which is another misguided search for unity in *Light in August*. Here, the fire provides unity: Young speculates perversely, against the sense of the novel, that the fire was not started by Brown, but self-born—by the hand of Fate, which governs the actions of the characters.

*Zink, Karl E. "William Faulkner: Form as Experience." *South Atlantic Quarterly*, 53 (July 1954), 384-403. Stimulating appraisal of Faulkner's "technique of accretion," the continuity of his style, which transcends the sentence form in his ample prose, his immediacy in the simple direct prose.

*————. "Faulkner's Garden: Woman and the Immemorial Earth." *Modern Fiction Studies*, 2 (Autumn 1956), 139-49. Good article on Faulkner's women (identified with the fecund earth). Men's frequent hostility toward them.